Reading Perspectives

Reading Perspectives

2019년 3월 1일 초판1쇄 발행
2020년 3월 1일 초판2쇄 발행
2021년 3월 1일 초판3쇄 발행

편저자 | 안필규, 이철, 최은영, 구자혁, 류승구, 이선우, 채수경, 박근영, 김향일
펴낸이 | 이찬규
펴낸곳 | 북코리아
등록번호 | 제03-01240호
주소 | 13209 경기도 성남시 중원구 사기막골로 45번길 14
　　　우림2차 A동 1007호
전화 | 02-704-7840
팩스 | 02-704-7848
이메일 | sunhaksa@korea.com
홈페이지 | www.북코리아.kr
ISBN | 978-89-6324-644-4 (93740)

값 15,000원

Reading Perspectives

안필규, 이철, 최은영, 구자혁, 류승구, 이선우, 채수경, 박근영, 김향일

북코리아

Contents

Contents

Part IV Poem

Part I
Public Speech

1

Inauguration Speech

John F. Kenney[1]

1   Vice President Johnson, Mr. Speaker, Mr. Chief Justice, President Eisenhower, Vice President Nixon, President Truman, reverend clergy, fellow citizens:

We observe today not a victory of party,[2] but a celebration of
5   freedom — symbolizing an end, as well as a beginning — signifying renewal, as well as change. For I have sworn[3] before you and Almighty God the same solemn oath[4] our forebears prescribed nearly a century and three-quarters ago.

The world is very different now. For man holds in his mortal hands
10 the power to abolish all forms of human poverty and all forms of human

---

1) 존 에프 케네디(John F. Kennedy, 1917-1963): 미국 역대 대통령 가운데 가장 뛰어난 달변가 중 한 명이다. 케네디는 1963년 11월 22일 텍사스주 댈러스에서 저격범의 손에 의하여 뜻하지 않게 비극적으로 생을 마감했다. 1961년 1월 20일 대통령 취임사에서 그는 시대의 여러 도전에 대처하기 위해 결단과 희생의 정신을 가질 것을 요구했다.

2) party: 정당

3) sworn: swear의 과거분사. 맹세하다

4) solemn oath: 엄숙한 맹세

1 life. And yet the same revolutionary beliefs for which our forebears[5] fought are still at issue around the globe — the belief that the rights of man come not from the generosity of the state, but from the hand of God.

5   We dare not forget[6] today that we are the heirs of that first revolution. Let the word go forth from this time and place, to friend and foe alike, that the torch has been passed to a new generation of Americans — born in this century, tempered by war, disciplined by a hard and bitter peace, proud of our ancient heritage,[7] and unwilling
10 to witness or permit the slow undoing of those human rights to which this nation has always been committed, and to which we are committed today at home and around the world.

    Let every nation know, whether it wishes us well or ill, that we shall pay any price, bear any burden, meet any hardship, support any friend,
15 oppose any foe, to assure the survival and the success of liberty.

    This much we pledge — and more.

    To those old allies[8] whose cultural and spiritual origins we share, we pledge the loyalty of faithful friends. United there is little we cannot do in a host of cooperative ventures. Divided there is little we can do — for
20 we dare not meet a powerful challenge at odds[9] and split asunder.

    To those new states whom we welcome to the ranks of the free, we pledge our word that one form of colonial control[10] shall not have passed

---

5)   forebears: 선조
6)   We dare not forget: 감히 잊지 않습니다
7)   ancient heritage: 오래된 유산
8)   old allies: 오래된 동맹국들
9)   at odds: 다투어, 불화하여
10)   colonial control: 식민통치

away merely to be replaced by a far more iron tyranny.[11] We shall not always expect to find them supporting our view. But we shall always hope to find them strongly supporting their own freedom — and to remember that, in the past, those who foolishly sought power by riding the back of the tiger ended up inside.[12]

To those people in the huts and villages of half the globe struggling to break the bonds of mass misery, we pledge our best efforts to help them help themselves, for whatever period is required — not because the Communists[13] may be doing it, not because we seek their votes, but because it is right. If a free society cannot help the many who are poor, it cannot save the few who are rich.

To our sister republics[14] south of our border, we offer a special pledge: to convert our good words into good deeds, in a new alliance for progress,[15] to assist free men and free governments in casting off the chains of poverty. But this peaceful revolution of hope cannot become the prey of hostile powers. Let all our neighbors know that we shall join with them to oppose aggression or subversion anywhere in the Americas. And let every other power know that this hemisphere intends to remain the master of its own house.

To that world assembly of sovereign states,[16] the United Nations, our last best hope in an age where the instruments of war have far outpaced the instruments of peace, we renew our pledge of support — to

---

11) iron tyranny: 가혹한 독재정권
12) ended up inside: 결국은 안에 들어가고 말았다. (본문의 문맥상) 호랑이 밥이 되고 말았다
13) Communists: 공산주의자들
14) sister republics: 자매 공화국들
15) alliance for progress: 진보를 위한 동맹
16) world assembly of sovereign states: 주권국들의 세계적 회합

¹ prevent it from becoming merely a forum for invective,[17] to strengthen its shield of the new and the weak, and to enlarge the area in which its writ may run.

Finally, to those nations who would make themselves our adversary, ⁵ we offer not a pledge but a request: that both sides begin anew the quest for peace, before the dark powers of destruction unleashed by science engulf all humanity in planned or accidental self−destruction.

We dare not tempt them with weakness. For only when our arms[18] are sufficient beyond doubt[19] can we be certain beyond doubt that they ¹⁰ will never be employed.

But neither can two great and powerful groups of nations take comfort from our present course — both sides overburdened by the cost of modern weapons, both rightly alarmed by the steady spread of the deadly atom,[20] yet both racing to alter that uncertain balance of terror ¹⁵ that stays the hand of mankind's final war.

So let us begin anew — remembering on both sides that civility is not a sign of weakness, and sincerity is always subject to proof. Let us never negotiate out of fear, but let us never fear to negotiate.

Let both sides explore what problems unite us instead of belaboring ²⁰ those problems which divide us.

Let both sides, for the first time, formulate serious and precise proposals for the inspection and control of arms, and bring the absolute power to destroy other nations under the absolute control of all nations.

---

17) a forum for invective: 독설의 광장

18) arms: 무력

19) beyond doubt: 의심할 여지 없이

20) the steady spread of the deadly atom: 치명적 핵무기의 지속적 확산

1   Let both sides seek to invoke the wonders of science instead of its terrors. Together let us explore the stars, conquer the deserts, eradicate disease, tap the ocean depths, and encourage the arts and commerce.

    Let both sides unite to heed, in all corners of the earth, the
5 command of Isaiah[21] — to "undo the heavy burdens, and [to] let the oppressed go free."

    And, if a beachhead[22] of cooperation may push back the jungle of suspicion, let both sides join in creating a new endeavor — not a new balance of power, but a new world of law — where the strong are just,
10 and the weak secure, and the peace preserved.

    All this will not be finished in the first one hundred days. Nor will it be finished in the first one thousand days; nor in the life of this Administration; nor even perhaps in our lifetime on this planet. But let us begin.

15   In your hands, my fellow citizens, more than mine, will rest the final success or failure of our course. Since this country was founded, each generation of Americans has been summoned to give testimony to its national loyalty. The graves of young Americans who answered the call to service surround the globe.

20   Now the trumpet summons us again — not as a call to bear arms, though arms we need — not as a call to battle, though embattled we are — but a call to bear the burden of a long twilight struggle, year in and year out, "rejoicing in hope; patient in tribulation," a struggle against the common enemies of man: tyranny, poverty, disease, and war itself.

---

21) Isaiah: 성경의 선지자, 이사야
22) beachhead: 발판

1   Can we forge[23]) against these enemies a grand and global alliance, North and South, East and West, that can assure a more fruitful life for all mankind? Will you join in that historic effort?

     In the long history of the world, only a few generations have been
5   granted the role of defending freedom in its hour of maximum danger. I do not shrink from this responsibility — I welcome it. I do not believe that any of us would exchange places with any other people or any other generation. The energy, the faith, the devotion which we bring to this endeavor will light our country and all who serve it. And the glow from
10   that fire can truly light the world.

     And so, my fellow Americans, ask not what your country can do for you; ask what you can do for your country.

     My fellow citizens of the world, ask not what America will do for you, but what together we can do for the freedom of man.

15   Finally, whether you are citizens of America or citizens of the world, ask of us here the same high standards of strength and sacrifice which we ask of you. With a good conscience our only sure reward, with history the final judge of our deeds, let us go forth to lead the land we love, asking His blessing and His help, but knowing that here on earth God's
20   work must truly be our own.

---

23) forge: 서서히 나아가다

2

I Have a Dream!

Martin Luther King, Jr.[1]

1   I am happy to join with you today in what will go down in history as the greatest demonstration for freedom in the history of our nation. Fivescore[2] years ago, a great American, in whose symbolic shadow we stand today, signed the Emancipation Proclamation.[3] This momentous

---

1) 마틴 루서 킹(Martin Luther King Jr., 1928-1968):
1929년 미국 남부 조지아주 애틀랜다시에서 출생하여
1968년 암살로 생을 마친 미국의 목사이자 20세기의
대표적 인권운동가 중 한 명이다. 미국 내에서 백인과
동등한 흑인의 권리 획득을 위해 그가 지도했던 공민권
운동은 1963년 8월 28일 '일자리와 자유를 위한 워싱
턴 대행진(March on Washington)'을 통해서 세상에
널리 알려져 있다. 1963년 그가 워싱턴 D.C의 링컨기
념관 앞에서 행한 연설인 "I Have a Dream"은 미국 사
회의 흑인에 대한 차별과 그에 대한 비폭력적 저항, 그

리고 평화공존에 대한 그의 소망과 신념을 담은 유명한 연설이 되었으며, 1964년 그는 비폭력주의
저항운동에 대한 공로를 인정받아 노벨평화상을 수상하였다. 그는 베트남전에 대한 반대 활동도 벌
였으나 테네시주 멤피스시에서 암살당하였다. 미국에서는 그의 생일(1월 15일)에 가까운 1월의 세
번째 월요일을 공휴일로 지정하여 그와 그의 업적을 기리고 있다.

2) Fivescore: 100의

3) Emancipation Proclamation: 노예 해방령(1862년 링컨 대통령이 선언; 1863년 1월 1일부터 발효)

¹ decree came as a great beacon light⁴⁾ of hope to millions of Negro slaves who had been seared in the flames of withering injustice. It came as a joyous daybreak to end the long night of their captivity.

But one hundred years later, the Negro still is not free. One hundred ⁵ years later, the life of the Negro is still sadly crippled by the manacles of segregation⁵⁾ and the chains of discrimination. One hundred years later, the Negro lives on a lonely island of poverty in the midst of a vast ocean of material prosperity. One hundred years later, the Negro is still languished⁶⁾ in the corners of American society and finds himself an exile ¹⁰ in his own land. And so we've come here today to dramatize⁷⁾ a shameful condition. In a sense we've come to our nation's capital to cash a check.⁸⁾

When the architects of our republic wrote the magnificent words of the Constitution and the Declaration of Independence,⁹⁾ they were signing a promissory note to which every American was to fall heir.¹⁰⁾ ¹⁵ This note was a promise that all men, yes, black men as well as white men, would be guaranteed the "unalienable Rights"¹¹⁾ of "Life, Liberty and the pursuit of Happiness."

It is obvious today that America has defaulted on this promissory note, insofar as¹²⁾ her citizens of color are concerned. Instead of honoring

---

4)　beacon light: 표지등, 신호빛

5)　segregation: (인종 · 종교 · 성별에 따른) 분리(차별) 정책

6)　languish: (강요를 받아 어디에서) 머물다, (오랫동안 불쾌한 일을) 겪다

7)　dramatize: 각색하다

8)　cash a check: 수표를 현금으로 바꾸다

9)　the Constitution and the Declaration of Independence: 헌법과 독립선언서

10)　fall heir: 상속인이 되다

11)　unalienable Rights: 양도할 수 없는 권리

12)　insofar as ~: ~하는 한에 있어서(는)

1 this sacred obligation,[13] America has given the Negro people a bad
check, a check which has come back marked "insufficient funds." But we
refuse to believe that the bank of justice is bankrupt. We refuse to believe
that there are insufficient funds in the great vaults[14] of opportunity of
5 this nation. So, we've come to cash this check, a check that will give us
upon demand the riches of freedom and the security of justice. We have
also come to this hallowed spot to remind America of the fierce urgency
of now. This is no time to engage in the luxury of cooling off or to take
the tranquilizing drug[15] of gradualism.[16]

10   Now is the time to make real the promises of democracy. Now is
the time to rise from the dark and desolate valley of segregation to the
sunlit path[17] of racial justice. Now is the time to lift our nation from the
quicksands of racial injustice to the solid rock of brotherhood.[18] Now is
the time to make justice a reality for all of God's children.

15   It would be fatal for the nation to overlook the urgency of the
moment. This sweltering summer of the Negro's legitimate[19] discontent
will not pass until there is an invigorating[20] autumn of freedom and
equality. Nineteen sixty‐three is not an end, but a beginning. And those
who hope that the Negro needed to blow off steam and will now be
20 content will have a rude awakening, if the nation returns to business as

---

13) sacred obligation: 신성한 의무

14) vault: 금고

15) tranquilizing drug: 안정제

16) gradualism: 점진주의(반대어: radicalism, 급진주의)

17) sunlit path: 양지바른 길

18) brotherhood: 인류애, 형제애

19) legitimate: 정당한, 타당한

20) invigorating: (공기·미풍 등이) 상쾌한, 기운 나게 하는

1 usual.

There will be neither rest nor tranquility in America until the Negro is granted his citizenship rights.[21] The whirlwinds of revolt[22] will continue to shake the foundations of our nation until the bright day of 5 justice emerges. But there is something that I must say to my people who stand on the warm threshold[23] which leads into the palace of justice.

In the process of gaining our rightful place we must not be guilty of wrongful deeds. Let us not seek to satisfy our thirst for freedom by drinking from the cup of bitterness and hatred.[24] We must forever 10 conduct our struggle on the high plane[25] of dignity and discipline. We must not allow our creative protest to degenerate[26] into physical violence. Again and again we must rise to the majestic heights of meeting physical force with soul force. The marvelous new militancy[27] which has engulfed[28] the Negro community must not lead us to distrust of all white 15 people, for many of our white brothers, as evidenced by their presence here today, have come to realize that their destiny is tied up with our destiny. They have come to realize that their freedom is inextricably[29] bound to our freedom.

We cannot walk alone. And as we walk, we must make the pledge 20 that we shall always march ahead. We cannot turn back. There are

---

21) citizenship rights: 시민권
22) whirlwinds of revolt: 저항의 회오리바람
23) threshold: 문지방, 문턱, 입구
24) bitterness and hatred: 비통과 증오
25) on the high plane of dignity and discipline: 위엄과 절제의 고귀한 수준으로
26) degenerate: 악화되다
27) militancy: 투지
28) engulf: 완전히 에워싸다, 휩싸다
29) inextricably: 불가분하게, 떼려야 뗄 수 없게

¹ those who are asking the devotees of civil rights,³⁰⁾ "When will you be satisfied?"

We can never be satisfied as long as the Negro is the victim of the unspeakable horrors of police brutality.³¹⁾ We can never be satisfied as ⁵ long as our bodies, heavy with the fatigue of travel, cannot gain lodging in the motels of the highways and the hotels of the cities. We cannot be satisfied as long as the Negro's basic mobility³²⁾ is from a smaller ghetto³³⁾ to a larger one. We can never be satisfied as long as our children are stripped of³⁴⁾ their selfhood and robbed of their dignity by signs stating ¹⁰ "for white only." We cannot be satisfied as long as a Negro in Mississippi cannot vote and a Negro in New York believes he has nothing for which to vote. No, no, we are not satisfied, and we will not be satisfied until justice rolls down like waters, and righteousness like a mighty stream.

I am not unmindful³⁵⁾ that some of you have come here out of ¹⁵ great trials and tribulations. Some of you have come fresh from narrow jail cells. And some of you have come from areas where your quest for freedom³⁶⁾ left you battered³⁷⁾ by the storms of persecution and staggered by the winds of police brutality. You have been the veterans of creative suffering. Continue to work with the faith that unearned suffering is ²⁰ redemptive. Go back to Mississippi, go back to Alabama, go back to

---

30) devotees of civil rights: 인권운동가들

31) police brutality: 경찰의 만행

32) basic mobility: 이주의 권리

33) ghetto: (흔히 소수 민족들이 모여 사는) 빈민가(게토)

34) are stripped of ~: ~이 박탈되다

35) unmindful: 무관심한

36) quest for freedom: 자유에 대한 추구, 자유 추구

37) battered: 구타당한, 매 맞는

1 South Carolina, go back to Georgia, go back to Louisiana, go back to the slums and ghettos of our northern cities, knowing that somehow this situation can and will be changed.

Let us not wallow[38] in the valley of despair, I say to you today, 5 my friends. And so even though we face the difficulties of today and tomorrow, I still have a dream. It is a dream deeply rooted in the American dream.

I have a dream that one day this nation will rise up and live out the true meaning of its creed,[39] "We hold these truths to be self-evident, 10 that all men are created equal."

I have a dream that one day on the red hills of Georgia, the sons of former slaves and the sons of former slave owners will be able to sit down together at the table of brotherhood.

I have a dream that one day even the state of Mississippi, a state 15 sweltering with the heat of injustice, sweltering with the heat of oppression, will be transformed into[40] an oasis of freedom and justice.

I have a dream that my four little children will one day live in a nation where they will not be judged by the color of their skin but by the content of their character.

20 I have a dream today.

I have a dream that one day, down in Alabama, with its vicious racists, with its governor having his lips dripping with the words of

---

38) wallow: 뒹굴다, 몸부림치다

39) creed: 신념

40) be transformed into ~: ~로 변하다

1 "interposition"[41] and "nullification",[42] one day right there in Alabama little black boys and black girls will be able to join hands with little white boys and white girls as sisters and brothers. I have a dream today.

I have a dream that one day every valley shall be exalted, and every
5 hill and mountain shall be made low, the rough places will be made plain, and the crooked[43] places will be made straight, and the glory of the Lord shall be revealed, and all flesh shall see it together.

This is our hope, and this is the faith that I go back to the South with. With this faith, we will be able to hew[44] out of the mountain of
10 despair a stone of hope. With this faith, we will be able to transform the jangling discords[45] of our nation into a beautiful symphony of brotherhood. With this faith, we will be able to work together, to pray together, to struggle together, to go to jail together, to stand up for freedom together, knowing that we will be free one day. And this will
15 be the day, this will be the day when all of God's children will be able to sing with new meaning.

My country 'tis[46] of thee, sweet land of liberty, of thee I sing. Land where my fathers died, land of the pilgrim's pride,[47] from every mountainside, let freedom ring. And if America is to be a great nation,
20 this must become true. And so let freedom ring from the prodigious

---

41) interposition: 주권 우위설(각 주는 연방정부의 조치에 반대할 수 있다는 주의)

42) nullification: 무효, 파기, 주의 연방법령 실시 거부

43) crooked: 굽어진, 휘어진

44) hew: (도구를 써서 큰 것을) 자르다

45) jangling discords: 쨍그랑거리는 다툼, 불협화음

46) 'tis: it is의 축약형

47) land of the Pilgrim's pride: 개척자의 자부심이 있는 땅

¹ hilltops[48] of New Hampshire. Let freedom ring from the mighty
mountains of New York. Let freedom ring from the heightening
Alleghenies of Pennsylvania. Let freedom ring from the snow－capped
Rockies of Colorado. Let freedom ring from the curvaceous slopes[49] of
⁵ California. But not only that. Let freedom ring from Stone Mountain
of Georgia. Let freedom ring from Lookout Mountain of Tennessee. Let
freedom ring from every hill and molehill of Mississippi. From every
mountainside, let freedom ring.

And when this happens, when we allow freedom ring, when we let it
¹⁰ ring from every village and every hamlet, from every state and every city,
we will be able to speed up that day when all of God's children, black
men and white men, Jews and Gentiles, Protestants and Catholics, will
be able to join hands and sing in the words of the old Negro spiritual,

"Free at last! Free at last!
¹⁵ Thank God Almighty,[50] we are free at last."

---

48) prodigious hilltops: 경이로운 언덕
49) curvaceous slopes: 굽이진 비탈길
50) God Almighty: 전능하신 하나님

3

Remembering Robert Frost

John F. Kennedy[1]

1   This day, devoted to the memory of Robert Frost,[2] offers an
opportunity for reflection which is prized[3] by politicians as well as
by others and even by poets. For Robert Frost was one of the granite
figures[4] of our time in America. He was supremely two things — an
5   artist and an American.

A nation reveals itself not only by the men it produces but also by
the men it honors, the men it remembers. In America our heroes have
customarily run to men of large accomplishments. But today this college
and country honors a man whose contribution was not to our size but to
10   our spirit; not to our political beliefs but to our insight; not to our self −

---

1)   우리 교재에 실린 「가지 않은 길」("The Road Not Taken")로 유명한 로버트 프로스트는 1963년에
     사망한 미국의 국민 시인이다. 당시 대통령이었던 존 에프 케네디는 그를 추도하는 연설(1963. 10.
     27.)을 한 바 있는데, 이 자리에서 그는 미국의 나아갈 길을 제시함으로써 큰 공감을 얻었다. 그의 유
     명한 말 "비단 힘 때문만이 아니라 그 문명 때문에 전 세계로부터 존경받는 미국을 고대합니다."는
     미국이 그 패권을 유지하는 것만큼이나 문화적으로 융성한 나라가 되길 바라는 마음을 담고 있다.

2)   This day, devoted to the memory of Robert Frost: 로버트 프로스트를 추모하는 오늘은

3)   be prized: 귀하게 여기다

4)   granite figures: 화강암과 같은 인물들

¹ esteem but to our self – comprehension.

In honoring Robert Frost we therefore can pay honor to the deepest sources of our national strength. That strength takes many forms, and the most obvious forms are not always the most significant.

⁵ The men who create power make an indispensable⁵⁾ contribution to the nation's greatness. But the men who question power make a contribution just as indispensable, especially when that questioning is disinterested,⁶⁾ for they determine whether we use power or power uses us. Our national strength matters; but the spirit which informs ¹⁰ and controls our strength matters just as much. This was the special significance of Robert Frost. He brought an unsparing instinct for reality to bear on the platitudes and pieties of society.⁷⁾ His sense of the human tragedy fortified⁸⁾ him against self – deception⁹⁾ and easy consolation.

"I have been," he wrote, "one acquainted with the night."¹⁰⁾ And ¹⁵ because he knew the midnight as well as the high noon, because he understood the ordeal as well as the triumph of the human spirit, he gave his age strength with which to overcome despair.

At bottom he held a deep faith in the spirit of man. And it's hardly an accident that Robert Frost coupled¹¹⁾ poetry and power, for he saw ²⁰ poetry as the means of saving power from itself.

---

5)   indispensable: 없어서는 안 될, 필수적인

6)   disinterested: 사심이 없는

7)   platitudes and pieties of society: 사회의 진부하고 경건한 태도들

8)   fortify: 굳세게 하다

9)   self – deception: 자기기만

10) I have been one acquainted with the night: 나는 밤을 아는 사람이었다. "Acquainted with the Night"은 프로스트의 시 중 하나이다.

11) couple: 결합하다

1　　When power leads man toward arrogance, poetry reminds him of his limitations. When power narrows the areas of man's concern, poetry reminds him of the richness and diversity of his existence. When power corrupts, poetry cleanses, for art establishes the basic human truths which
5　must serve as the touchstones of our judgment.[12] The artist, however faithful to his personal vision of reality, becomes the last champion of the individual mind and sensibility against an intrusive[13] society and an officious[14] state.

　　The great artist is thus a solitary[15] figure. He has, as Frost said, "a
10　lover's quarrel with the world."[16] In pursuing his perceptions of reality, he must often sail against the currents of his time. This is not a popular role.

　　If Robert Frost was much honored during his lifetime, it was because a good many preferred to ignore his darker truths. Yet in retrospect we
15　see how the artist's fidelity[17] has strengthened the fiber[18] of our national life. If sometimes our great artists have been the most critical of our society, it is because their sensitivity and their concern for justice, which must motivate any true artist, makes him aware that our nation falls short of[19] its highest potential.

20　　I see little of more importance to the future of our country and our

---

12) the touchstones of our judgment: 판단의 시금석

13) intrusive: 거슬리는

14) officious: 위세를 부리는

15) solitary: 혼자 있기를 좋아하는, 고독한

16) a lover's quarrel with the world: 세상과의 사랑싸움. "I had a lover's quarrel with the world"는 프로스트의 시의 제목이면서 프로스트의 묘비명이기도 하다.

17) fidelity: 충실함

18) fiber: 기질, 정신력, 핵심

19) falls short of: (예상되는 필요한 기준인) ~에 미치지 못하다

civilization than full recognition of the place of the artist. If art is to nourish the roots of our culture, society must set the artist free to follow his vision wherever it takes him.

We must never forget that art is not a form of propaganda;[20] it is a form of truth. And as Mr. MacLeish once remarked of poets, "There is nothing worse for our trade than to be in style."[21]

In free society, art is not a weapon and it does not belong to the sphere of polemics and ideology.[22] Artists are not engineers of the soul. It may be different elsewhere. But democratic society — in it — the highest duty of the writer, the composer, the artist is to remain true to himself and to let the chips fall where they may.

In serving his vision of the truth, the artist best serves his nation. And the nation which disdains[23] the mission of art invites the fate of Robert Frost's hired man — "the fate of having nothing to look backward to with pride and nothing to look forward to with hope."[24] I look forward to a great future for America — a future in which our country will match its military strength with our moral restraint, its wealth with our wisdom, its power with our purpose.

I look forward to an America which will not be afraid of grace and beauty, which will protect the beauty of our national environment, which will preserve the great old American houses and squares and parks of our

---

20) a form of propaganda: (정치 지도자, 정당 등에 대한 허위, 과장된) 선전의 형식

21) There is nothing worse for our trade than to be in style.: 업으로 치자면 시를 쓰는 것보다 더 나쁜 것은 없다. 아치볼드 매클리시(Archibald Macleish)의 "Invocation to the Social Muse"라는 시의 한 구절.

22) the sphere of polemics and ideology: 논쟁과 이데올로기의 영역

23) disdain: 업신여기다, 무시하다

24) 프로스트의 "The Death of the Hired Man"이라는 시의 한 구절.

¹ national past and which will build handsome and balanced cities for our future.

I look forward to an America which will reward achievement in the arts as we reward achievement in business or statecraft. I look
⁵ forward to an America which will steadily raise the standards of artistic accomplishment and which will steadily enlarge cultural opportunities for all of our citizens.

And I look forward to an America which commands respect throughout the world not only for its strength but for its civilization
¹⁰ as well. And I look forward to a world which will be safe not only for democracy and diversity but also for personal distinction.

Robert Frost was often skeptical about projects for human improvement. Yet I do not think he would disdain this hope. As he wrote during the uncertain days of the Second War:
¹⁵

> Take human nature altogether since time began...
> And it must be a little more in favor of man,
> Say a fraction of one percent at the very least...
> Our hold on the planet wouldn't have so increased.

²⁰

Because of Mr. Frost's life and work, because of the life and work of this college, our hold on this planet has increased.

4

Yes, We Can!

Barack Hussein Obama[1]

1   If there is anyone out there who still doubts that America is a place where all things are possible; who still wonders if the dream of our founders[2] is alive in our time; who still questions the power of our democracy, tonight is your answer.

5   It's the answer told by lines that stretched around schools and churches in numbers this nation has never seen; by people who waited three hours and four hours, many for the very first time in their lives,

---

1)   버락 후세인 오바마(Barack Hussein Obama, 1961-): 1961년 아프리카 케냐에서 하와이로 유학 온 최초의 흑인 학생인 아버지와 미국 백인 어머니 사이에서 태어났다. 그는 인권변호사 출신으로 일리노이주 상원의원(3선)을 거쳐 연방 상원의원을 지냈으며, 2008년 민주당 대통령 후보로 출마하여 공화당의 존 매케인 후보에 압승하고 제44대 미국 대통령에 당선됨으로써 미국 최초의 흑인(혼혈) 대통령이 되었다. "Yes, We Can"은 그의 대통령 선거 캠페인의 슬로건(slogan)이었으며, 2008년 당선 확정 후 시카고에서 이 슬로건을 주제로 연설하였다.

2)   founder: 설립자, 개척자

1 because they believed that this time must be different; that their voices could be that difference.

It's the answer spoken by young and old, rich and poor, Democrat and Republican,[3] black, white, Hispanic, Asian, Native American, gay,
5 straight,[4] disabled and not disabled — Americans who sent a message to the world that we have never been just a collection of individuals or a collection of red states and blue states; we are, and always will be, the United States of America.

It's the answer that led those who have been told for so long by so
10 many to be cynical,[5] and fearful, and doubtful of what we can achieve to put their hands on the arc of history[6] and bend it once more toward the hope of a better day.

It's been a long time coming, but tonight, because of what we did on this day, in this election, at this defining moment, change has come to
15 America.

A little bit earlier this evening, I received an extraordinarily gracious call from Senator McCain.[7] Senator McCain fought long and hard in this campaign, and he's fought even longer and harder for the country that he loves. He has endured sacrifices for America that most of us
20 cannot begin to imagine, (and) we are better off for the service rendered by this brave and selfless leader. I congratulate him and I congratulate Governor Palin[8] for all they have achieved, and I look forward to

---

3) Democrat and Republican: 민주당원과 공화당원
4) straight: 이성애자
5) cynical: 냉소적인
6) on the arc of history: 역사의 전환점에서
7) Sen. McCain: 매케인 상원의원
8) Gov. Palin: 페일린 주지사

1 working with them to renew this nation's promise in the months ahead.

I want to thank my partner in this journey, a man who campaigned from his heart and spoke for the men and women he grew up with on the streets of Scranton and rode with on that train home to Delaware,

5 the vice‒president‒elect of the United States, Joe Biden.

And I would not be standing here tonight without the unyielding support of my best friend for the last 16 years, the rock of our family, the love of my life, the nation's next first lady, Michelle Obama. Sasha and Malia, I love you both more than you can imagine, and you have earned

10 the new puppy that's coming with us to the White House. And while she's no longer with us, I know my grandmother is watching, along with the family that made me who I am. I miss them tonight, I know that my debt to them is beyond measure. To my sister Maya, my sister Alma, all my other brothers and sisters, thank you so much for all the support that

15 you've given me. I'm grateful to them.

To my campaign manager, David Plouffe the unsung hero of this campaign, who built the best, best political campaign, I think, in the history of the United States of America. To my chief strategist, David Axelrod who's been a partner with me every step of the way. To the best

20 campaign team ever assembled in the history of politics — you made this happen, and I am forever grateful for what you've sacrificed to get it done.

But above all, I will never forget who this victory truly belongs to — it belongs to you. It belongs to you.

25 I was never the likeliest candidate for this office.[9] We didn't start

_____

9) office: 직무

¹ with much money or many endorsements. Our campaign was not hatched in the halls of Washington — it began in the backyards of Des Moines and the living rooms of Concord and the front porches of Charleston.

⁵ It was built by working men and women who dug into what little savings they had to give $5, $10, $20 to the cause. It grew strength from the young people who rejected the myth of their generation's apathy who left their homes and their families for jobs that offered little pay and less sleep. It drew strength from the not‑so‑young people who braved the
¹⁰ bitter cold and scorching heat to knock on the doors of perfect strangers, and from the millions of Americans who volunteered and organized and proved that more than two centuries later, a government of the people, by the people, and for the people has not perished from the Earth. This is your victory.

¹⁵ I know you didn't do this just to win an election. I know you didn't do it for me. You did it because you understand the enormity[10] of the task that lies ahead. For even as we celebrate tonight, we know the challenges that tomorrow will bring are the greatest of our lifetime — two wars, a planet in peril, the worst financial crisis in a century. Even
²⁰ as we stand here tonight, we know there are brave Americans waking up in the deserts of Iraq and the mountains of Afghanistan to risk their lives for us. There are mothers and fathers who will lie awake after the children fall asleep and wonder how they'll make the mortgage or pay their doctors' bills or save enough for their child's college education.
²⁵ There is new energy to harness, new jobs to be created, new schools to

---

10) enormity: 심각함, 위중함

1 build, and threats to meet, alliances to repair.

The road ahead will be long. Our climb will be steep. We may not get there in one year or even in one term. But, America, I have never been more hopeful than I am tonight that we will get there. I promise

5 you, we as a people will get there.

There will be setbacks[11] and false starts. There are many who won't agree with every decision or policy I make as president. And we know that government can't solve every problem. But I will always be honest with you about the challenges we face. I will listen to you, especially

10 when we disagree. And, above all, I will ask you to join in the work of remaking this nation, the only way it's been done in America for 221 years — block by block, brick by brick, callused hand by callused hand.[12]

What began 21 months ago in the depths of winter must not end

15 on this autumn night. This victory alone is not the change we seek — it is only the chance for us to make that change. And that cannot happen if we go back to the way things were. It cannot happen without you, without a new spirit of service, a new spirit of sacrifice.

So let us summon a new spirit of patriotism, of responsibility, where

20 each of us resolves to pitch in and work harder and look after not only ourselves but each other. Let us remember that if this financial crisis taught us anything, it's that we cannot have a thriving Wall Street while Main Street suffers. In this country, we rise or fall as one nation, as one people.

---

11) setback: 차질
12) callused hand by callused hand: 굳은살이 박힌 손에 손을 잡고

1 Let's resist the temptation to fall back[13] on the same partisanship[14] and pettiness and immaturity that has poisoned our politics for so long. Let's remember that it was a man from this state who first carried the banner of the Republican Party[15] to the White House, a party founded

5 on the values of self‑reliance and individual liberty and national unity. Those are values that we all share. And while the Democratic Party[16] has won a great victory tonight, we do so with a measure of humility and determination to heal the divides that have held back our progress.

As Lincoln said to a nation far more divided than ours, "We are

10 not enemies, but friends. Though passion may have strained, it must not break our bonds of affection." To those Americans whose support I have yet to earn, I may not have won your vote tonight, but I hear your voices, I need your help. And I will be your president, too.

And (to) all those watching tonight from beyond our shores, from

15 parliaments and palaces, to those who are huddled around radios in the forgotten corners of our world, our stories are singular, but our destiny is shared, and a new dawn of American leadership is at hand. To those, to those who would tear the world down: We will defeat you. To those who seek peace and security: We support you. And to all those who have

20 wondered if America's beacon still burns as bright: Tonight, we proved once more that the true strength of our nation comes not from the might of our arms or the scale of our wealth, but from the enduring power of our ideals: democracy, liberty, opportunity and unyielding hope.

---

13) fall back: 후퇴하다, 물러나다
14) partisanship: 당파심, 당파근성
15) Republican Party: 공화당
16) Democratic Party: 민주당

1   That's the true genius of America: that America can change. Our union can be perfected. What we've already achieved gives us hope for what we can and must achieve tomorrow.

This election had many firsts and many stories that will be told for generations. But one that's on my mind tonight's about a woman who cast her ballot in Atlanta. She's a lot like the millions of others who stood in line to make their voice heard in this election except for one thing: Ann Nixon Cooper is 106 years old.

She was born just a generation past slavery; a time when there were no cars on the road or planes in the sky; when someone like her couldn't vote for two reasons — because she was a woman and because of the color of her skin.

And tonight, I think about all that she's seen throughout her century in America — the heartache and the hope; the struggle and the progress; the times we were told that we can't, and the people who pressed on with that American creed: Yes, we can.

At a time when women's voices were silenced and their hopes dismissed, she lived to see them stand up and speak out and reach for the ballot. Yes, we can.

When there was despair in the Dust Bowl[17] and depression across the land, she saw a nation conquer fear itself with a New Deal,[18] new jobs, and a new sense of common purpose. Yes, we can.

When the bombs fell on our harbor and tyranny threatened the world, she was there to witness a generation rise to greatness and a

---

17) Dust Bowl: 미국의 중남부 지역
18) New Deal: 뉴딜정책. 미국 제32대 대통령 루스벨트의 지도 아래 대공황 극복을 위하여 추진하였던 제반 정책.

¹ democracy was saved. Yes, we can.

    She was there for the buses in Montgomery, the hoses in Birmingham, a bridge in Selma, and a preacher from Atlanta who told a people that "We Shall Overcome." Yes, we can.

⁵   A man touched down on the moon, a wall came down in Berlin, a world was connected by our own science and imagination. And this year, in this election, she touched her finger to a screen, and cast her vote, because after 106 years in America, through the best of times and the darkest of hours, she knows how America can change. Yes, we can.

¹⁰   America, we have come so far. We have seen so much. But there is so much more to do. So tonight, let us ask ourselves: If our children should live to see the next century; if my daughters should be so lucky to live as long as Ann Nixon Cooper, what change will they see? What progress will we have made?

¹⁵   This is our chance to answer that call. This is our moment. This is our time, to put our people back to work and open doors of opportunity for our kids; to restore prosperity and promote the cause of peace; to reclaim the American Dream and reaffirm that fundamental truth, that, out of many, we are one;[19] that while we breathe, we hope. And where ²⁰ we are met with cynicism and doubts, and those who tell us that we can't, we will respond with that timeless creed that sums up the spirit of a people: Yes, we can.

    Thank you, God bless you. And may God bless the United States of America.

---

19) out of many, we are one: 많은 수이기는 하지만, 우리는 하나입니다

Part II

Essay & Science

1

1833 Factory Act[1]

The National Archives[2]

1   In 1833 the Government passed a Factory Act to improve conditions for children working in factories. Young children were working very long hours in workplaces where conditions were often terrible. The basic act was as follows:

5
- no child workers under nine years of age
- employers must have an age certificate for their child workers
- children of 9 – 13 years to work no more than nine hours a day
- children of 13 – 18 years to work no more than 12 hours a day
- children are not to work at night

10
- two hours schooling each day for children
- four factory inspectors appointed to enforce the law

---

1)   1833 Factory Act: 1833년에 제정된 영국의 공장법
2)   국립보존기록관(The National Archives). 이 글의 출처는 영국의 국립보존기록관에 보관된 문서이며 수업용으로 수정 · 재편집되었다.

1　However, the passing of this act did not mean that the mistreatment[3] of children stopped overnight.

Using these sources, investigate how the far the act had solved the problems of child labour.

5　As the Industrial Revolution[4] gathered pace thousands of factories sprang up all over the country. There were no laws relating to the running of factories as there had been no need for them before. As a result, dangerous machinery was used that could, and frequently did, cause serious injuries to workers. To add to these dangers, people were required
10　to work incredibly long hours – often through the night. Perhaps one of the worst features of this new industrial age was the use of child labour. Very young children worked extremely long hours[5] and could be severely punished for any mistakes. Arriving late for work could lead to a large fine and possibly a beating. Dozing at a machine could result in the
15　accidental loss of a limb.[6]

People began to realise how bad these conditions were in many factories and started to campaign for improvements.[7] There was a lot of resistance[8] from factory owners who felt it would slow down the running of their factories and make their products more expensive. Many people
20　also did not like the government interfering in their lives. Some parents, for instance, needed their children to go out to work from a young age, as they needed the money to help feed the family.

---

3) mistreatment: 학대
4) Industrial Revolution: 산업혁명
5) extremely long hours: 엄청나게 긴 시간
6) limb: 사지, 팔다리
7) improvement: 개선
8) resistance: 저항

1 Not all factory owners kept their workers in bad conditions however. Robert Owen, who owned a cotton mill in Lanark, Scotland, built the village of New Lanark for his workers. Here they had access to schools, doctors and there was a house for each family who worked in his mills.

5 By 1833, the Government passed what was to be the first of many acts dealing with working conditions and hours. At first, there was limited power to enforce these acts but as the century progressed the rules were enforced[9] more strictly. Nonetheless, the hours and working conditions were still very tough by today's standards, and no rules were

10 in place to protect adult male workers.

An extract[10] from a Factory Inspectors report – British Parliamentary Papers (1836) No. 353

My Lord, in the case of Taylor, Ibbotson & Co. I took the evidence from the mouths of the boys themselves. They stated to me that they commenced working on Friday morning, the 27th of May last, at six A.M., and that, with the exception of meal hours and one hour at midnight extra, they did not cease working till four o'clock on Saturday evening, having been two days and a night thus engaged. Believing the case scarcely possible, I asked every boy the same questions, and from each received the same answers. I then went into the house to look at the time book, and, in the presence of one of the masters, referred to the cruelty of the case, and stated that I should certainly punish it with all the severity in my power. Mr. Rayner, the certificating surgeon of Bastile, was with me at the time.

---

9) enforce: 집행하다
10) extract: 발췌문

2

Where I Lived,
and What I Lived For

Henry David Thoreau[1]

1   At a certain season of our life we are accustomed to consider every
spot as the possible site of a house. I have thus surveyed the country on
every side within a dozen miles of where I live. In imagination I have
bought all the farms in succession,[2] for all were to be bought, and I
5 knew their price. I walked over each farmer's premises,[3] tasted his wild
apples, discoursed on husbandry[4] with him, took his farm at his price,

---

1)   헨리 데이비드 소로(Henry David Thoreau, 1817-1862): 소로는 에머슨(Emerson)의 『자연』(*Na-ture*)을 읽고 감명받아 평생을 순수한 초절주의자(transcendentalist)로 살았다. 미국 정부가 남부에서의 노예제도를 인정한 것과 멕시코와 전쟁을 벌인 데에 대한 항거로 세금 납부를 거절하기도 했다. "우리는 첫째, 인간이어야 하고, 그 다음이 신민이다."라는 말로 톨스토이, 간디, 마틴 루서 킹 등에게 큰 영향을 미쳤다. 대표작으로는 『월든』(*Walden*)(1854)이 있는데, 1845년부터 1847년까지 콩코드로부터 몇 마일 떨어져 있는 월든 호수(Walden Pond)에서 오두막을 짓고 홀로 살았던 경험을 토대로 쓴 것이다. 이 책은 "책이라기보다는 훌륭한 것이 많이 쌓여 있는 더미"라는 평을 들을 정도로, 콩코드강의 물고기 목록, 호머의 시, 인디언과의 싸움, 소리에 대한 초절주의적 의미 등의 다양한 내용이 포함되어 있다. 교재에 실린 위의 글은 『월든』의 일부를 발췌한 것이다.

2)   in succession: 잇달아, 계속하여

3)   I walked over each farmer's premises: 나는 그 농장들을 하나하나 둘러보았다

4)   husbandry: 농사

at any price, mortgaging it to him in my mind;[5] even put a higher price on it — took everything but a deed of it — took his word for his deed, for I dearly love to talk — cultivated it, and him too to some extent, I trust, and withdrew when I had enjoyed it long enough, leaving him to carry it on. This experience entitled me to be regarded as a sort of real-estate broker by my friends. Wherever I sat, there I might live, and the landscape radiated[6] from me accordingly. What is a house but a *sedes*, a seat? — better if a country seat.[7] I discovered many a site for a house not likely to be soon improved,[8] which some might have thought too far from the village, but to my eyes the village was too far from it. Well, there I might live, I said; and there I did live, for an hour, a summer and a winter life; saw how I could let the years run off,[9] buffet[10] the winter through, and see the spring come in. The future inhabitants of this region, wherever they may place their houses, may be sure that they have been anticipated.[11] An afternoon sufficed[12] to lay out the land into orchard, wood-lot,[13] and pasture, and to decide what fine oaks or pines should be left to stand before the door, and whence each blasted tree[14] could be seen to the best advantage; and then I let it lie, fallow,

---

5) mortgaging it to him in my mind: 나의 마음속에서 그에게 그것을 저당 잡혔다

6) radiate: 내뿜다, 뿜어져 나오다

7) better if a country seat: 만약 자리가 시골에 있으면 더욱 좋은 것이다

8) not likely to be soon improved: 쉽게 개발될 것으로 보이지 않는

9) let the years run off: 몇 년이란 세월을 흘려보내다

10) buffet: ~와 싸우다

11) may be sure that they have been anticipated: 먼저 그곳을 집터로 생각한 사람이 있었다는 것을 믿어도 좋을 것이다

12) suffice: 충분하다

13) wood-lot: 식림지, 나무숲

14) blasted tree: 고목나무

¹ perchance, for a man is rich in proportion to the number of things which he can afford to let alone.

My imagination carried me so far that I even had the refusal¹⁵⁾ of several farms — the refusal was all I wanted — but I never got my
⁵ fingers burned¹⁶⁾ by actual possession. The nearest that I came to actual possession was when I bought the Hollowell place, and had begun to sort my seeds, and collected materials with which to make a wheelbarrow to carry it on or off with; but before the owner gave me a deed of it, his wife — every man has such a wife — changed her mind and wished to keep
¹⁰ it, and he offered me ten dollars to release him. Now, to speak the truth, I had but ten cents in the world, and it surpassed my arithmetic to tell, if I was that man who had ten cents, or who had a farm, or ten dollars, or all together. However, I let him keep the ten dollars and the farm too, for I had carried it far enough; or rather, to be generous, I sold him
¹⁵ the farm for just what I gave for it, and, as he was not a rich man, made him a present of ten dollars, and still had my ten cents, and seeds, and materials for a wheelbarrow left. I found thus that I had been a rich man without any damage to my poverty. But I retained the landscape, and I have since annually carried off¹⁷⁾ what it yielded without a wheelbarrow.
²⁰ With respect to landscapes,

> "I am monarch of all I *survey*,
> My right there is none to dispute."¹⁸⁾

---

15) refusal: 우선권

16) got my fingers burned: 나쁜 경험을 하다, 따끔한 맛을 보다

17) carry off: 해내다

18) 영국의 시인이자 찬송가 작가인 윌리엄 쿠퍼(William Cowper, 1731-1800)의 시에서 가져옴.

1   I have frequently seen a poet withdraw, having enjoyed the most valuable part of a farm, while the crusty[19] farmer supposed that he had got a few wild apples only. Why, the owner does not know it for many years when a poet has put his farm in rhyme, the most admirable kind of invisible fence, has fairly impounded[20] it, milked it, skimmed it, and got all the cream, and left the farmer only the skimmed milk.[21]

    The real attractions of the Hollowell farm, to me, were: its complete retirement,[22] being, about two miles from the village, half a mile from the nearest neighbor, and separated from the highway by abroad field; its bounding on the river,[23] which the owner said protected it by its fogs from frosts in the spring, though that was nothing to me; the gray color and ruinous state of the house and barn, and the dilapidated fences,[24] which put such an interval between me and the last occupant; the hollow and lichen – covered apple trees,[25] gnawed by rabbits, showing what kind of neighbors I should have; but above all, the recollection I had of it from my earliest voyages up the river, when the house was concealed behind a dense grove of red maples, through which I heard the house – dog bark. I was in haste to buy it, before the proprietor[26] finished getting out some rocks, cutting down the hollow apple trees, and grubbing up some young birches which had sprung up in the pasture,[27] or, in short,

---

19) crusty: 신경질적인, 화를 잘 내는, 무뚝뚝한

20) impounded: 압수하다, 가둬두다

21) skimmed milk: 탈지유, 찌꺼기 우유

22) its complete retirement: 그곳이 완전히 외진 곳에 있다는 것

23) its bounding on the river: 강을 끼고 있다는 것

24) the dilapidated fences: 다 허물어져가는 울타리

25) the hollow and lichen – covered apple trees: 속이 비고 이끼로 덮여 있는 사과나무들

26) proprietor: 소유주, 집주인

27) grubbing up some young birches which had sprung up in the pasture: 풀밭에 자라고 있던 어린 자

¹ had made any more of his improvements.²⁸⁾ To enjoy these advantages I was ready to carry it on; like Atlas, to take the world on my shoulders, — I never heard what compensation he received for that, — and do all those things which had no other motive or excuse but that I might pay for it
⁵ and be unmolested²⁹⁾ in my possession of it; for I knew all the while that it would yield the most abundant crop of the kind I wanted, if I could only afford to let it alone. But it turned out as I have said.

All that I could say, then, with respect to farming on a large scale — I have always cultivated a garden — was, that I had had my seeds
¹⁰ ready. Many think that seeds improve with age. I have no doubt that time discriminates between the good and the bad; and when at last I shall plant, I shall be less likely to be disappointed. But I would say to my fellows, once for all, As long as possible live free and uncommitted. It makes but little difference whether you are committed to a farm or the
¹⁵ county jail.

Old Cato, whose *De Re Rusticâ*³⁰⁾ is my "Cultivator",³¹⁾ says — and the only translation I have seen makes sheer nonsense of the passage — "When you think of getting a farm turn it thus in your mind, not to buy greedily; nor spare your pains to look at it, and do not think it enough to
²⁰ go round it once. The oftener you go there the more it will please you, if it **is** good." I think I shall not buy greedily, but go round and round it as

---

작나무를 파내다

28) improvements: 농장 개량 작업

29) unmolested: 방해받지 않는

30) *De Re Rusticâ*: 『전원생활론』. 로마의 역사가이자 정치가인 카토(Marcus Porcius Cato, 234-149 B.C.)의 작품.

31) "Cultivator": 소로 당시 간행되던 (Boston Cultivator, New England Cultivator 등과 같은) 농사지침서 를 가리킴.

long as I live, and be buried in it first, that it may please me the more at
last.

The present was my next experiment of this kind, which I purpose
to describe more at length, for convenience putting the experience of
two years into one. As I have said, I do not propose to write an ode
to dejection,[32] but to brag as lustily as chanticleer[33] in the morning,
standing on his roost,[34] if only to wake my neighbors up.

When first I took up my abode in the woods, that is, began to spend
my nights as well as days there, which, by accident, was on Independence
Day, or the Fourth of July, 1845, my house was not finished for winter,
but was merely a defence against the rain,[35] without plastering or
chimney, the walls being of rough, weather‒stained boards,[36] with wide
chinks,[37] which made it cool at night. The upright white hewn studs and
freshly planed door and window casings gave it a clean and airy look,
especially in the morning, when its timbers were saturated with dew,[38]
so that I fancied that by noon some sweet gum would exude from them.
To my imagination it retained throughout the day more or less of this
auroral character, reminding me of a certain house on a mountain which
I had visited a year before. This was an airy and unplastered[39] cabin,
fit to entertain a travelling god, and where a goddess might trail her

---

32) dejection: 실의, 낙담

33) chanticleer: 수탉

34) standing on his roost: 횃대 위에 올라앉은

35) was merely a defence against the rain: 비만 겨우 막아주고 있었다

36) the walls being of rough, weather‒stained boards: 벽은 비바람에 시달리고 햇빛에 바랜 거친 판자
들로 되어 있었다

37) with wide chinks: 넓은 틈들이 있어서

38) when its timbers were saturated with dew: 재목들이 이슬에 젖어 있을 때

39) unplastered: 회반죽을 바르지 않은

¹ garments. The winds which passed over my dwelling were such as sweep over the ridges of mountains, bearing the broken strains, or celestial parts[40] only, of terrestrial music.[41] The morning wind forever blows, the poem of creation is uninterrupted; but few are the ears that hear it.[42]

⁵ Olympus is but the outside of the earth everywhere.

The only house I had been the owner of before, if I except a boat, was a tent, which I used occasionally when making excursions in the summer, and this is still rolled up in my garret;[43] but the boat, after passing from hand to hand, has gone down the stream of time. With ¹⁰ this more substantial shelter about me, I had made some progress toward settling in the world. This frame, so slightly clad, was a sort of crystallization[44] around me, and reacted on the builder. It was suggestive somewhat as a picture in outlines.[45] I did not need to go outdoors to take the air, for the atmosphere within had lost none of its freshness. It ¹⁵ was not so much within doors as behind a door where I sat,[46] even in the rainiest weather. The Harivansa says, "An abode without birds is like a meat without seasoning." Such was not my abode, for I found myself suddenly neighbor to the birds; not by having imprisoned one, but having caged myself near them. I was not only nearer to some of those ²⁰ which commonly frequent the garden and the orchard, but to those

---

40) celestial parts: 천상의 부분

41) terrestrial music: 지상의 음악

42) few are the ears that hear it: 그것을 듣는 귀를 가진 사람은 드물다

43) this is still rolled up in my garret: 이것은 다락방에서 여전히 돌돌 말려 있다

44) a sort of crystallization: 일종의 결정체

45) as a picture in outlines: 윤곽만을 그린 그림처럼

46) It was not so much within doors as behind a door where I sat: 집 안에 있었다기보다는 차라리 문 뒤에 앉아 있었다

¹ smaller and more thrilling songsters of the forest which never, or rarely, serenade a villager, — the wood‐thrush, the veery, the scarlet tanager, the field‐sparrow, the whip‐poor‐will, and many others.⁴⁷⁾

⁵ I was seated by the shore of a small pond, about a mile and a half south of the village of Concord and somewhat higher than it, in the midst of an extensive wood between that town and Lincoln, and about two miles south of that our only field known to fame, Concord Battle Ground; but I was so low in the woods that the opposite shore, half a mile off, like the rest, covered with wood, was my most distant horizon.

¹⁰ For the first week, whenever I looked out on the pond it impressed me like a tarn⁴⁸⁾ high up on the side of a mountain, its bottom far above the surface of other lakes, and, as the sun arose, I saw it throwing off its nightly clothing of mist, and here and there, by degrees, its soft ripples or its smooth reflecting surface was revealed, while the mists, like ghosts,

¹⁵ were stealthily⁴⁹⁾ withdrawing in every direction into the woods, as at the breaking up of some nocturnal conventicle.⁵⁰⁾ The very dew seemed to hang upon the trees later into the day than usual, as on the sides of mountains.

This small lake was of most value as a neighbor in the intervals of a

²⁰ gentle rain‐storm in August, when, both air and water being perfectly still, but the sky overcast, mid‐afternoon had all the serenity of evening, and the wood thrush sang around, and was heard from shore to shore. A lake like this is never smoother than at such a time; and the clear portion

---

47) the wood‐thrush, the veery, the scarlet tanager, the field‐sparrow, the whip‐poor‐will: 티티새, 개똥지빠귀, 붉은 풍금조, 바위종다리, 쏙독새

48) tarn: 호수

49) stealthily: 몰래, 은밀히

50) conventicle: 비밀집회

of the air above it being shallow and darkened by clouds, the water, full of light and reflections, becomes a lower heaven itself so much the more important. From a hill－top near by, where the wood had been recently cut off, there was a pleasing vista southward across the pond, through a wide indentation in the hills which form the shore there, where their opposite sides sloping toward each other suggested a stream flowing out in that direction through a wooded valley, but stream there was none. That way I looked between and over the near green hills to some distant and higher ones in the horizon, tinged with blue.[51] Indeed, by standing on tiptoe[52] I could catch a glimpse of some of the peaks of the still bluer and more distant mountain ranges in the northwest, those true－blue coins from heaven's own mint,[53] and also of some portion of the village. But in other directions, even from this point, I could not see over or beyond the woods which surrounded me. It is well to have some water in your neighborhood, to give buoyancy to and float the earth. One value even of the smallest well is, that when you look into it you see that earth is not continent but insular. This is as important as that it keeps butter cool. When I looked across the pond from this peak toward the Sudbury meadows, which in time of flood I distinguished elevated perhaps by a mirage in their seething[54] valley, like a coin in a basin, all the earth beyond the pond appeared like a thin crust insulated and floated even by this small sheet of intervening water,[55] and I was reminded that this on

---

51) tinged with blue: 푸른빛을 띠고 있는

52) by standing on tiptoe: 발돋움을 해서 보면

53) those true－blue coins from heaven's own mint: 하늘의 조폐국에서 찍어낸 진청색의 동전들

54) seething: 소용돌이치는

55) like a thin crust insulated and floated even by this small sheet of intervening water: 그 사이에 있는 이 작은 수면 때문에 고립되어 둥둥 떠 있는 빵 조각처럼

1 which I dwelt was but *dry land.*

    Though the view from my door was still more contracted, I did not feel crowded or confined in the least. There was pasture enough for my imagination. The low shrub oak plateau to which the opposite shore
5 arose stretched away toward the prairies of the West and the steppes of Tartary, affording ample room for all the roving families of men.[56] "There are none happy in the world but beings who enjoy freely a vast horizon" — said Damodara,[57] when his herds required new and larger pastures.

    Both place and time were changed, and I dwelt nearer to those parts
10 of the universe and to those eras in history which had most attracted me. Where I lived was as far off as many a region viewed nightly by astronomers. We are wont to imagine rare and delectable[58] places in some remote and more celestial corner of the system, behind the constellation of Cassiopeia's Chair,[59] far from noise and disturbance. I
15 discovered that my house actually had its site in such a withdrawn, but forever new and unprofaned,[60] part of the universe. If it were worth the while to settle in those parts near to the Pleiades or the Hyades, to Aldebaran or Altair,[61] then I was really there, or at an equal remoteness from the life which I had left behind, dwindled and twinkling with as
20 fine a ray to my nearest neighbor, and to be seen only in moonless nights by him. Such was that part of creation where I had squatted;

---

56) all the roving families of men: 방황하는 모든 인간 가족들

57) Damodara: 다모다라. 힌두교의 신 크리슈나의 또 다른 이름.

58) delectable: 매력이 넘치는

59) Cassiopeia's Chair: 카시오페이아의 의자

60) unprofaned: 더럽혀지지 않은, 신성을 모독당하지 않은

61) near to the Pleiades or the Hyades, to Aldebaran or Altair: 플레이아데스 성좌, 히아데스 성좌, 알데
    바란 성이나 견우성 가까이에

¹ "There was a shepherd that did live,

And held his thoughts as high

As were the mounts whereon his flocks

Did hourly feed him by."

⁵

What should we think of the shepherd's life if his flocks⁶²⁾ always wandered to higher pastures than his thoughts?

Every morning was a cheerful invitation to make my life of equal simplicity, and I may say innocence, with Nature herself. I have been as ¹⁰ sincere a worshipper of Aurora⁶³⁾ as the Greeks. I got up early and bathed in the pond; that was a religious exercise, and one of the best things which I did. They say that characters were engraven on the bathing tub of King Tching‐thang to this effect: "Renew thyself completely each day; do it again, and again, and forever again." I can understand that. ¹⁵ Morning brings back the heroic ages. I was as much affected by the faint burn of a mosquito making its invisible and unimaginable tour through my apartment at earliest dawn, when I was sailing with door and windows open, as I could be by any trumpet that ever sang of fame. It was Homer's requiem; itself an Iliad and Odyssey in the air, singing ²⁰ its own wrath and wanderings. There was something cosmical about it; a standing advertisement, till forbidden, of the everlasting vigor and fertility of the world.⁶⁴⁾ The morning, which is the most memorable season of the day, is the awakening hour. Then there is least somnolence⁶⁵⁾

---

62) his flocks: 그의 양떼들

63) Aurora: 여명의 여신. 그리스 신화의 에오스(Eos)에 해당.

64) of the everlasting vigor and fertility of the world: 세계의 끝없는 생장력과 번식력에 대한

65) somnolence: 졸림, 비몽사몽

1 in us; and for an hour, at least, some part of us awakes which slumbers all the rest of the day and night. Little is to be expected of that day, if it can be called a day, to which we are not awakened by our Genius, but by the mechanical nudgings of some servitor, are not awakened by our own

5 newly acquired force and aspirations from within, accompanied by the undulations of celestial music, instead of factory bells, and a fragrance filling the air — to a higher life than we fell asleep from; and thus the darkness bear its fruit, and prove itself to be good, no less than the light.[66] That man who does not believe that each day contains an earlier,

10 more sacred, and auroral hour than he has yet profaned, has despaired of life, and is pursuing a descending and darkening way. After a partial cessation of his sensuous life,[67] the soul of man, or its organs rather, are reinvigorated each day, and his Genius tries again what noble life it can make. All memorable events, I should say, transpire[68] in morning time

15 and in a morning atmosphere. The Vedas[69] say, "All intelligences awake with the morning." Poetry and art, and the fairest and most memorable of the actions of men, date from such an hour. All poets and heroes, like Memnon,[70] are the children of Aurora, and emit their music at sunrise. To him whose elastic and vigorous thought keeps pace with the sun,

20 the day is a perpetual morning. It matters not what the clocks say or the attitudes and labors of men. Morning is when I am awake and there is a dawn in me. Moral reform is the effort to throw off sleep. Why is

---

66) no less than the light: 빛에 못지않게

67) a partial cessation of his sensuous life: 인간의 감각적인 생활의 부분적 중단, 즉 수면

68) transpire: 일어나다, 발생하다

69) The Vedas: 베다(고대 브라만교 경전)

70) Memnon: 멤논. 그리스 신화에 나오는 에티오피아의 왕. 새벽의 여신인 에오스의 아들로 이집트에 있는 그의 석상이 아침 햇살에 울림소리를 낸다는 전설이 있다.

1 it that men give so poor an account of their day if they have not been
slumbering? They are not such poor calculators.[71] If they had not been
overcome with drowsiness, they would have performed something. The
millions are awake enough for physical labor; but only one in a million
5 is awake enough for effective intellectual exertion, only one in a hundred
millions to a poetic or divine life. To be awake is to be alive. I have never
yet met a man who was quite awake. How could I have looked him in
the face?

We must learn to reawaken and keep ourselves awake, not by
10 mechanical aids, but by an infinite expectation of the dawn, which does
not forsake[72] us in our soundest sleep. I know of no more encouraging
fact than the unquestionable ability of man to elevate his life by a
conscious endeavor. It is something to be able to paint a particular
picture, or to carve a statue, and so to make a few objects beautiful; but it
15 is far more glorious to carve and paint the very atmosphere and medium
through which we look, which morally we can do. To affect the quality of
the day,[73] that is the highest of arts. Every man is tasked to make his life,
even in its details, worthy of the contemplation of his most elevated and
critical hour. If we refused, or rather used up, such paltry information as
20 we get, the oracles would distinctly inform us how this might be done.

I went to the woods because I wished to live deliberately, to front
only the essential facts of life, and see if I could not learn what it had
to teach, and not, when I came to die, discover that I had not lived. I
did not wish to live what was not life, living is so dear; nor did I wish to

---

71) They are not such poor calculators: 그들은 그렇게 계산에 서툰 사람들은 아니다

72) forsake: 저버리다

73) To affect the quality of the day: 하루의 본질에 영향을 미치는 것

practise resignation, unless it was quite necessary. I wanted to live deep and suck out all the marrow of life, to live so sturdily and Spartan – like as to put to rout[74] all that was not life, to cut a broad swath and shave close, to drive life into a corner, and reduce it to its lowest terms, and, if it proved to be mean, why then to get the whole and genuine meanness of it, and publish its meanness to the world; or if it were sublime, to know it by experience, and be able to give a true account of it in my next excursion. For most men, it appears to me, are in a strange uncertainty about it, whether it is of the devil or of God, and have *somewhat hastily* concluded that it is the chief end of man here to "glorify God and enjoy him forever."

Still we live meanly, like ants; though the fable tells us that we were long ago changed into men; like pygmies we fight with cranes;[75] it is error upon error, and clout upon clout, and our best virtue has for its occasion a superfluous and evitable wretchedness. Our life is frittered away by detail. An honest man has hardly need to count more than his ten fingers, or in extreme cases he may add his ten toes, and lump the rest. Simplicity, simplicity, simplicity! I say, let your affairs be as two or three, and not a hundred or a thousand; instead of a million count half a dozen, and keep your accounts on your thumb – nail. In the midst of this chopping sea of civilized life, such are the clouds and storms and quicksands and thousand – and – one items to be allowed for, that a man has to live, if he would not founder[76] and go to the bottom and not make

---

74) put to rout: 완패시키다

75) pygmies: 난쟁이 부족. 호머의 『일리아드』는 트로이 사람들을 난쟁이 부족과 싸우는 학들로 비유
했다.

76) founder: 침몰하다

1   his port at all, by dead reckoning,[77] and he must be a great calculator indeed who succeeds. Simplify, simplify. Instead of three meals a day, if it be necessary eat but one; instead of a hundred dishes, five; and reduce other things in proportion. Our life is like a German Confederacy,[78]

5   made up of petty states, with its boundary forever fluctuating, so that even a German cannot tell you how it is bounded at any moment. The nation itself, with all its so‐called internal improvements, which, by the way are all external and superficial, is just such an unwieldy and overgrown establishment, cluttered with furniture and tripped up by its

10   own traps, ruined by luxury and heedless expense, by want of calculation and a worthy aim, as the million households in the land; and the only cure for it, as for them, is in a rigid economy, a stern and more than Spartan simplicity of life and elevation of purpose. It lives too fast. Men think that it is essential that the *Nation* have commerce, and export ice,

15   and talk through a telegraph, and ride thirty miles an hour, without a doubt, whether *they* do or not; but whether we should live like baboons or like men, is a little uncertain. If we do not get out sleepers,[79] and forge rails, and devote days and nights to the work, but go to tinkering upon our *lives* to improve *them*, who will build railroads? And if railroads are

20   not built, how shall we get to heaven in season?[80] But if we stay at home and mind our business, who will want railroads? We do not ride on the railroad; it rides upon us. Did you ever think what those sleepers are

---

77) dead reckoning: 추측 항법. 위치를 알고 있는 출발점에서 현재 위치까지의 여행 거리 및 방향을 계산하여 현재의 위치를 추적하는 위치추적기술.

78) German Confederacy: 독일연방은 1871년 비스마르크가 통일하기 전까지 39개의 군소국가가 난립해 있었다.

79) sleeper: (철도의) 침목

80) in season: 때가 왔을 때

that underlie the railroad? Each one is a man, an Irishman, or a Yankee man. The rails are laid on them, and they are covered with sand, and the cars run smoothly over them. They are sound sleepers, I assure you. And every few years a new lot is laid down and run over; so that, if some have the pleasure of riding on a rail, others have the misfortune to be ridden upon.[81] And when they run over a man that is walking in his sleep, a supernumerary[82] sleeper in the wrong position, and wake him up, they suddenly stop the cars, and make a hue and cry[83] about it, as if this were an exception. I am glad to know that it takes a gang of men for every five miles to keep the sleepers down and level in their beds as it is, for this is a sign that they may sometime get up again.

Why should we live with such hurry and waste of life? We are determined to be starved before we are hungry. Men say that a stitch in time saves nine,[84] and so they take a thousand stitches today to save nine tomorrow. As for *work*, we haven't any of any consequence. We have the Saint Vitus' dance,[85] and cannot possibly keep our heads still. If I should only give a few pulls at the parish bell – rope, as for a fire, that is, without setting the bell, there is hardly a man on his farm in the outskirts of Concord, notwithstanding that press of engagements which was his excuse so many times this morning, nor a boy, nor a woman, I might almost say, but would forsake all and follow that sound, not mainly to save property from the flames, but, if we will confess the truth,

---

81) be ridden upon: 깔리다

82) supernumerary: 여분의

83) hue and cry: 강력한 항의

84) a stitch in time saves nine: 제때의 바늘 한 번이 아홉 바느질을 덜어준다. (호미로 막을 것을 가래로 막는다.)

85) Saint Vitus' dance: 무도병

1 much more to see it burn, since burn it must, and we, be it known, did not set it on fire — or to see it put out, and have a hand in it, if that is done as handsomely; yes, even if it were the parish church itself. Hardly a man takes a half‑hour's nap after dinner, but when he wakes he holds

5 up his head and asks, "What's the news?" as if the rest of mankind had stood his sentinels. Some give directions to be waked every half‑hour, doubtless for no other purpose; and then, to pay for it, they tell what they have dreamed. After a night's sleep the news is as indispensable as the breakfast. "Pray tell me anything new that has happened to a man

10 anywhere on this globe," — and he reads it over his coffee and rolls, that a man has had his eyes gouged out[86] this morning on the Wachito River; never dreaming the while that he lives in the dark unfathomed mammoth cave of this world, and has but the rudiment of an eye himself.

    For my part, I could easily do without the post‑office. I think that

15 there are very few important communications made through it. To speak critically, I never received more than one or two letters in my life — I wrote this some years ago — that were worth the postage. The penny‑post[87] is, commonly, an institution through which you seriously offer a man that penny for his thoughts which is so often safely offered in jest.[88]

20 And I am sure that I never read any memorable news in a newspaper. If we read of one man robbed, or murdered, or killed by accident, or one house burned, or one vessel wrecked, or one steamboat blown up, or one cow run over on the Western Railroad, or one mad dog killed, or one lot of grasshoppers in the winter — we never need read of another.

---

86) gouge out: (눈알을) 후벼내다

87) penny‑post: 1페니 우편제

88) in jest: 농담으로

One is enough. If you are acquainted with the principle, what do you care for a myriad instances and applications? To a philosopher all news, as it is called, is gossip, and they who edit and read it are old women over their tea. Yet not a few are greedy after this gossip. There was such a rush, as I hear, the other day at one of the offices to learn the foreign news by the last arrival, that several large squares of plate glass belonging to the establishment were broken by the pressure — news which I seriously think a ready wit might write a twelve‑month, or twelve years, beforehand with sufficient accuracy. As for Spain, for instance, if you know how to throw in Don Carlos and the Infanta, and Don Pedro and Seville and Granada, from time to time in the right proportions — they may have changed the names a little since I saw the papers — and serve up a bull‑fight when other entertainments fail, it will be true to the letter, and give us as good an idea of the exact state or ruin of things in Spain as the most succinct and lucid reports under this head in the newspapers: and as for England, almost the last significant scrap of news from that quarter was the revolution of 1649; and if you have learned the history of her crops for an average year, you never need attend to that thing again, unless your speculations are of a merely pecuniary character. If one may judge who rarely looks into the newspapers, nothing new does ever happen in foreign parts, a French revolution not excepted.[89]

What news! how much more important to know what that is which was never old! "Kieou‑he‑yu(great dignitary of the state of Wei)[90] sent a man to Khoung‑tseu[91] to know his news. Khoung‑tseu caused the messenger

---

89) a French revolution not excepted: 프랑스에서 자주 일어나는 혁명을 포함해서

90) Kieou‑he‑yu(great dignitary of the state of Wei): 거백옥. 위나라의 고위 관리

91) Khoung‑tseu: 공자

¹ to be seated near him, and questioned him in these terms: What is your master doing? The messenger answered with respect: My master desires to diminish the number of his faults, but he cannot come to the end of them. The messenger being gone, the philosopher remarked: What

⁵ a worthy messenger! What a worthy messenger!" The preacher, instead of vexing the ears of drowsy farmers on their day of rest at the end of the week — for Sunday is the fit conclusion of an ill‑spent week, and not the fresh and brave beginning of a new one — with this one other draggle‑tail of a sermon, should shout with thundering voice, "Pause!

¹⁰ Avast! Why so seeming fast, but deadly slow?"

Shams and delusions are esteemed for soundest truths, while reality is fabulous. If men would steadily observe realities only, and not allow themselves to be deluded, life, to compare it with such things as we know, would be like a fairy tale and the Arabian Nights' Entertainments.

¹⁵ If we respected only what is inevitable and has a right to be, music and poetry would resound along the streets. When we are unhurried and wise, we perceive that only great and worthy things have any permanent and absolute existence, that petty fears and petty pleasures are but the shadow of the reality. This is always exhilarating and sublime. By closing

²⁰ the eyes and slumbering, and consenting to be deceived by shows, men establish and confirm their daily life of routine and habit everywhere,⁹²⁾ which still is built on purely illusory foundations. Children, who play life, discern its true law and relations more clearly than men, who fail to live it worthily, but who think that they are wiser by experience, that

²⁵ is, by failure. I have read in a Hindoo book, that "there was a king's son,

---

92) men establish and confirm their daily life of routine and habit everywhere: 사람들은 도처에 자신들의 인습적인 일상생활을 확립시킨다

who, being expelled in infancy from his native city, was brought up by a forester, and, growing up to maturity in that state, imagined himself to belong to the barbarous race with which he lived. One of his father's ministers having discovered him, revealed to him what he was, and the misconception of his character[93] was removed, and he knew himself to be a prince. So soul," continues the Hindoo philosopher, "from the circumstances in which it is placed, mistakes its own character, until the truth is revealed to it by some holy teacher, and then it knows itself to be *Brahme*." I perceive that we inhabitants of New England live this mean life that we do because our vision does not penetrate the surface of things. We think that that *is* which *appears* to be. If a man should walk through this town and see only the reality, where, think you, would the "Mill‐dam" go to? If he should give us an account of the realities he beheld there, we should not recognize the place in his description. Look at a meeting‐house,[94] or a court‐house, or a jail, or a shop, or a dwelling‐house, and say what that thing really is before a true gaze, and they would all go to pieces in your account of them.[95] Men esteem truth remote, in the outskirts of the system, behind the farthest star, before Adam and after the last man. In eternity there is indeed something true and sublime. But all these times and places and occasions are now and here. God himself culminates in the present moment, and will never be more divine in the lapse of all the ages. And we are enabled to apprehend at all what is sublime and noble only by the perpetual instilling and drenching of the reality that surrounds us. The universe constantly and

---

93) the misconception of his character: 그의 신분에 대한 오해

94) meeting‐house: 예배당

95) in your account of them: 그것들에 대해 말하는 도중

1 obediently answers to our conceptions; whether we travel fast or slow, the track is laid for us. Let us spend our lives in conceiving then. The poet or the artist never yet had so fair and noble a design but some of his posterity at least could accomplish it.

5   Let us spend one day as deliberately as Nature, and not be thrown off the track[96] by every nutshell and mosquito's wing that falls on the rails. Let us rise early and fast, or break fast, gently and without perturbation; let company come and let company go, let the bells ring and the children cry — determined to make a day of it. Why should we knock under[97]

10 and go with the stream? Let us not be upset and overwhelmed in that terrible rapid and whirlpool called a dinner, situated in the meridian shallows. Weather this danger[98] and you are safe, for the rest of the way is down hill. With unrelaxed nerves, with morning vigor, sail by it, looking another way, tied to the mast like Ulysses. If the engine whistles, let it

15 whistle till it is hoarse for its pains. If the bell rings, why should we run? We will consider what kind of music they are like. Let us settle ourselves, and work and wedge our feet downward through the mud and slush of opinion, and prejudice, and tradition, and delusion, and appearance, that alluvion[99] which covers the globe, through Paris and London, through

20 New York and Boston and Concord, through Church and State, through poetry and philosophy and religion, till we come to a hard bottom and rocks in place, which we can call *reality*, and say, This is, and no mistake;

---

96) be thrown off the track: 선로에서 탈선하다

97) knock under: 굴복하다, 항복하다

98) Weather this danger: 이 위험을 이겨내다

99) alluvion: 충적층

1 and then begin, having a *point d'appui*,[100] below freshet and frost and
fire,[101] a place where you might found a wall or a state, or set a lamp –
post safely, or perhaps a gauge, not a Nilometer, but a Realometer, that
future ages might know how deep a freshet of shams and appearances
5 had gathered from time to time.[102] If you stand right fronting and face
to face to a fact, you will see the sun glimmer on both its surfaces, as if it
were a cimeter,[103] and feel its sweet edge dividing you through the heart
and marrow, and so you will happily conclude your mortal career.[104] Be
it life or death, we crave only reality. If we are really dying, let us hear the
10 rattle in our throats[105] and feel cold in the extremities;[106] if we are alive,
let us go about our business.

Time is but the stream I go a – fishing in. I drink at it; but while
I drink I see the sandy bottom and detect how shallow it is. Its thin
current slides away, but eternity remains.[107] I would drink deeper; fish in
15 the sky, whose bottom is pebbly with stars. I cannot count one. I know
not the first letter of the alphabet. I have always been regretting that
I was not as wise as the day I was born. The intellect is a cleaver;[108] it
discerns and rifts its way into the secret of things.[109] I do not wish to be

---

100) *point d'appui:* 지점, 근거지, 거점

101) below freshet and frost and fire: 돌발홍수와 서리와 불 아래

102) that future ages might know how deep a freshet of shams and appearances had gathered from time
to time: 미래의 세대들이 가식과 겉치레의 홍수가 때때로 얼마나 깊게 모였는가를 알 수 있도록

103) as if it were a cimeter: 마치 그것이 아랍인의 신월도이기라도 한 것처럼

104) conclude your mortal career: 당신의 유한한 삶을 마치다

105) the rattle in our throats: 목 안에서의 가래 끓는 소리

106) extremities: 사지

107) Its thin current slides away, but eternity remains: 시간의 얕은 물은 흘러가 버리지만 영원은 남아
있다

108) cleaver: 식칼

109) it discerns and rifts its way into the secret of things: 그것은 사물의 비밀을 식별하고 그 길을 헤쳐

1 any more busy with my hands than is necessary. My head is hands and
   feet. I feel all my best faculties concentrated in it. My instinct tells me
   that my head is an organ for burrowing, as some creatures use their snout
   and fore paws, and with it I would mine and burrow my way through
5 these hills. I think that the richest vein is somewhere hereabouts; so by
   the divining－rod[110] and thin rising vapors I judge; and here I will begin
   to mine.

나아간다

110) divining－rod: (수맥 등을 찾는) 점 막대기

3

The San Francisco Earthquake
This chapter excerpted from Mark Twain's *Roughing It.*

Mark Twain[1]

1   A month afterward I enjoyed my first earthquake. It was one which was long called the "great" earthquake, and is doubtless so distinguished till this day. It was just after noon, on a bright October day. I was coming down Third Street. The only objects in motion anywhere in sight in that
5   thickly built and populous quarter, were a man in a buggy[2] behind me, and a street car wending[3] slowly up the cross street.[4] Otherwise, all was

---

1)   마크 트웨인(Mark Twain, 1835-1910): 본명은 새뮤얼 클레멘스(Samuel Clemens)로 "전 미국적 문학"을 만들어 낸 작가 중 한 명이다. 트웨인에게 미시시피강은 중요한데 이 강은 그에게 "온전한 실체"이고 "인간여정"에 대한 중요한 상징물로 이 강에서의 삶 그 자체가 그에게 영향을 주었다. 주요작품으로는 『유명한 멀리 뛰는 개구리』(*The Celebrated Jumping Frog*), 『톰 소여의 모험』(*Adventures of Tom Sawyer*), 『허클베리 핀의 모험』(*The Adventures of Huckleberry Finn*) 등이 있다. 그는 미국 민주주의의 위대한 소설 작가로 여겨지며, 그의 작품은 "많은 후기의 서부 작가들의 산실", "모든 미국 문학은 허클베리 핀으로부터 나온다."는 등의 찬사를 받았다. 그의 작품은 인간의 삶에서 직면하는 도덕적 문제, 민주주의에 관한 문제, 인간의 사악함에 대해 사유하게 하며, 미국인들이 갖고 있는 이상과 금욕 사이의 갈등에 대해서도 파헤친다.
2)   buggy: (말 한 필이 끄는, 1~2인용) 마차
3)   wend: (천천히) 가다
4)   cross street: (다른 도로와 교차하는) 교차 도로

solitude and a Sabbath[5] stillness. As I turned the corner, around a frame house[6], there was a great rattle and jar,[7] and it occurred to me that here was an item! — no doubt a fight in that house. Before I could turn and seek the door, there came a really terrific shock; the ground seemed to roll under me in waves, interrupted by a violent joggling up and down, and there was a heavy grinding noise as of brick houses rubbing together. I fell up against the frame house and hurt my elbow. I knew what it was, now, and from mere reportorial instinct, nothing else, took out my watch and noted the time of day; at that moment a third and still severer shock came, and as I reeled[8] about on the pavement trying to keep my footing, I saw a sight! The entire front of a tall four‑story brick building in Third street sprung outward like a door and fell sprawling across the street, raising a dust like a great volume of smoke! And here came the buggy — overboard went the man,[9] and in less time than I can tell it the vehicle was distributed in small fragments along three hundred yards of street.

One could have fancied that somebody had fired a charge of chair‑rounds and rags down the thoroughfare. The street car had stopped, the horses were rearing and plunging, the passengers were pouring out at both ends, and one fat man had crashed half way through a glass window on one side of the car, got wedged fast and was squirming[10] and screaming like an impaled[11] madman.

---

5) Sabbath: 안식일

6) a frame house: (판자를 댄) 목조 가옥

7) a great rattle and jar: 크게 덜커덕거리는 소리와 충격

8) reel: 비틀거리다, 휘청거리다

9) overboard went the man: = the man went overboard. 그 남자는 잔뜩 흥분했다

10) squirm: 꿈틀대다, 몹시 당혹해하다

11) impale: 찌르다

1   Every door, of every house, as far as the eye could reach, was vomiting a stream of human beings; and almost before one could execute a wink and begin another, there was a massed multitude of people stretching in endless procession down every street my position
5   commanded. Never was solemn solitude turned into teeming life quicker.

Of the wonders wrought by "the great earthquake," these were all that came under my eye; but the tricks it did, elsewhere, and far and wide over the town, made toothsome gossip for nine days.

The destruction of property was trifling — the injury to it was
10 wide‑spread and somewhat serious.

The "curiosities" of the earthquake were simply endless. Gentlemen and ladies who were sick, or were taking a siesta, or had dissipated till a late hour and were making up lost sleep, thronged into[12] the public streets in all sorts of queer apparel, and some without any at all. One
15 woman who had been washing a naked child, ran down the street holding it by the ankles as if it were a dressed turkey. Prominent citizens who were supposed to keep the Sabbath strictly, rushed out of saloons in their shirt‑sleeves, with billiard cues in their hands. Dozens of men with necks swathed in[13] napkins, rushed from barber ‑ shops, lathered[14]
20 to the eyes or with one cheek clean shaved and the other still bearing a hairy stubble. Horses broke from stables, and a frightened dog rushed up a short attic ladder and out on to a roof, and when his scare was over had not the nerve to[15] go down again the same way he had gone up.

---

12) throng into: 몰려들다, 우르르 들어가다

13) swathe in: ~로 싸다

14) lather: 비누거품 칠을 하다

15) have the nerve to ~: ~할 용기를 내다

1   A prominent editor flew down stairs, in the principal hotel, with nothing on but one brief undergarment — met a chambermaid,[16] and exclaimed:

"Oh, what shall I do! Where shall I go!"

5   She responded with naive serenity:

"If you have no choice, you might try a clothing–store!"

A certain foreign consul's lady was the acknowledged leader of fashion, and every time she appeared in anything new or extraordinary, the ladies in the vicinity made a raid on their husbands' purses and
10   arrayed themselves similarly. One man who had suffered considerably and growled accordingly, was standing at the window when the shocks came, and the next instant the consul's wife, just out of the bath, fled by with no other apology for clothing than — a bath‒towel! The sufferer rose superior to[17] the terrors of the earthquake, and said to his wife:

15   "Now that is something like! Get out your towel my dear!"

The plastering that fell from ceilings in San Francisco that day, would have covered several acres of ground. For some days afterward, groups of eyeing and pointing men stood about many a building, looking at long zig‒zag cracks that extended from the eaves to the ground. Four feet
20   of the tops of three chimneys on one house were broken square off and turned around in such a way as to completely stop the draft.

A crack a hundred feet long gaped open six inches wide in the middle of one street and then shut together again with such force, as to ridge up the meeting earth like a slender grave. A lady sitting in her
25   rocking and quaking parlor, saw the wall part at the ceiling, open and

---

16) chambermaid: 호텔의 객실 · 침실 담당 여종업원
17) rise superior to: ~을 초월하다, ~의 영향을 받지 않다

1 shut twice, like a mouth, and then — drop the end of a brick on the floor like a tooth. She was a woman easily disgusted with foolishness, and she arose and went out of there. One lady who was coming down stairs was astonished to see a bronze Hercules lean forward on its pedestal[18] as if
5 to strike her with its club. They both reached the bottom of the flight at the same time, — the woman insensible from the fright. Her child, born some little time afterward, was club‑footed.[19] However — on second thought, — if the reader sees any coincidence in this, he must do it at his own risk.[20]

10 The first shock brought down two or three huge organ‑pipes in one of the churches. The minister, with uplifted hands, was just closing the services. He glanced up, hesitated, and said:

"However, we will omit the benediction!"[21] — and the next instant there was a vacancy in the atmosphere where he had stood.

15 After the first shock, an Oakland minister said:

"Keep your seats! There is no better place to die than this." —

And added, after the third:

"But outside is good enough!" He then skipped out at the back door.

Such another destruction of mantel ornaments and toilet bottles as
20 the earthquake created, San Francisco never saw before. There was hardly a girl or a matron in the city but suffered losses of this kind. Suspended pictures were thrown down, but oftener still, by a curious freak of the earthquake's humor, they were whirled completely around with their

---

18) pedestal: 기둥
19) club‑footed: 내반족, 만곡족을 가진
20) at his own risk: 그의 책임하에
21) benediction: (축복의) 기도

1 faces to the wall! There was great difference of opinion, at first, as to the course or direction the earthquake traveled, but water that splashed out of various tanks and buckets settled that. Thousands of people were made so sea‑sick by the rolling and pitching of floors and streets that
5 they were weak and bed‑ridden for hours, and some few for even days afterward. — Hardly an individual escaped nausea entirely.

The queer earthquake–episodes that formed the staple San Francisco gossip for the next week would fill a much larger book than this, and so I will diverge from the subject.

4

On Umbrella Morals

Alfred George Gardiner[1]

1   A sharp shower came on as I walked along the Strand,[2] but I did not put up my umbrella. The truth is I couldn't put up my umbrella. The frame would not work for one thing, and if it had worked, I would not have put the thing up, for I would no more be seen under such a

5   travesty[3] of an umbrella than Falstaff[4] would be seen marching through Coventry[5] with his regiment of ragamuffins.[6] The fact is, the umbrella is not my umbrella at all. It is the umbrella of some person who I hope will read these lines. He has got my silk umbrella. I have got the cotton one

---

1) 앨프리드 조지 가디너(Alfred George Gardiner, 1865-1946): 영국 저널리스트, 편집자 겸 저자. 그는 1915년부터 필명으로 『별』(*The Star*)에 기고했다. 그의 글은 일정하게 우아하고 유머러스하다. 그는 에세이에서 삶의 기본적 진리를 가르친다. 작품으로는 『사회의 기둥』(*Pillars of Society*), 『해변의 자갈』(*Pebbles on the Shore*), 『바람의 많은 고랑과 잎』(*Many Furrows and Leaves in the Wind*) 등이 있다.

2) the Strand: 스트랜드가

3) travesty: 졸렬한 모방

4) Falstaff: 폴스타프. 셰익스피어의 『헨리 4세』(*Henry IV*)와 『윈저의 즐거운 아낙네들』(*The Merry Wives of Windsor*)에 등장하는 쾌활하고 재치 있는 허풍쟁이 뚱뚱보 기사.

5) Coventry: 코번트리[영국 워릭셔(Warwickshire) 지방의 도시]

6) with his regiment of ragamuffins: 남루한 차림의 일단의 군대를 이끌고

1   he left in exchange. I imagine him flaunting along the Strand under my umbrella, and throwing a scornful glance at the fellow who was carrying his abomination[7] and getting wet into the bargain.[8] I daresay the rascal chuckled as he eyed the said abomination. "Ah," he said gaily to himself, "I

5   did you in that time, old boy. I know that thing. It won't open for nuts.[9] And it folds up like a sack. Now, this umbrella...."

    But I leave him to his unrighteous communings. He is one of those people who have what I may call an umbrella conscience. You know the sort of person I mean. He would never put his hand in another's pocket,

10   or forge a cheque or rob a till — not even if he had the chance. But he will swop[10] umbrellas, or forget to return a book, or take a rise out of the railway company.[11] In fact he is a thoroughly honest man who allows his honesty the benefit of the doubt.[12] Perhaps he takes your umbrella at random from the barber's stand. He knows he can't get a worse one than

15   his own. He may get a better. He doesn't look at it very closely until he is well on his way. Then, "Dear me! I've taken the wrong umbrella," he says, with an air of surprise, for he likes really to feel that he has made a mistake. "Ah, well, it's no use going back now. He'd be gone. And I've left him mine!"

20   It is thus that we play hide‐and‐seek with our own conscience. It is not enough not to be found out by others; we refuse to be found out

---

7)   abomination: 혐오스러운 것

8)   into the bargain: 또한, 게다가

9)   for nuts: 아무리 해도, 전혀, 조금도

10)   swop: = swap. (어떤 것을 주고 그 대신 다른 것으로) 바꾸다

11)   take a rise out of the railway company: 철도회사를 약 올리다. take a rise out of: ~을 굴복시키다, 한 방 먹이다

12)   allow his honesty the benefit of the doubt: (증거 불충분의 경우) 그의 정직에 유리하게 해석하다, 정직의 의심스러운 점은 선의로 해석하다

¹ by ourselves. Quite impeccable¹³⁾ people, people who ordinarily seem unspotted from the world, are afflicted with¹⁴⁾ umbrella morals. It was a well‑known preacher who was found dead in a first‑class railway carriage with a third‑class ticket in his pocket.

⁵   And as for books, who has any morals where they are concerned? I remember some years ago the library of a famous divine and literary critic, who had died, being sold. It was a splendid library of rare books, chiefly concerned with seventeenth‑century writers, about whom he was a distinguished authority. Multitudes of the books had the marks of ¹⁰ libraries all over the country. He had borrowed them and never found a convenient opportunity of returning them. They clung to him like precedents¹⁵⁾ to law. Yet he was a holy man and preached admirable sermons, as I can bear witness.¹⁶⁾ And, if you press me on the point, I shall have to own that it is hard to part with¹⁷⁾ a book you have come to ¹⁵ love.

    Indeed, the only sound rule about books is that adopted by the man who was asked by a friend to lend him a certain volume. "I'm sorry," he said, "but I can't." "Haven't you got it?" asked the other. "Yes, I've got it," he said, "but I make it a rule never to lend books. You see, nobody ever ²⁰ returns them. I know it is so from my own experience. Here, come with me." And he led the way to his library. "There," said he, "four thousand volumes. Every‑one‑of‑'em‑borrowed." No, never lend books. You

---

13) impeccable: 완전무결한, 흠 잡을 데 없는
14) are afflicted with: ~에 시달리다, ~에 대해 고민하다
15) precedent: 선례, 판례
16) bear witness: 증명하다, 증언하다
17) part with: (특히 자기가 계속 갖고 있고 싶은) ~을 주다

1 can't trust your dearest friend there. I know. Where is that Gil Blas gone? Eh? And that Silvio Pellico? And.... But why continue the list.... He knows. HE KNOWS.

And hats. There are people who will exchange hats. Now that is
5 unpardonable.[18] That goes outside that dim borderland of conscience where honesty and dishonesty dissemble.[19] No one can put a strange hat on without being aware of the fact. Yet it is done. I once hung a silk hat up in the smoking – room of the House of Commons.[20] When I wanted it, it was gone. And there was no silk hat left in its place. I had to go out
10 bareheaded through Palace Yard and Whitehall to buy another. I have often wondered who was the gentleman who put my hat on and carried his own in his hand. Was he a Tory?[21] Was he a Radical?[22] It can't have been a Labour man,[23] for no Labour man could put a silk hat on in a moment of abstraction.[24] The thing would scorch his brow. Fancy Will
15 Crooks in a silk hat![25] One would as soon dare to play with the fancy of the Archbishop of Canterbury in a bowler[26] — a thought which seems almost impious. It is possible, of course, that the gentleman who took my silk umbrella did really make a mistake. Perhaps if he knew the owner he would return it with his compliments. The thing has been done. Let

---

18) unpardonable: 용서할 수 없는, 변명의 여지가 없는

19) dissemble: (진짜 감정 · 의도를) 숨기다, 가식적으로 꾸미다

20) the House of Commons: 하원

21) a Tory: (영국의 보수당인) 토리당원

22) a Radical: 급진파 사람

23) a Labour man: 노동당원

24) in a moment of abstraction: 깜박 잊고서, 정신이 딴 데 팔려 있는 사이에

25) Fancy Will Crooks in a silk hat: 윌 크룩스가 실크 모자를 쓴 모습을 상상해 보라. Will Crooks: the 1899 London Docks Strike의 리더 중 한 명.

26) the Archbishop of Canterbury in a bowler: 캔터베리 대주교가 중산모를 쓴 모습

1 me give an illustration. I have myself exchanged umbrellas — often. I hope I have done it honestly, but one can never be quite sure. Indeed, now I come to think of it,[27] that silk umbrella itself was not mine. It was one of a long series of exchanges in which I had sometimes gained
5 and sometimes lost. My most memorable exchange was at a rich man's house where I had been invited to dine with some politicians. It was summer – time, and the weather being dry I had not occasion for some days afterwards to carry an umbrella. Then one day a sensation reigned[28] in our household. There had been discovered in the umbrella – stand
10 an umbrella with a gold band and a gold tassel,[29] and the name of a certain statesman engraved upon it. There had never been such a super – umbrella in our house before. Before its golden splendours we were at once humbled and terrified — humbled by its magnificence, terrified by its presence. I felt as though I had been caught in the act of stealing the
15 British Empire.[30] I wrote a hasty letter to the owner, told him I admired his politics, but had never hoped to steal his umbrella; then hailed a cab, and took the umbrella and the note to the nearest dispatch office.[31]

He was very nice about it, and in returning my own umbrella took all the blame on himself. "What," he said, "between the noble – looking
20 gentleman who thrust a hat on my head, and the second noble – looking gentleman who handed me a coat, and the third noble – looking gentleman who put an umbrella in my hand, and the fourth noble –

---

27) now I come to think of it: 이제 생각해보니

28) a sensation reigned: 소동이 벌어졌다

29) tassel: 술(여러 가닥의 실)

30) as though I had been caught in the act of stealing the British Empire: 대영제국을 훔치려다 잡힌 것 처럼

31) dispatch office: 긴급 공문 취급소, 속달 화물 취급소

1 looking gentleman who flung me into a carriage, I hadn't the least idea what I was taking. I was too bewildered by all the noble flunkeys[32] to refuse anything that was offered me."

Be it observed,[33] it was the name on the umbrella that saved the
5 situation in this case. That is the way to circumvent[34] the man with an umbrella conscience. I see him eyeing his exchange with a secret joy;[35] then he observes the name and address and his solemn conviction that he is an honest man does the rest. After my experience today, I think I will engrave my name on my umbrella. But not on that baggy thing standing
10 in the corner. I do not care who relieves me of that. It is anybody's for the taking.[36]

---

32) flunkeys: (제복을 입은) 하인들
33) Be it observed: 앞에서 본 것처럼
34) circumvent: 피하다
35) with a secret joy: 남몰래 기뻐하면서
36) for the taking: (원한다면) 마음대로, 무료로

5

The Special Theory of Relativity
Physical Meaning of Geometrical Propositions

Albert Einstein[1]

1   In your schooldays most of you who read this book made acquaintance with the noble building of Euclid's geometry,[2] and you remember — perhaps with more respect than love — the magnificent structure, on the lofty staircase[3] of which you were chased about for

5   uncounted hours by conscientious teachers.[4] By reason of our past experience, you would certainly regard everyone with disdain[5] who should pronounce even the most out–of–the–way proposition[6] of this

---

1) 알베르트 아인슈타인(Albert Einstein, 1879-1955): 독일 태생의 이론물리학자로 광양자설, 브라운 운동의 이론, 특수상대성이론을 연구하여 1905년에 발표하였으며, 1916년 일반상대성이론을 발표 하였다. 미국의 원자폭탄 연구인 맨해튼계획의 시초를 이루었으며, 통일장이론을 더욱 발전시켰다. 위의 본문은 1916년 발표된 그의 저서 『상대성이론』(*Relativity: The Special and General Theory*)의 한 부분이다.

2) Euclid's geometry: 유클리드의 기하학. 유클리드(Euclid)는 기원전 300년경의 알렉산드리아의 기 하학자.

3) lofty staircase: 높은 계단

4) conscientious teachers: 성실한 교사들, 열심히 가르치는 교사들

5) with disdain: 경멸을 가지고, 경멸의 눈으로

6) the most out–of–the–way proposition: 가장 특이한 명제

¹ science to be untrue. But perhaps this feeling of proud certainty would leave you immediately if some one were to ask you: "What, then, do you mean by the assertion that these propositions are true?" Let us proceed to give this question a little consideration.[7]

⁵   Geometry sets out form certain conceptions such as "plane," "point," and "straight line,"[8] with which we are able to associate more or less definite ideas, and from certain simple propositions (axioms)[9] which, in virtue of these ideas, we are inclined to accept as "true." Then, on the basis of a logical process, the justification of which we feel ourselves
¹⁰ compelled to admit, all remaining propositions are shown to follow from those axioms, i.e. they are proven. A proposition is then correct ("true") when it has been derived in the recognised manner from the axioms. The question of "truth" of the individual geometrical propositions is thus reduced to one of the "truth" of the axioms. Now it has long been
¹⁵ known that the last question is not only unanswerable by the methods of geometry, but that it is in itself entirely without meaning. We cannot ask whether it is true that only one straight line goes through two points. We can only say that Euclidean geometry deals with things called "straight lines," to each of which is ascribed the property of being uniquely
²⁰ determined by two points situated on it. The concept "true" does not tally with the assertions of pure geometry, because by the word "true" we are eventually in the habit of designating always the correspondence with a "real" object; geometry, however, is not concerned with the relation of the ideas involved in it to objects of experience, but only with the logical

---

7)   give this question a little consideration: 이 문제에 대한 고찰을 하다
8)   "plane," "point," and "straight line": 면, 점, 직선
9)   axiom: 자명한 이치, 공리

1 connection[10] of these ideas among themselves.

It is not difficult to understand why, in spite of this, we feel constrained to call the propositions of geometry "true." Geometrical ideas correspond to more or less exact objects in nature, and these last are

5 undoubtedly the exclusive cause of the genesis of those ideas.[11] Geometry ought to refrain from such a course, in order to give to its structure the largest possible logical unity. The practice, for example, of seeing in a "distance" two marked positions on a practically rigid body is something which is lodged deeply in our habit of thought. We are accustomed

10 further to regard three points as being situated on a straight line, if their apparent positions can be made to coincide for observation with one eye, under suitable choice of our place of observation.

If, in pursuance of our habit of thought,[12] we now supplement[13] the propositions of Euclidean geometry by the single proposition that

15 two points on a practically rigid body always correspond to the same distance (line–interval),[14] independently of any changes in position to which we may subject the body, the propositions of Euclidean geometry then resolve themselves into propositions on the possible relative position of practically rigid bodies. Geometry which has been supplemented

20 in this way is then to be treated as a branch of physics.[15] We can now legitimately ask as to the "truth" of geometrical propositions interpreted in this way, since we are justified in asking whether these propositions

---

10) logical connection: 논리적 관계

11) the exclusive cause of the genesis of those ideas: 기하학적 관념을 생성시킨 배타적인 원인

12) in pursuance of our habit of thought: 우리의 사고습관에 따라

13) supplement: 보충하다

14) line – interval: 선 간격

15) a branch of physics: 물리학의 한 분과

1 are satisfied for those real things we have associated with the geometrical ideas. In less exact terms we can express this by saying that by the "truth" of a geometrical proposition in this sense we understand its validity for a construction with rule and compasses.

5   Of course the conviction of the "truth" of geometrical propositions in this sense is founded exclusively on rather incomplete experience. For the present we shall assume the "truth" of the geometrical propositions, then at a later stage (in the general theory of relativity) we shall see that this "truth" is limited, and we shall consider the extent of its limitation.

Part **III**

Short Story

1

The Invisible Lover
The Story of Cupid and Psyche Told by Apuleius

Lucius Apuleius[1]

1   Once upon a time a king and queen had three very beautiful daughters, but much the most beautiful was the youngest, Psyche. People came from many lands to admire her, in the belief that she was Venus,[2] or had succeeded her as goddess of love. This caused the rites of Venus

5   to be neglected, and the goddess angrily bade her son Cupid[3] wound Psyche so as to make her fall in love with some completely degraded creature. Venus then went on her way across the sea to her sacred island of Cyprus.[4] But Psyche received no benefit from all the honours paid to

---

1) 루치우스 아풀레이우스(Lucius Apuleius, 123-170): 북 아프리카의 철학자 · 수사학자. 카르타고 와 아테네에서 교육을 받고 지식이 많은 학자로 존경을 받았다. 이집트를 여행하고 나서 쓴 『변명』 은 그때의 풍습을 살필 수 있는 매우 재미있는 책이다. 그 밖에도 예리한 풍자 이야기 『황금 당나귀』 (*Asiuns Aureus*)등의 걸작이 있다.

2) Venus: 비너스. 그리스 신화에 나오는 사랑과 미(美)와 풍요(豊饒)의 여신. 아프로디테 등과 동일시 되면서 모성과 아름다운 여성성을 상징하게 되었다.

3) Cupid: 큐피드. 로마 신화 속 사랑의 신. 비너스의 아들로 아모르(Amor, 사랑)라고도 한다. 아풀레 이우스의 『황금 당나귀』에는 미소녀 프시케와의 유명한 연애 이야기가 있다.

4) Cyprus: 키프로스 섬, 혹은 사이프러스 섬(지중해 동부의 섬; 공화국). 지중해 동부에 있는 섬나라로

1 her. Her sisters had married kings, yet no one courted Psyche, and she sat
   alone at home, feeling ill and miserable.

     Her father, suspecting divine anger, inquired from the oracle
   of Apollo[5] at Miletus[6] where he might find a husband for her. The
5 answer, however, came that Psyche's husband was no human being but
   a winged serpent of whom even Jupiter[7] was afraid ; she must put on
   black mourning and go to a mountain–top for her deathly marriage. To
   the accompaniment of funeral music and lamentation, she headed the
   procession like a woman going to her grave.

10   Sending away her parents, who shut themselves in their palace to
   grieve, Psyche climbed to the very top of the hill. A breeze came, and
   lifted her off the ground, and carried her down to a valley beneath, where
   she found herself laid upon a bed of flowery grass. After sleeping for a
   while there, she rose and walked beside a stream into the depths of a
15 wood, and she came upon a palace so radiant with gold and gems and
   precious woods that she knew it was a god's. When she finally ventured
   to cross the threshold of this heavenly abode,[8] Psyche found within its
   doors unbelievably valuable treasures, with no guard to watch over them.

     But the voice of an unseen maidservant guided her to her bedroom

---

소아시아와 인접해 있다. 지리적 중요성 때문에 제1차 세계대전 개전 시 영국의 식민지가 되었다.
그 후 1925년 로잔조약으로 영국의 정식 직할 식민지가 되었지만, 그리스와 터키의 갈등을 잠재우
기 위해 1959년 영국이 런던에서 미국의 중재 아래 키프로스 독립협정에 서명하였다. 그 후 1960년
8월 16일 정식으로 독립을 선언하였다.

5) Apollo: 아폴론. 그리스 신화에 나오는 올림포스 12신 중 한 명으로 태양, 음악, 시, 예언, 의술, 궁술
을 관장하는 신이다. 델포이 섬에 있는 아폴론 신전은 앞일을 예언하는 신탁으로 유명하다. 종종 '밝
게 빛나는 자'라는 뜻을 지닌 '포이보스'라는 별칭으로 불린다.

6) Miletus: 밀레토스[소아시아 이오니아(그리스 아테네를 중심으로 하는 지방)의 고대 도시]

7) Jupiter: 유피테르. 그리스 신화의 제우스에 해당한다.

8) abode: 거처, 주소, 체류

¹ and bathroom. First she found her bedroom and dozed off again for a while, then she went to the bath, where invisible hands undressed her, washed her, anointed her and dressed her again in her bridal costume. As she wandered out of the bathroom she noticed a semi–circular table ⁵ with a comfortable chair in front of it; it was laid for a banquet, though there was nothing yet on it to eat or drink. She sat down expectantly — and at once nectarous[9] wines and appetizing dishes appeared by magic, floating up to her of their own accord. She saw nobody at all, the waiters were mere voices, and when someone came in and sang and someone ¹⁰ else accompanied him on the lyre, she saw neither of them, nor the lyre either. Then a whole invisible choir burst into song.

When this delightful banquet was over, Psyche thought it must be about time to go to bed, so she went to her bedroom again and undressed and lay awake for a long time. Towards midnight she heard a ¹⁵ gentle whispering near her, and began to feel lonely and scared. Anything might happen in a vast uninhabited[10] place like this, and she had fears for her chastity.[11] But no, it was the whisper of her unknown husband. He came and lay with her, without being seen, and left before daybreak; and the next two nights he visited her again. Meanwhile Psyche's ²⁰ parents, joined by her sisters, were still lamenting her as lost, but her unseen husband warned her not to answer her sisters if she heard them mourning. When, however, she pleaded to be allowed their company, he reluctantly relented,[12] but on the condition that she must not, however

---

9)   nectarous: 과즙의, 감미로운
10) uninhabited: 사람이 살지 않는, 무인의
11) chastity: (육체적) 순결
12) relent: 상냥스러워지다, 약해지다, 누그러지다

1 much they importuned[13] her, try to find out what he looked like. So the West Wind brought her sisters to the palace, and Psyche, drawing upon her imagination, told them her husband was a handsome young man with his first beard, who liked hunting.

5 When they were alone with one another on their way back to their father's house, the elder sisters indulged in[14] jealousy. One of them complained that her own husband was bald, feeble and miserly. The other grumbled that she was married to a man who suffered so badly from sciatica[15] and gout[16] that his wife was no more than[17] a nurse,

10 whose hands were ruined by his plasters[18] and poultices.[19] So they returned to their homes, full of malicious intentions; and now Psyche's husband again warned her of the danger from them, this time with the assurance that she was to have a baby by him — a god if she kept his secret, but only a mortal if she talked.

15 But next time she saw her sisters, Psyche was not sufficiently on her guard. She was very simple–minded and, forgetting what story she had told them before, invented a new one. She said that he was a middle– aged merchant from the next province, very rich, with slightly grizzled hair. Then, breaking the conversation off short, she loaded them with

20 valuable presents and sent them away. As they rode home, the younger

---

13) importune: 성가시게 조르다

14) indulge in: (특히 좋지 않다고 여겨지는 것을) 마음껏 하다

15) sciatica: 좌골 신경통, 좌골통

16) gout: 통풍(痛風), 응혈

17) no more than: = only. 단지 ~에 지나지 않다, ~일 뿐

18) plaster: 고약, 경고(硬膏)

19) poultice: 찜질약, 습포

1 sister said: "Now, what do you make of[20] the monstrous lies she tells us? First the silly creature says that her husband is a very young man with a downy beard, and then she says that he's middle-aged with grizzled hair! Quick work, eh? You may depend upon it that the beast is either hiding 5 something from us, or else she doesn't know herself what her husband looks like." "Whatever the truth may be," said the elder sister, "we must ruin her as soon as possible."

And so, correctly guessing the unwelcome prospect that Psyche's baby was destined to be a god, they deliberately frightened her by 10 suggesting that her husband was a fiendish[21] reptile. Accordingly, at their proposal, next time she was in bed with him she got up and took a lamp, and took also a carving knife to kill him. But by the light she saw he was Cupid himself in all his glory. She tried the point of one of his arrows, which pricked her, and the lamp she was carrying spilt a drop of burning 15 oil upon his shoulder. He woke, and immediately departed from her, and flew to the top of a cypress-tree. After pausing there with a reproachful[22] message, he soared up into the air and was gone.

After vainly trying to down herself — the river set her ashore — Psyche wandered off in aimless misery, and came to the city where one 20 of her elder sisters lived. She told this woman what had happened, but deceitfully[23] added: "As he flew away, he said that he would have you in my place as his wife." So, like Psyche before her, the sister jumped off the rock too, shouting confidently: "Here I come, Cupid, a woman

---

20) what do you make of ~?: ~에 대해 어떻게 생각해?

21) fiendish: 사악한, 기괴한

22) reproachful: 비난하는

23) deceitfully: 속여서, 기만하여

¹ worthy of your love. West Wind, convey your mistress to the Palace at
once." Then she took a head–long leap; but she never reached the valley,
either dead or alive, because the rocks cut her to pieces as she fell and
scattered her flesh and guts all over the mountain–side. So she got what
⁵ she deserved, and the birds and beasts feasted on her remains. Soon
afterwards the other sister met with the same fate.

Meanwhile, in his mother's celestial house, Cupid lay groaning with
pain. Venus, who was bathing in the sea, was told of his affair by a sea–
gull, and furiously complained to her stepmother Juno²⁴⁾ and Ceres²⁵⁾
¹⁰ about what had happened; but they, in fear of cupid's arrows, tried to
excuse him. Psyche, looking everywhere for her lover, came to their
shrines²⁶⁾ for protection. But although they would have liked to help
her, they dared not offend Venus. After announcing a reward for anyone
who could find Psyche, Venus — through her servant Custom — soon
¹⁵ tracked her down. After two of her other women, Anxiety and Sadness,
had whipped the girl, the goddess leapt on her, tore her clothes to rags,²⁷⁾
pulled out handfuls of her hair, and shook her repeatedly.

Then she imposed a series of formidable²⁸⁾ tasks. First, before
nightfall, Psyche must sort out an enormous heap of wheat, barley,
²⁰ millet, lentils, beans and the seeds of poppy and vetch. "You look such
a dreadful sight, slave," said Venus, "that the only way that you are ever
likely to get a lover is by hard work" — and she flew off to a wedding–

---

24) Juno: 주노[주피터(Jupiter)의 아내로 결혼한 여성의 수호신; 그리스 신화의 헤라(Hera)]

25) Ceres: 케레스[풍작의 여신; 그리스 신화의 데메테르(Demeter)에 해당]

26) shrine: 성지, 사당

27) to rags: 갈기갈기

28) formidable: 가공할, 어마어마한

party, from which she returned at midnight, scented and slightly drunk. But Psyche, helped by an army of ants, had completed her task. She was then set a second and more dreadful task, of bringing Venus a piece of wool from some fiercely dangerous golden sheep on the bank of a stream.
5 But this too, with the help of a green reed, she was able to achieve, and she brought Venus back a whole lap–full[29] of the golden wool.

Yet even her performance of this second perilous task did not satisfy the goddess, who frowned and told her with a cruel smile: "Someone has been helping you again, that's quite clear. But now I'll put your courage
10 and prudence to a still severer test. Do you see the summit of that high mountain over there? You'll find that a dark–coloured stream cascades down its precipitous[30] sides into a gorge below and then floods the Stygian[31] marshes and feeds the hoarse River of Wailing. Here is a little jar. Go off at once and bring it back to me brimful of ice–cold water
15 fetched from the very middle of the cascade where it bursts out of the rock." Psyche was horrified by the fierce dragons guarding the stream, but Providence came to her aid and sent her Jupiter's eagle, which owed Cupid a debt of gratitude for helping him carry Ganymede[32] to heaven to be Jupiter's cup–bearer. With critical words for Psyche's silly simplicity,
20 the eagle took the jar and induced the stream to give up its water.

Declaring Psyche was a witch, Venus now bade her take a box down to the Underworld itself, and hand it to Proserpina,[33] with the request

---

29) lap－full: 앞치마 그득한 분량

30) precipitous: 가파른, 깎아지른 듯한

31) Stygian: (무섭도록) 새까만, 몹시 어두운

32) Ganymede: 가니메데스(제우스의 술 시중을 든 트로이의 미소년)

33) Proserpina: 프로세르피나[제우스와 케레스의 딸; 플루토(하데스)에게 납치되어 저승의 여왕이 됨]

1 that the queen should put a little of her beauty inside the box, and send
   it back for Venus, who had expended some of her own beauty in looking
   after her sick son, and needed further supplies for a theatre–party that
   evening. Psyche was now desperate, and went up a high tower, resolved
5 to throw herself from its top and reach the Underworld by killing herself.
   But the tower broke into speech, and dissuaded her. "Listen to me. The
   famous Greek city of Lacedaemon (Sparta) is not far from here. Go there
   at once and ask to be directed to Taenarus,[34] which is rather an out–
   of–the–way[35] place to find. It's on a peninsula to the south. Once you
10 get there you'll find one of the ventilation holes of the Underworld. Put
   your head through it and you'll see a road running down hill, but there'll
   be no traffic on it. Climb through at once and the road will lead you
   straight to Pluto's[36] palace. But don't forget to take with you two pieces
   of barley–bread soaked in honey water, one in each hand, and two coins
15 in your mouth.

   "When you have gone a good way along the road you'll meet a lame
   ass loaded with wood, and its lame driver will ask you to hand him some
   pieces of rope for tying up part of the load which the ass has dropped.
   Pass him by in silence. Then hurry forward until you reach the river of
20 the dead, where Charon[37] will at once ask you for his fee and ferry you
   across in his patched boat among crowds of ghosts. It seems that the God
   Avarice lives thereabouts,[38] because neither Charon nor his great father

---

34) Taenarus: 테나루스 (펠로폰네소스 반도 최남단의 곳)

35) out–of–the–way: 외딴

36) Pluto: 플루토 (저승의 신 하데스의 별칭)

37) Charon: 카론. 그리스 신화에 나오는 인물. 저승으로 가는 내의 나루터를 지키는 늙은 뱃사공으로,
   스틱스(Styx)와 아케론(Acheron)의 강을 건너 저승에 이르도록 해준다고 한다.

38) thereabouts: 그 근처에, 그 부근에

1 **Pluto does anything for nothing.** (A poor man on the point of[39] death is expected to have his passage–fee ready; but if he can't get hold of a coin, he isn't allowed to achieve true death, but must wander about disconsolately[40] for ever on this side of Styx.) **Anyhow, give the dirty ruffian**[41] **one of your coins, but let him take it from your mouth not**
5 **from your hand.**

"While you are being ferried across the sluggish[42] stream, the corpse of an old man will float by. He will raise a putrid[43] hand and beg you to haul him into the boat. But you must be careful not to yield to any feeling of pity for him; that is forbidden. Once ashore, you will meet
10 three women some distance away from the bank. They will be weaving cloth and will ask you to help them. To touch the cloth is also forbidden. All these apparitions,[44] and others like them, are snares set for you by Venus; her object is to make you let go one of the sops you are carrying, and you must understand that the loss of even one of them would be
15 fatal — it would prevent your return to this world. They are for you to give to Cerberus,[45] the huge, fierce, formidable hound with three heads on three necks, all barking in unison, who terrifies the dead; though of course the dead have no need to be frightened by him because they are only shadows and he can't injure shadows." After dealing with Cerberus,
20 Psyche would be welcomed by Proserpina. But on her way back she must take care not to open or even look at the box. Its treasure was not for her.

---

39) on the point of ~: ~이 임박한

40) disconsolately: 절망적으로

41) ruffian: 악당

42) sluggish: 느릿느릿 움직이는

43) putrid: 부패하는, 썩는, 악취가 나는

44) apparition: 유령

45) Cerberus: 케르베로스(지옥을 지키는 개; 머리가 셋에 꼬리는 뱀 모양), 엄중한 문지기

All went well upon her dangerous quest, and she obeyed every instruction, until she was on her return journey and had left the Underworld behind. But then, out of a foolish desire to have some of the beauty for herself, she opened the box; and at once she fell down in a fatal sleep, as if she were dead.

But Cupid, now recovered, came to rouse and rescue her, and Psyche was able to rise to her feet[46] and deliver Proserpina's present to Venus. Meanwhile her lover pleaded with Jupiter, who summoned[47] the gods and goddesses to Council and told them Cupid had best stop roving and settle down with Psyche. Assuring Venus that this would be no disgrace for herself, he sent Mercury to bring Psyche up to heaven, and gave her a cup of nectar to make her immortal, and to keep Cupid, for all time, from flying away from her again.

Then Jupiter ordered a great wedding–banquet, at which, to the accompaniment of flute and pipe–music, the Muses chanted the marriage–hymn, and Apollo sang to his own lyre. And, as he sang, Venus performed a lively dance.

So Cupid and Psyche were married; and their child was a daughter called Pleasure.

---

46) rise to her feet: 일어서다
47) summon: 소환하다

2

The Tell–Tale Heart

Edgar Allan Poe[1]

1   TRUE! — nervous — very, very dreadfully nervous I had been and am; but why will you say that I am mad? The disease had sharpened my senses[2] — not destroyed — not dulled[3] them. Above all was the sense of hearing[4] acute. I heard all things in the heaven and in the earth. I heard

5 many things in hell. How, then, am I mad? Hearken![5] and observe how healthily — how calmly I can tell you the whole story.

It is impossible to say how first the idea entered my brain; but once

---

1) 에드거 앨런 포(Edgar Allan Poe, 1809-1849): 미국의 시인 · 평론가 · 단편소설 작가. 18세에 시집 『태머레인 외(外)』(*Tamerlane, and Other Poems*)를 출간했으며, 『그로테스크하고 아라베스크한 이야기들』(*Tales of the Grotesque and Arabesque*), 「모르드가의 살인사건」("The Murders in the Rue Morgue"), 「황금 풍뎅이」("The Gold Bug"), 「까마귀」("The Raven") 등의 소설과 시를 발표했다. 자전적 시로 평가받는 「애너벨 리」("Annabel Lee")는 포의 1849년 발표작이다.

2) sense: 감각

3) dull: 무디게 만들다, 둔하게 만들다

4) the sense of hearing: 청각

5) Hearken: 귀를 기울이고 듣다

Part III. Short Story 95

conceived,[6] it haunted[7] me day and night. Object there was none.[8] Passion there was none. I loved the old man. He had never wronged me. He had never given me insult. For his gold I had no desire. I think it was his eye! yes, it was this! He had the eye of a vulture[9] — a pale blue eye, with a film over it.[10] Whenever it fell upon me, my blood ran cold;[11] and so by degrees — very gradually — I made up my mind to take the life of the old man, and thus rid myself of the eye forever.

Now this is the point. You fancy[12] me mad. Madmen know nothing. But you should have seen me. You should have seen how wisely I proceeded — with what caution — with what foresight — with what dissimulation[13] I went to work! I was never kinder[14] to the old man than during the whole week before I killed him. And every night, about midnight, I turned the latch[15] of his door and opened it — oh so gently! And then, when I had made an opening sufficient for my head, I put in a dark lantern, all closed, closed, that no light shone out, and then I thrust in[16] my head. Oh, you would have laughed to see how cunningly I thrust it in! I moved it slowly — very, very slowly, so that I might not disturb the old man's sleep. It took me an hour to place my whole head

---

6) conceive: 생각을 품다

7) haunt: (특히 불쾌한 생각이) 뇌리에서 떠나지 않다, 계속해서 떠오르다

8) Object there was none: 목적도 없었다

9) vulture: 독수리

10) with a film over it: 얇은 막이 덮여 있는

11) my blood ran cold: 내 피가 얼어붙었다

12) fancy: 생각하다

13) dissimulation: 위장

14) was never kinder: 더없이 친절하게 대했다

15) latch: 자물쇠

16) thrust in: 밀어 넣다, 찔러 넣다

within the opening so far that I could see him as he lay upon his bed. Ha! would a madman have been so wise as this, And then, when my head was well in the room, I undid the lantern cautiously — oh, so cautiously — cautiously (for the hinges creaked)[17] — I undid it just so much that a single thin ray fell upon the vulture eye. And this I did for seven long nights — every night just at midnight — but I found the eye always closed; and so it was impossible to do the work; for it was not the old man who vexed[18] me, but his Evil Eye. And every morning, when the day broke, I went boldly into the chamber,[19] and spoke courageously to him, calling him by name in a hearty tone, and inquiring how he has passed the night. So you see he would have been a very profound old man, indeed, to suspect that every night, just at twelve, I looked in upon him while he slept.

Upon the eighth night I was more than usually cautious in opening the door. A watch's minute hand[20] moves more quickly than did mine. Never before that night had I felt the extent of my own powers — of my sagacity.[21] I could scarcely contain my feelings of triumph. To think that there I was, opening the door, little by little, and he not even to dream of my secret deeds or thoughts. I fairly chuckled at[22] the idea; and perhaps he heard me; for he moved on the bed suddenly, as if startled. Now you may think that I drew back[23] — but no. His room was as black as

---

17) for the hinges creaked: 문이 삐걱거렸으므로
18) vex: 성가시게 하다, 짜증나게 하다
19) chamber: 침실
20) A watch's minute hand: 시계의 분침
21) sagacity: 총명함, 기민함
22) chuckle at: ~에 빙그레(싱긋) 웃다
23) draw back: 뒤로 물러서다

1   pitch²⁴⁾ with the thick darkness, (for the shutters were close fastened, through fear of robbers,) and so I knew that he could not see the opening of the door, and I kept pushing it on steadily, steadily.

    I had my head in, and was about to open the lantern, when my
5 thumb slipped upon the tin fastening, and the old man sprang up in bed, crying out — "Who's there?"

    I kept quite still and said nothing. For a whole hour I did not move a muscle, and in the meantime I did not hear him lie down. He was still sitting up in the bed listening; — just as I have done, night after night,
10 hearkening to the death watches²⁵⁾ in the wall.

    Presently I heard a slight groan, and I knew it was the groan of mortal terror.²⁶⁾ It was not a groan of pain or of grief — oh, no! — it was the low stifled²⁷⁾ sound that arises from the bottom of the soul when overcharged with awe. I knew the sound well. Many a night, just
15 at midnight, when all the world slept, it has welled up from my own bosom,²⁸⁾ deepening, with its dreadful echo, the terrors that distracted²⁹⁾ me. I say I knew it well. I knew what the old man felt, and pitied him, although I chuckled at heart. I knew that he had been lying awake ever since the first slight noise, when he had turned in the bed. His fears
20 had been ever since growing upon him. He had been trying to fancy them causeless,³⁰⁾ but could not. He had been saying to himself — "It is

---

24) as black as pitch: 새까만, 깜깜한
25) the death watch: 죽음의 파수꾼
26) mortal: 죽음을 두려워하는 공포
27) stifled: 억눌러진
28) welled up from my own bosom: 가슴속에서 솟아나다
29) distract: (정신이) 집중이 안 되게 하다, 산만·산란하게 하다, (주의를) 딴 데로 돌리다
30) causeless: 이유가 없는

¹ nothing but the wind in the chimney — it is only a mouse crossing the floor," or "It is merely a cricket which has made a single chirp."³¹⁾ Yes, he had been trying to comfort himself with these suppositions:³²⁾ but he had found all in vain. All in vain; because Death, in approaching him had

⁵ stalked³³⁾ with his black shadow before him, and enveloped the victim. And it was the mournful influence of the unperceived shadow³⁴⁾ that caused him to feel — although he neither saw nor heard — to feel the presence of my head within the room.

When I had waited a long time, very patiently, without hearing him

¹⁰ lie down, I resolved to open a little — a very, very little crevice in the lantern. So I opened it — you cannot imagine how stealthily, stealthily — until, at length a simple dim ray, like the thread of the spider, shot from out the crevice and fell full upon the vulture eye.

It was open — wide, wide open — and I grew furious as I gazed

¹⁵ upon it. I saw it with perfect distinctness — all a dull blue, with a hideous veil over it that chilled the very marrow in my bones;³⁵⁾ but I could see nothing else of the old man's face or person: for I had directed the ray as if by instinct,³⁶⁾ precisely upon the damned spot.

And have I not told you that what you mistake for madness is but

²⁰ over–acuteness of the sense?³⁷⁾ — now, I say, there came to my ears a low, dull, quick sound, such as a watch makes when enveloped in cotton. I

---

31) made a single chirp: 한 번 운 것(소리를 낸 것)

32) suppositions: 가정들

33) stalk: (공격 대상에게) 몰래 접근하다

34) unperceived shadow: 알아차릴 수 없는 그림자

35) that chilled the very marrow in my bones: 뼛속까지 얼어붙게 하는

36) as if by instinct: 마치 본능에 의한 것인 것처럼

37) but over–acuteness of the sense: 감각이 지나치게 예민한 것일 뿐

knew that sound well, too. It was the beating of the old man's heart. It increased my fury, as the beating of a drum stimulates[38] the soldier into courage.

But even yet I refrained[39] and kept still. I scarcely breathed. I held the lantern motionless. I tried[40] how steadily I could maintain the ray upon the eye. Meantime[41] the hellish tattoo of the heart[42] increased. It grew quicker and quicker, and louder and louder every instant. The old man's terror must have been extreme! It grew louder, I say, louder every moment! — do you mark[43] me well I have told you that I am nervous:[44] so I am. And now at the dead hour of the night,[45] amid the dreadful silence of that old house, so strange a noise as this excited me to uncontrollable terror. Yet, for some minutes longer I refrained and stood still. But the beating grew louder, louder! I thought the heart must burst. And now a new anxiety seized me — the sound would be heard by a neighbour! The old man's hour had come! With a loud yell, I threw open the lantern and leaped into the room. He shrieked[46] once — once only. In an instant I dragged him to the floor, and pulled the heavy bed over him. I then smiled gaily,[47] to find the deed so far done.[48] But, for

---

38) stimulate: 자극하다, 증폭시키다
39) refrain: (특히 하고 싶은 것을) 삼가다
40) try: 시도하다, 시험해보다
41) Meantime: 그러는 동안에
42) the hellish tattoo of the heart: 심장의 지독히 기분 나쁜 박동 소리
43) mark: (구식) 유의해서 듣다
44) nervous: 신경과민의, 신경질적인
45) at the dead hour of the night: 한밤중에
46) shriek: (흥분, 공포감 등으로 날카롭게) 소리 · 비명을 지르다
47) gaily: 화사하게, 명랑하게
48) to find the deed so far done: 이제까지 했던 일들을 생각하며

many minutes, the heart beat on with a muffled sound.[49] This, however, did not vex me; it would not be heard through the wall. At length[50] it ceased. The old man was dead. I removed the bed and examined the corpse. Yes, he was stone, stone dead.[51] I placed my hand upon the heart and held it there many minutes. There was no pulsation. He was stone dead. His eye would trouble me no more.

If still you think me mad, you will think so no longer when I describe the wise precautions[52] I took for the concealment[53] of the body. The night waned,[54] and I worked hastily, but in silence. First of all I dismembered[55] the corpse. I cut off the head and the arms and the legs.

I then took up three planks[56] from the flooring of the chamber, and deposited all between the scantlings.[57] I then replaced the boards so cleverly, so cunningly, that no human eye — not even his — could have detected any thing wrong. There was nothing to wash out — no stain of any kind — no blood–spot whatever. I had been too wary for[58] that. A tub had caught all — ha! ha!

When I had made an end of these labors, it was four o'clock — still dark as midnight. As the bell sounded the hour, there came a knocking at

---

49) with a muffled sound: 둔탁한 소리를 내며
50) At length: 한참 있다가
51) stone dead: 완전히 죽은
52) precaution: 예방책, 예방 조치
53) concealment: 은폐
54) wane: 약해지다
55) dismember: (사람의) 시신을 훼손하다, 자르다
56) took up three planks: 널빤지를 뜯어냈다
57) scantling: 각목
58) too wary for: 극도로 경계하는

the street door. I went down to open it with a light heart,[59] — for what had I now to fear? There entered three men, who introduced themselves, with perfect suavity,[60] as officers of the police. A shriek had been heard by a neighbour during the night; suspicion of foul play[61] had been
5 aroused; information had been lodged at the police office, and they (the officers) had been deputed to search the premises.[62]

I smiled, — for what had I to fear? I bade[63] the gentlemen welcome. The shriek, I said, was my own in a dream. The old man, I mentioned, was absent in the country. I took my visitors all over the house. I bade
10 them search — search well. I led them, at length, to his chamber. I showed them his treasures, secure, undisturbed. In the enthusiasm of my confidence, I brought chairs into the room, and desired them here to rest from their fatigues, while I myself, in the wild audacity[64] of my perfect triumph, placed my own seat upon the very spot beneath which reposed
15 the corpse of the victim.

The officers were satisfied. My manner had convinced them. I was singularly at ease.[65] They sat, and while I answered cheerily, they chatted of familiar things. But, ere long,[66] I felt myself getting pale and wished them gone. My head ached, and I fancied a ringing[67] in my ears: but
20 still they sat and still chatted. The ringing became more distinct: — It

---

59) with a light heart: 가벼운 마음으로
60) suavity: 유화, 온화
61) foul play: 폭행치사, 살인
62) premises: 부지, 지역, 구내
63) bid: (인사 등을) 말하다, 명령하다
64) audacity: 뻔뻔함
65) at ease: 마음이 편안한
66) ere long: 머지않아, 이윽고
67) a ringing: 소리의 울림

¹ continued and became more distinct: I talked more freely to get rid of the feeling: but it continued and gained definiteness — until, at length, I found that the noise was not within my ears.

No doubt I now grew very pale; — but I talked more fluently, and
⁵ with a heightened voice. Yet the sound increased — and what could I do? It was a low, dull, quick sound — much such a sound as a watch makes when enveloped in cotton. I gasped for breath — and yet the officers heard it not. I talked more quickly — more vehemently;[68] but the noise steadily increased. I arose and argued about trifles, in a high key and
¹⁰ with violent gesticulations; but the noise steadily increased. Why would they not be gone? I paced the floor to and fro with heavy strides, as if excited to fury by the observations of the men — but the noise steadily increased. Oh God! what could I do? I foamed — I raved[69] — I swore! I swung the chair upon which I had been sitting, and grated it upon the
¹⁵ boards, but the noise arose over all and continually increased. It grew louder — louder — louder! And still the men chatted pleasantly, and smiled. Was it possible they heard not? Almighty God! — no, no! They heard! — they suspected! — they knew! — they were making a mockery of my horror! — this I thought, and this I think. But anything was better
²⁰ than this agony! Anything was more tolerable than this derision![70] I could bear those hypocritical smiles no longer! I felt that I must scream or die! and now — again! — hark! louder! louder! louder! louder!

"Villains!" I shrieked, "dissemble no more! I admit the deed! — tear up the planks! here, here! — It is the beating of his hideous heart!"

---

68) vehemently: 열정적으로, 격렬하게

69) rave: 열변을 토하다

70) derision: 조롱, 조소

3

The Black Cat

Edgar Allan Poe

1   For the most wild, yet most homely[1] narrative which I am about to pen, I neither expect nor solicit belief. Mad indeed would I be to expect it, in a case where my very senses reject their own evidence. Yet, mad am I not — and very surely do I not dream. But to–morrow I die, and to–

5 day I would unburthen[2] my soul. My immediate purpose is to place before the world, plainly,[3] succinctly,[4] and without comment, a series of mere household events. In their consequences, these events have terrified — have tortured — have destroyed me. Yet I will not attempt to expound[5] them. To me, they have presented little but Horror — to many[6] they

10 will seem less terrible than barroques.[7] Hereafter, perhaps, some intellect

---

1) homely: 단순한
2) unburthen: = unburden. 짐을 내려놓다
3) plainly: 있는 그대로, 솔직하게
4) succinctly: 간결하게, 간단명료하게
5) expound: 자세히 설명하다
6) to many: 사람들에게는
7) less terrible than barroques: 무섭다기보다는 기괴한

¹ may be found which will reduce my phantasm to the common–place —
some intellect more calm, more logical, and far less excitable than my
own, which will perceive, in the circumstances I detail with awe, nothing
more than an ordinary succession of very natural causes and effects.

⁵   From my infancy I was noted for the docility⁸⁾ and humanity⁹⁾ of
my disposition.¹⁰⁾ My tenderness of heart was even so conspicuous as to
make me the jest of my companions.¹¹⁾ I was especially fond of animals,
and was indulged by my parents with a great variety of pets. With these
I spent most of my time, and never was so happy as when feeding and
¹⁰ caressing them. This peculiarity of character grew with my growth,
and, in my manhood, I derived from it one of my principal sources of
pleasure. To those who have cherished an affection for a faithful and
sagacious dog, I need hardly be at the trouble of explaining the nature or
the intensity of the gratification thus derivable. There is something in the
¹⁵ unselfish and self–sacrificing love of a brute, which goes directly to the
heart of him who has had frequent occasion to test the paltry friendship
and gossamer fidelity of mere Man.

      I married early, and was happy to find in my wife a disposition not
uncongenial¹²⁾ with my own. Observing my partiality for domestic pets,
²⁰ she lost no opportunity of procuring¹³⁾ those of the most agreeable kind.
We had birds, gold–fish, a fine dog, rabbits, a small monkey, and a cat.

      This latter was a remarkably large and beautiful animal, entirely

---

8)   docility: 유순함

9)   humanity: 인간적임, 정이 많음

10) disposition: 기질, 성향

11) the jest of my companions: 친구들의 농담거리, 장난의 대상

12) not uncongenial with: ~와 마음이 맞는

13) procure: 구입하다

black, and sagacious[14] to an astonishing degree. In speaking of his intelligence, my wife, who at heart was not a little tinctured with superstition,[15] made frequent allusion to the ancient popular notion, which regarded all black cats as witches in disguise. Not that she was ever
5 serious upon this point — and I mention the matter at all for no better reason than that it happens, just now, to be remembered.

Pluto — this was the cat's name — was my favorite pet and playmate. I alone fed him, and he attended me wherever I went about the house. It was even with difficulty that I could prevent him from
10 following me through the streets.

Our friendship lasted, in this manner, for several years, during which my general temperament and character[16] — through the instrumentality of the Fiend Intemperance[17] — had (I blush to confess it) experienced a radical alteration for the worse. I grew, day by day, more moody, more
15 irritable, more regardless of the feelings of others. I suffered myself to use intemperate language[18] to my wife. At length,[19] I even offered her personal violence. My pets, of course, were made to feel the change in my disposition. I not only neglected, but ill–used them. For Pluto, however, I still retained sufficient regard to restrain me from maltreating
20 him, as I made no scruple of[20] maltreating the rabbits, the monkey, or

---

14) sagacious: 영리한, 현명한
15) was not a little tinctured with superstition: 적지 않게 미신을 믿었던
16) temperament and character: 기질 및 성격
17) through the instrumentality of the Fiend Intemperance: 술이라는 악마의 도구를 통해서, 술이라는 악마의 도구 때문에
18) intemperate language: 바른 언어
19) at length: 한참 후에
20) made no scruple of: ~하는 것을 망설이지 않다

1 even the dog, when by accident, or through affection, they came in my way. But my disease grew upon me — for what disease is like Alcohol! — and at length even Pluto, who was now becoming old, and consequently somewhat peevish[21] — even Pluto began to experience the effects of my
5 ill temper.

One night, returning home, much intoxicated,[22] from one of my haunts about town, I fancied that the cat avoided my presence. I seized him; when, in his fright at my violence, he inflicted a slight wound upon my hand with his teeth. The fury of a demon instantly possessed me.
10 I knew myself no longer.[23] My original soul seemed, at once, to take its flight from my body; and a more than fiendish malevolence, gin–nurtured, thrilled every fibre of my frame. I took from my waistcoat–pocket a pen–knife, opened it, grasped the poor beast by the throat, and deliberately cut one of its eyes from the socket ! I blush, I burn, I
15 shudder, while I pen the damnable atrocity.[24]

When reason returned with the morning — when I had slept off the fumes of the night's debauch[25] — I experienced a sentiment half of horror, half of remorse,[26] for the crime of which I had been guilty; but it was, at best, a feeble and equivocal feeling, and the soul remained
20 untouched. I again plunged into excess, and soon drowned in wine all memory of the deed.

In the meantime the cat slowly recovered. The socket of the lost eye

---

21) peevish: 짜증을 잘 내는, 화를 잘 내는
22) much intoxicated: 술이 많이 취해서
23) I knew myself no longer: 나는 이성을 잃었다
24) atrocity: 잔혹행위
25) the fumes of the night's debauch: 그날 밤의 술기운
26) remorse: 후회

presented, it is true, a frightful appearance,[27] but he no longer appeared to suffer any pain. He went about the house as usual, but, as might be expected, fled in extreme terror at my approach. I had so much of my old heart left, as to be at first grieved by this evident dislike on the part of a creature which had once so loved me. But this feeling soon gave place to irritation. And then came, as if to my final and irrevocable overthrow, the spirit of PERVERSENESS.[28] Of this spirit philosophy takes no account.[29] Yet I am not more sure that my soul lives, than I am that perverseness is one of the primitive impulses of the human heart — one of the indivisible primary faculties, or sentiments, which give direction to the character of Man. Who has not, a hundred times, found himself committing a vile or a silly action, for no other reason than because he knows he should not? Have we not a perpetual inclination, in the teeth of our best judgment, to violate that which is Law, merely because we understand it to be such? This spirit of perverseness, I say, came to my final overthrow. It was this unfathomable longing of the soul to vex itself — to offer violence to its own nature — to do wrong for the wrong's sake only — that urged me to continue and finally to consummate the injury I had inflicted upon the unoffending brute. One morning, in cool blood,[30] I slipped a noose[31] about its neck and hung it to the limb of a tree; — hung it with the tears streaming from my eyes, and with the bitterest remorse at my heart; — hung it because I knew that it had loved

---

27) a frightful appearance: 소름끼치는 몰골
28) the spirit of perverseness: 악마성
29) takes no account: 설명할 수 없다
30) in cool blood: 태연하게, 냉정하게
31) slip a noose: 올가미를 걸다

me, and because I felt it had given me no reason of offence; — hung it because I knew that in so doing I was committing a sin — a deadly sin that would so jeopardize[32] my immortal soul as to place it — if such a thing were possible — even beyond the reach of[33] the infinite mercy of the Most Merciful and Most Terrible God.

On the night of the day on which this cruel deed was done, I was aroused from sleep by the cry of fire. The curtains of my bed were in flames. The whole house was blazing. It was with great difficulty that my wife, a servant, and myself, made our escape from the conflagration.[34] The destruction was complete. My entire worldly wealth was swallowed up, and I resigned myself thenceforward[35] to despair.

I am above the weakness of seeking to establish a sequence of cause and effect, between the disaster and the atrocity. But I am detailing a chain of facts — and wish not to leave even a possible link imperfect. On the day succeeding the fire, I visited the ruins. The walls, with one exception, had fallen in. This exception was found in a compartment wall, not very thick, which stood about the middle of the house, and against which had rested the head of my bed. The plastering had here, in great measure, resisted the action of the fire — a fact which I attributed to its having been recently spread. About this wall a dense crowd[36] were collected, and many persons seemed to be examining a particular portion of it with very minute and eager attention. The words

---

32) jeopardize: 위태롭게 하다
33) even beyond the reach of: ~의 손길이 닿을 수 없을 정도로
34) conflagration: 대화재, 큰불
35) thenceforward: 그 이후로
36) a dense crowd: 많은 구경꾼들

1 "strange!" "singular!" and other similar expressions, excited my curiosity. I approached and saw, as if graven in bas relief[37] upon the white surface, the figure of a gigantic cat. The impression was given with an accuracy truly marvellous. There was a rope about the animal's neck.

5   When I first beheld this apparition[38] — for I could scarcely regard it as less — my wonder and my terror were extreme. But at length reflection came to my aid. The cat, I remembered, had been hung in a garden adjacent to the house. Upon the alarm of fire, this garden had been immediately filled by the crowd — by some one of whom the
10 animal must have been cut from the tree and thrown, through an open window, into my chamber. This had probably been done with the view of arousing me from sleep. The falling of other walls had compressed the victim of my cruelty into the substance of the freshly–spread plaster; the lime of which, with the flames, and the ammonia from the carcass, had
15 then accomplished the portraiture[39] as I saw it.

    Although I thus readily accounted to my reason, if not altogether to my conscience, for the startling fact just detailed, it did not the less fail to make a deep impression upon my fancy. For months I could not rid myself of the phantasm of the cat; and, during this period, there came
20 back into my spirit a half–sentiment that seemed, but was not, remorse. I went so far as to regret the loss of the animal, and to look about me, among the vile haunts which I now habitually frequented, for another pet of the same species, and of somewhat similar appearance, with which to supply its place.

---

37) as if graven in bas relief: 마치 돋을새김(조각품)이라도 한 듯이

38) apparition: 유령

39) portraiture: 그림, 초상화

One night as I sat, half stupified,[40] in a den of more than infamy, my attention was suddenly drawn to some black object, reposing upon the head of one of the immense hogsheads of Gin, or of Rum[41], which constituted the chief furniture of the apartment. I had been looking steadily at the top of this hogshead for some minutes, and what now caused me surprise was the fact that I had not sooner perceived the object thereupon. I approached it, and touched it with my hand. It was a black cat — a very large one — fully as large as Pluto, and closely resembling him in every respect but one. Pluto had not a white hair upon any portion of his body; but this cat had a large, although indefinite splotch[42] of white, covering nearly the whole region of the breast.

Upon my touching him, he immediately arose, purred loudly, rubbed against my hand, and appeared delighted with my notice. This, then, was the very creature of which I was in search. I at once offered to purchase it of the landlord; but this person made no claim to it — knew nothing of it — had never seen it before.

I continued my caresses,[43] and, when I prepared to go home, the animal evinced a disposition to accompany me. I permitted it to do so; occasionally stooping and patting it as I proceeded. When it reached the house it domesticated[44] itself at once, and became immediately a great favorite with my wife.

For my own part, I soon found a dislike to it arising within me. This

---

40) half stupified: 얼큰하게 술에 취해서
41) one of the immense hogsheads of Gin, or of Rum: 진이나 럼을 담는 큰 술통 중의 하나
42) indefinite splotch: 윤곽이 확실하지 않은 점, 얼룩
43) caress: 어루만짐
44) domesticated: 친숙해지다, 길들여지다

¹ was just the reverse of what I had anticipated; but — I know not how or why it was — its evident fondness for myself rather disgusted and annoyed. By slow degrees, these feelings of disgust and annoyance rose into the bitterness of hatred. I avoided the creature; a certain sense of

⁵ shame, and the remembrance of my former deed of cruelty, preventing me from physically abusing it. I did not, for some weeks, strike, or otherwise violently ill use it; but gradually — very gradually — I came to look upon it with unutterable loathing, and to flee silently from its odious presence, as from the breath of a pestilence.

¹⁰   What added, no doubt, to my hatred of the beast, was the discovery, on the morning after I brought it home, that, like Pluto, it also had been deprived of one of its eyes. This circumstance, however, only endeared it to my wife, who, as I have already said, possessed, in a high degree, that humanity of feeling which had once been my distinguishing trait, and

¹⁵ the source of many of my simplest and purest pleasures.

With my aversion to this cat, however, its partiality for myself seemed to increase. It followed my footsteps with a pertinacity which it would be difficult to make the reader comprehend. Whenever I sat, it would crouch beneath my chair, or spring upon my knees, covering

²⁰ me with its loathsome caresses. If I arose to walk it would get between my feet and thus nearly throw me down, or, fastening its long and sharp claws in my dress, clamber, in this manner, to my breast. At such times, although I longed to destroy it with a blow, I was yet withheld from so doing, partly by a memory of my former crime, but chiefly — let me

²⁵ confess it at once — by absolute dread of the beast.

This dread was not exactly a dread of physical evil — and yet I should be at a loss how otherwise to define it. I am almost ashamed to own — yes, even in this felon's cell, I am almost ashamed to own — that the terror and horror with which the animal inspired me, had been heightened by one of the merest chimæras it would be possible to conceive. My wife had called my attention, more than once, to the

5   character of the mark of white hair, of which I have spoken, and which constituted the sole visible difference between the strange beast and the one I had destroyed. The reader will remember that this mark, although large, had been originally very indefinite; but, by slow degrees[45] — degrees nearly imperceptible,[46] and which for a long time my Reason

10 struggled to reject as fanciful — it had, at length, assumed a rigorous distinctness of outline. It was now the representation of an object that I shudder to name — and for this, above all, I loathed,[47] and dreaded, and would have rid myself of the monster had I dared — it was now, I say, the image of a hideous — of a ghastly thing — of the GALLOWS ! —

15 oh, mournful and terrible engine of Horror and of Crime — of Agony and of Death !

And now was I indeed wretched beyond the wretchedness of mere Humanity. And a brute beast — whose fellow I had contemptuously destroyed — a brute beast to work out for me — for me a man,

20 fashioned in the image of the High God — so much of insufferable wo! Alas! neither by day nor by night knew I the blessing of Rest any more! During the former the creature left me no moment alone; and, in the latter, I started, hourly, from dreams of unutterable fear, to find the hot breath of the thing upon my face, and its vast weight — an incarnate

---

45) by slow degrees: 아주 천천히
46) imperceptible: 감지할 수 없을 정도의
47) loathe: 혐오하다

¹ Night–Mare that I had no power to shake off — incumbent eternally upon my heart !

Beneath the pressure of torments such as these, the feeble remnant of the good within me succumbed. Evil thoughts became my sole intimates
⁵ — the darkest and most evil of thoughts. The moodiness of my usual temper increased to hatred of all things and of all mankind; while, from the sudden, frequent, and ungovernable outbursts of a fury⁴⁸⁾ to which I now blindly abandoned myself, my uncomplaining wife, alas! was the most usual and the most patient of sufferers.

¹⁰ One day she accompanied me, upon some household errand, into the cellar of the old building which our poverty compelled us to inhabit. The cat followed me down the steep stairs, and, nearly throwing me headlong, exasperated⁴⁹⁾ me to madness. Uplifting an axe, and forgetting, in my wrath, the childish dread which had hitherto stayed my hand,
¹⁵ I aimed a blow at the animal which, of course, would have proved instantly fatal had it descended as I wished. But this blow was arrested by the hand of my wife. Goaded,⁵⁰⁾ by the interference, into a rage more than demoniacal, I withdrew my arm from her grasp and buried the axe in her brain. She fell dead upon the spot, without a groan.

²⁰ This hideous murder accomplished, I set myself forthwith, and with entire deliberation, to the task of concealing the body. I knew that I could not remove it from the house, either by day or by night, without the risk of being observed by the neighbors. Many projects entered my mind. At one period I thought of cutting the corpse into minute

---

48) ungovernable outbursts of a fury: 억누를 수 없는 분노의 발작
49) exasperate: 몹시 화나게 하다
50) Goaded: 자극이 되어

fragments, and destroying them by fire. At another, I resolved to dig a grave for it in the floor of the cellar. Again, I deliberated about casting it in the well in the yard — about packing it in a box, as if merchandize, with the usual arrangements, and so getting a porter to take it from the house. Finally I hit upon what I considered a far better expedient[51] than either of these. I determined to wall it up in the cellar — as the monks[52] of the middle ages are recorded to have walled up their victims.

For a purpose such as this the cellar was well adapted. Its walls were loosely constructed, and had lately been plastered throughout with a rough plaster, which the dampness of the atmosphere had prevented from hardening. Moreover, in one of the walls was a projection, caused by a false chimney, or fireplace, that had been filled up, and made to resemble the rest of the cellar. I made no doubt that I could readily displace the bricks at this point, insert the corpse, and wall the whole up as before, so that no eye could detect any thing suspicious.

And in this calculation I was not deceived. By means of a crow—bar I easily dislodged the bricks, and, having carefully deposited the body against the inner wall, I propped it in that position, while, with little trouble, I re–laid the whole structure as it originally stood. Having procured mortar, sand, and hair, with every possible precaution, I prepared a plaster which could not be distinguished from the old, and with this I very carefully went over the new brick–work. When I had finished, I felt satisfied that all was right. The wall did not present the slightest appearance of having been disturbed. The rubbish on the floor was picked up with the minutest care. I looked around triumphantly, and

---

51) expedient: 처방, 방편
52) monk: 수도승

1 said to myself — "Here at least, then, my labor has not been in vain."

My next step was to look for the beast which had been the cause of so much wretchedness; for I had, at length, firmly resolved to put it to death. Had I been able to meet with it, at the moment, there could have

5 been no doubt of its fate; but it appeared that the crafty animal had been alarmed at the violence of my previous anger, and forebore to present itself in my present mood. It is impossible to describe, or to imagine, the deep, the blissful sense of relief which the absence of the detested creature occasioned in my bosom. It did not make its appearance during the night

10 — and thus for one night at least, since its introduction into the house, I soundly and tranquilly[53] slept; aye, slept even with the burden of murder upon my soul!

The second and the third day passed, and still my tormentor came not. Once again I breathed as a freeman. The monster, in terror, had

15 fled the premises forever! I should behold it no more! My happiness was supreme! The guilt of my dark deed disturbed me but little. Some few inquiries had been made, but these had been readily answered. Even a search had been instituted — but of course nothing was to be discovered. I looked upon my future felicity as secured.

20 Upon the fourth day of the assassination, a party of the police came, very unexpectedly, into the house, and proceeded again to make rigorous investigation of the premises. Secure, however, in the inscrutability[54] of my place of concealment, I felt no embarrassment whatever. The officers bade me accompany them in their search. They left no nook or corner

25 unexplored. At length, for the third or fourth time, they descended into

---

53) soundly and tranquilly: 평안히
54) inscrutability: 헤아릴 수 없음, 불가사의

1 the cellar. I quivered not in a muscle. My heart beat calmly as that of one
   who slumbers in innocence. I walked the cellar from end to end. I folded
   my arms upon my bosom, and roamed easily to and fro. The police were
   thoroughly satisfied and prepared to depart. The glee at my heart was
5 too strong to be restrained. I burned to say if but one word, by way of
   triumph, and to render doubly sure their assurance of my guiltlessness.

   "Gentlemen," I said at last, as the party ascended the steps, "I delight
   to have allayed your suspicions. I wish you all health, and a little more
   courtesy. By the bye, gentlemen, this — this is a very well constructed
10 house." (In the rabid desire to say something easily, I scarcely knew what I uttered at all.) — "I
   may say an excellently well constructed house. These walls — are you
   going, gentlemen? — these walls are solidly put together;" and here,
   through the mere phrenzy of bravado,[55] I rapped heavily, with a cane
   which I held in my hand, upon that very portion of the brick–work
15 behind which stood the corpse of the wife of my bosom.

   But may God shield and deliver me from the fangs of the Arch–
   Fiend ![56] No sooner had the reverberation of my blows sunk into silence,
   than I was answered by a voice from within the tomb! — by a cry, at
   first muffled and broken, like the sobbing of a child, and then quickly
20 swelling into one long, loud, and continuous scream, utterly anomalous
   and inhuman[57] — a howl — a wailing shriek, half of horror and half of
   triumph, such as might have arisen only out of hell, conjointly from the
   throats of the dammed in their agony and of the demons that exult in
   the damnation.

   ---

   55) through the mere phrenzy of bravado: 허세로 똘똘 뭉쳐서
   56) the fangs of the Arch – Fiend: 악마의 독니
   57) utterly anomalous and inhuman: 완전히 이상하고 잔혹한

1   Of my own thoughts it is folly to speak. Swooning, I staggered to the opposite wall. For one instant the party[58] upon the stairs remained motionless, through extremity of terror and of awe. In the next, a dozen stout arms were toiling at the wall. It fell bodily. The corpse, already

5 greatly decayed and clotted with gore, stood erect before the eyes of the spectators. Upon its head, with red extended mouth and solitary eye of fire, sat the hideous beast whose craft had seduced me into murder, and whose informing voice had consigned[59] me to the hangman. I had walled the monster up within the tomb!

---

58) the party: 그 경찰의 무리

59) consign: (좋지 않은 상황에) 처하게 만들다

4

The Bet

Anton Chekhov[1]

1   It was a dark autumn night. The old banker was walking up and
down his study and remembering how, fifteen years before, he had given
a party one autumn evening. There had been many clever men there, and
there had been interesting conversations. Among other things they had
5 talked of capital punishment.[2] The majority of the guests, among whom
were many journalists and intellectual men, disapproved of the death
penalty. They considered that form of punishment out of date,[3] immoral,
and unsuitable for Christian States. In the opinion of some of them
the death penalty ought to be replaced everywhere by imprisonment

---

1) 안톤 체호프(Anton Chekhov, 1860-1904): 러시아의 소설가 겸 극작가. 객관주의 문학론을 주장하
였고 시대의 변화와 요구에 올바르게 반응하였다. 당시 러시아에는 다윈니즘, 실증주의, 유물론 등
이 소개되었는데 다양한 사상의 영향하에서 러시아를 대표하는 단편소설 작가로 자리 잡았다. 대표
작으로는 『지루한 이야기』, 『사할린 섬』 등 다수가 있다. 그가 문학사에 한 가장 큰 기여는 현대 단편
소설의 형식을 확립하는 데 중요한 역할을 했다는 것이다. 그는 평범한 일상 속의 면면들을 간결하
면서도 명료한 표현으로 묘사한다. 또한 날카롭고 엄정하게 인간을 그리면서도 그 내면에는 인간에
대한 연민의 감정을 지니고 있는 작품들이 많다.

2) capital punishment: 사형, 극형

3) out of date: = old-fashioned. 시대에 뒤떨어진, 구식의

1 for life.[4] "I don't agree with you," said their host the banker. "I have not tried either the death penalty or imprisonment for life, but if one may judge a priori,[5] the death penalty is more moral and more humane than imprisonment for life. Capital punishment kills a man at once, but

5 lifelong imprisonment kills him slowly. Which executioner is the more humane, he who kills you in a few minutes or he who drags the life out of you in the course of many years?"

"Both are equally immoral," observed one of the guests, "for they both have the same object — to take away life. The State is not God. It

10 has not the right to take away what it cannot restore when it wants to."[6] Among the guests was a young lawyer, a young man of five–and–twenty. When he was asked his opinion, he said: "The death sentence and the life sentence are equally immoral, but if I had to choose between the death penalty and imprisonment for life, I would certainly choose the second.

15 To live anyhow is better than not at all." A lively discussion arose. The banker, who was younger and more nervous in those days, was suddenly carried away by excitement; he struck the table with his fist and shouted at the young man:

"It's not true! I'll bet you two million you wouldn't stay in solitary

20 confinement[7] for five years."

"If you mean that in earnest," said the young man, "I'll take the bet, but I would stay not five but fifteen years."

"Fifteen? Done!" cried the banker. "Gentlemen, I stake two million!"

---

4) imprisonment for life: = life imprisonment. 종신형

5) if one may judge a priori: 선험적으로(경험과 상관없이) 판단해본다면

6) It has not the right to take away what it cannot restore when it wants to: 원한다 해도 다시 살릴 수 없는 생명을 국가가 빼앗을 권리는 없다

7) solitary confinement: = solitary imprisonment. 독방, 감금

"Agreed! You stake your millions and I stake my freedom!"[8] said the young man. And this wild, senseless bet was carried out! The banker, spoilt and frivolous, with millions beyond his reckoning, was delighted at the bet. At supper he made fun of the young man, and said: "Think better of it, young man, while there is still time. To me two million is a trifle, but you are losing three or four of the best years of your life. I say three or four, because you won't stay longer. Don't forget either, you unhappy man, that voluntary confinement[9] is a great deal harder to bear than compulsory. The thought that you have the right to step out in liberty at any moment will poison your whole existence in prison. I am sorry for you."

And now the banker, walking to and fro,[10] remembered all this, and asked himself: "What was the object of that bet?[11] What is the good of that man's losing fifteen years of his life and my throwing away two million? Can it prove that the death penalty is better or worse than imprisonment for life? No, no. It was all nonsensical and meaningless. On my part it was the caprice of a pampered man,[12] and on his part simple greed for money..."[13]

Then he remembered what followed that evening. It was decided that the young man should spend the years of his captivity under the strictest supervision[14] in one of the lodges in the banker's garden. It was

---

8) I stake my freedom: 내 자유를 걸겠다
9) voluntary confinement: 스스로 택한 감금
10) walking to and fro: 이리저리, 왔다 갔다 하면서
11) What was the object of that bet?: 무엇 때문에 이런 내기를 했을까?
12) On my part it was the caprice of a pampered man: 나로 말하자면 권태에 지친 인간의 변덕이었고
13) greed for money: 금전욕
14) under the strictest supervision: 가장 엄중한 감시 속에

1 agreed that for fifteen years he should not be free to cross the threshold[15]
of the lodge, to see human beings, to hear the human voice, or to receive
letters and newspapers. He was allowed to have a musical instrument and
books, and was allowed to write letters, to drink wine, and to smoke. By
5 the terms of the agreement,[16] the only relations he could have with the
outer world[17] were by a little window made purposely for that object.
He might have anything he wanted — books, music, wine, and so on
— in any quantity he desired by writing an order, but could only receive
them through the window. The agreement provided for every detail
10 and every trifle that would make his imprisonment strictly solitary, and
bound the young man to stay there exactly fifteen years, beginning from
twelve o'clock of November 14, 1870, and ending at twelve o'clock
of November 14, 1885. The slightest attempt on his part to break the
conditions,[18] if only two minutes before the end, released the banker
15 from the obligation to pay[19] him the two million.

For the first year of his confinement, as far as one could judge from
his brief notes,[20] the prisoner suffered severely from loneliness and
depression. The sounds of the piano could be heard continually day and
night from his lodge. He refused wine and tobacco. Wine, he wrote,
20 excites the desires, and desires are the worst foes of the prisoner; and
besides, nothing could be more dreary than drinking good wine and

---

15) he should not be free to cross the threshold: 그가 문지방을 넘게 놔두어서는 안 된다
16) By the terms of the agreement: 협약조건에 따르면
17) the only relations he could have with the outer world: 외부 세계와 가질 수 있는 유일한 접촉
18) The slightest attempt on his part to break the conditions: 경미하게라도 약정한 조건을 위반하는 시도를 하는 경우에는
19) released the banker from the obligation to pay: 은행가는 지불할 의무로부터 벗어나게 된다
20) as far as one could judge from his brief notes: 그의 짤막한 메모들로 미루어 판단한다면

seeing no one.[21] And tobacco spoilt the air of his room. In the first year the books he sent for were principally of a light character; novels with a complicated love plot, sensational and fantastic stories, and so on.

In the second year the piano was silent in the lodge, and the prisoner asked only for the classics. In the fifth year music was audible again, and the prisoner asked for wine. Those who watched him through the window said that all that year he spent doing nothing but eating and drinking and lying on his bed, frequently yawning and angrily talking to himself. He did not read books. Sometimes at night he would sit down to write; he would spend hours writing, and in the morning tear up all that he had written. More than once he could be heard crying.

In the second half of the sixth year the prisoner began zealously studying languages, philosophy, and history. He threw himself eagerly into[22] these studies — so much so that the banker had enough to do to get him the books he ordered.[23] In the course of four years some six hundred volumes were procured at his request. It was during this period that the banker received the following letter from his prisoner:

"My dear Jailer, I write you these lines in six languages. Show them to people who know the languages. Let them read them. If they find not one mistake I implore you to fire a shot in the garden. That shot will show me that my efforts have not been thrown away.[24] The geniuses of all ages and of all lands speak different languages, but the same flame

---

21) nothing could be more dreary than drinking good wine and seeing no one: 상대도 없이 좋은 술을 마시는 것처럼 따분한 일은 없다

22) throw oneself into: ~에 큰 노력을 기울이다, ~을 적극적으로 하다

23) so much so that the banker had enough to do to get him the books he ordered: 은행가는 책을 대주기가 벅찰 정도였다

24) that my efforts have not been thrown away: 내가 노력한 것들이 허사가 되지 않았다는 것

1 burns in them all. Oh, if you only knew what unearthly happiness my soul feels now from being able to understand them!"[25] The prisoner's desire was fulfilled. The banker ordered two shots to be fired in the garden.

5 Then after the tenth year, the prisoner sat immovably at the table and read nothing but the Gospel. It seemed strange to the banker that a man who in four years had mastered six hundred learned volumes should waste nearly a year over one thin book easy of comprehension.[26] Theology and histories of religion followed the Gospels. In the last 10 two years of his confinement the prisoner read an immense quantity of books quite indiscriminately.[27] At one time he was busy with the natural sciences, then he would ask for Byron or Shakespeare. There were notes in which he demanded at the same time books on chemistry, and a manual of medicine, and a novel, and some treatise on philosophy or 15 theology. His reading suggested a man swimming in the sea among the wreckage of his ship,[28] and trying to save his life by greedily clutching first at one spar and then at another.

The old banker remembered all this, and thought:

"To-morrow at twelve o'clock he will regain his freedom. By our 20 agreement I ought to pay him two million. If I do pay him, it is all over with me: I shall be utterly ruined."[29]

---

25) Oh, if you only knew what unearthly happiness my soul feels now from being able to understand them!: 내가 이들을 이해할 수 있음으로써 내 영혼이 누리는 천상의 행복을 당신이 알기나 할까요!

26) one thin book easy of comprehension: 이해하기 쉬운 얇은 책 한 권

27) read an immense quantity of books quite indiscriminately: 종류를 가리지 않고 엄청나게 많은 책들을 읽었다

28) swimming in the sea among the wreckage of his ship: 바다 위에 널린 그의 난파선의 잔해들 속에서 헤엄치면서

29) I shall be utterly ruined: 나는 깡그리 망하게 될 것이다, 여지없이 파산할 것이다

Fifteen years before, his millions had been beyond his reckoning; now he was afraid to ask himself which were greater, his debts or his assets.[30] Desperate gambling on the Stock Exchange,[31] wild speculation and the excitability which he could not get over even in advancing years,[32] had by degrees led to the decline of his fortune[33] and the proud, fearless, self–confident millionaire had become a banker of middling rank,[34] trembling at every rise and fall in his investments. "Cursed bet!" muttered the old man, clutching his head in despair "Why didn't the man die? He is only forty now. He will take my last penny from me, he will marry, will enjoy life, will gamble on the Exchange; while I shall look at him with envy like a beggar, and hear from him every day the same sentence: 'I am indebted to you for the happiness of my life, let me help you!' No, it is too much! The one means of being saved from bankruptcy and disgrace[35] is the death of that man!"

It struck three o'clock, the banker listened; everyone was asleep in the house and nothing could be heard outside but the rustling of the chilled trees. Trying to make no noise,[36] he took from a fireproof safe[37] the key of the door which had not been opened for fifteen years, put on his overcoat, and went out of the house.

---

30) he was afraid to ask himself which were greater, his debts or his assets: 그는 빚과 재산 중에 어느 것이 더 큰지 자문하기가 두려웠다

31) Desperate gambling on the Stock Exchange: 아슬아슬한 주식 놀음

32) he could not get over even in advancing years: 그는 나이가 들어서도 버릴 수 없었다

33) had by degrees led to the decline of his fortune: 서서히 그의 운이 기울게 되다

34) had become a banker of middling rank: 이류 은행가로 전락하고 말았다

35) The one means of being saved from bankruptcy and disgrace: 파산과 오욕으로부터 벗어날 수 있는 유일한 길

36) Trying to make no noise: 소리를 내지 않도록 주의하면서

37) a fireproof safe: 불에 타지 않는 금고

1   It was dark and cold in the garden. Rain was falling. A damp cutting wind[38] was racing about the garden, howling and giving the trees no rest. The banker strained his eyes,[39] but could see neither the earth nor the white statues, nor the lodge, nor the trees. Going to the spot where
5   the lodge stood, he twice called the watchman. No answer followed. Evidently the watchman had sought shelter from the weather, and was now asleep somewhere either in the kitchen or in the greenhouse.

"If I had the pluck to carry out my intention,"[40] thought the old man, "Suspicion would fall first upon the watchman."[41]

10   He felt in the darkness for the steps and the door, and went into the entry of the lodge. Then he groped his way[42] into a little passage and lighted a match. There was not a soul there. There was a bedstead with no bedding on it, and in the corner there was a dark cast–iron stove. The seals on the door leading to the prisoner's rooms were intact.

15   When the match went out[43] the old man, trembling with emotion, peeped through the little window. A candle was burning dimly in the prisoner's room. He was sitting at the table. Nothing could be seen but his back, the hair on his head, and his hands. Open books were lying on the table, on the two easy–chairs, and on the carpet near the table.

20   Five minutes passed and the prisoner did not once stir. Fifteen years' imprisonment had taught him to sit still. The banker tapped at the window with his finger, and the prisoner made no movement whatever

---

38) damp cutting wind: 매섭고 습기 찬 바람
39) strain one's eyes: 눈을 크게 뜨다
40) If I had the pluck to carry out my intention: 내게 만약 내 자신의 목적을 실행할 용기가 있다면
41) Suspicion would fall first upon the watchman: 누구보다도 경비원이 의심을 받게 될 것이다
42) grope one's way: 손으로 더듬어 나아가다, 암중모색하다
43) When the match went out: 성냥불이 꺼지자

in response. Then the banker cautiously broke the seals off the door[44] and put the key in the keyhole. The rusty lock gave a grating sound and the door creaked.[45] The banker expected to hear at once footsteps and a cry of astonishment, but three minutes passed and it was as quiet as ever in the room. He made up his mind to go in.

At the table a man unlike ordinary people was sitting motionless. He was a skeleton with the skin drawn tight over his bones,[46] with long curls like a woman's and a shaggy beard. His face was yellow with an earthy tint in it, his cheeks were hollow, his back long and narrow, and the hand on which his shaggy head was propped was so thin and delicate that it was dreadful to look at it. His hair was already streaked with silver, and seeing his emaciated, aged–looking face,[47] no one would have believed that he was only forty. He was asleep … In front of his bowed head there lay on the table a sheet of paper on which there was something written in fine handwriting.

"Poor creature!" thought the banker, "he is asleep and most likely dreaming of the millions. And I have only to take this half–dead man, throw him on the bed, stifle[48] him a little with the pillow, and the most conscientious expert would find no sign of a violent death.[49] But let us first read what he has written here..."

The banker took the page from the table and read as follows:

---

44) broke the seals off the door: 문의 봉인을 뜯었다

45) The rusty lock gave a grating sound and the door creaked: 녹슨 자물쇠에서는 긁히는 소리가 났고 문은 삐걱거렸다

46) a skeleton with the skin drawn tight over his bones: 뼈에 살가죽을 입혀놓은 해골

47) emaciated, aged – looking face: 수척해지고 나이 들어 보이는 얼굴

48) stifle: 질식시키다

49) the most conscientious expert would find no sign of a violent death: 아무리 꼼꼼한 전문가라도 피살의 흔적을 찾아내지 못할 것이다

1   "To-morrow at twelve o'clock I regain my freedom and the right to associate with other men, but before I leave this room and see the sunshine, I think it necessary to say a few words to you. With a clear conscience I tell you, as before God, who beholds me, that I despise

5   freedom and life and health, and all that in your books is called the good things of the world. "For fifteen years I have been intently studying earthly life. It is true I have not seen the earth nor men, but in your books I have drunk fragrant wine, I have sung songs, I have hunted stags and wild boars in the forests, have loved women ... Beauties as

10   ethereal as clouds,[50] created by the magic of your poets and geniuses, have visited me at night, and have whispered in my ears wonderful tales that have set my brain in a whirl. In your books I have climbed to the peaks of Elburz[51] and Mont Blanc,[52] and from there I have seen the sun rise and have watched it at evening flood the sky, the ocean, and the

15   mountain-tops with gold and crimson. I have watched from there the lightning flashing over my head and cleaving the storm-clouds. I have seen green forests, fields, rivers, lakes, towns. I have heard the singing of the sirens, and the strains of the shepherds' pipes; I have touched the wings of comely devils who flew down to converse with me of God...[53]

20   In your books I have flung myself into the bottomless pit,[54] performed miracles, slain, burned towns, preached new religions, conquered whole kingdoms....

---

50) Beauties as ethereal as clouds: 구름처럼 하늘거리는 미녀들

51) Elburz: 엘브루즈 산맥(카스피해 남쪽 해안을 따라 뻗은 이란 북부의 산맥)

52) Mont Blanc: 몽블랑산[알프스(Alps) 산계(山系)의 최고봉(4,810 m)]

53) converse with a person of a subject: ~와 ~에 관해 이야기하다

54) I have flung myself into the bottomless pit: 바닥 모를 심연에 내 자신을 던졌다

1   "Your books have given me wisdom. All that the unresting thought of man has created in the ages is compressed into a small compass in my brain. I know that I am wiser than all of you.

    "And I despise your books, I despise wisdom and the blessings of this
5 world. It is all worthless, fleeting, illusory, and deceptive, like a mirage. You may be proud, wise, and fine, but death will wipe you off the face of the earth as though you were no more than mice burrowing under the floor,[55] and your posterity, your history, your immortal geniuses will burn or freeze together with the earthly globe.

10   "You have lost your reason and taken the wrong path. You have taken lies for truth, and hideousness for beauty.[56] You would marvel if, owing to strange events of some sorts, frogs and lizards suddenly grew on apple and orange trees instead of fruit, or if roses began to smell like a sweating horse; so I marvel at you who exchange heaven for earth. I don't
15 want to understand you.

    "To prove to you in action how I despise all that you live by, I renounce the two million of which I once dreamed as of paradise and which now I despise.[57] To deprive myself of the right to the money[58] I shall go out from here five hours before the time fixed, and so break
20 the compact..." When the banker had read this he laid the page on the table, kissed the strange man on the head, and went out of the lodge,

---

55) death will wipe you off the face of the earth as though you were no more than mice burrowing under the floor: 죽음은 그대들을 마루 밑의 쥐들처럼 지상에서 쓸어버릴 것이다, 완전히 파괴할 것이다

56) take A for B: A를 B로 잘못 알다, 오해하다

57) which I once dreamed as of paradise and which now I despise: 한때는 낙원을 꿈꾸듯 갈망했으나 이제는 경멸하는

58) To deprive myself of the right to the money: 그 돈에 대한 나의 권리를 스스로 박탈하기 위하여

¹ weeping. At no other time, even when he had lost heavily on the Stock Exchange,[59] had he felt so great a contempt for himself. When he got home he lay on his bed, but his tears and emotion kept him for hours from sleeping. Next morning the watchmen ran in with pale faces, and

⁵ told him they had seen the man who lived in the lodge climb out of the window into the garden, go to the gate, and disappear. The banker went at once with the servants to the lodge and made sure of the flight of his prisoner. To avoid arousing unnecessary talk,[60] he took from the table the writing in which the millions were renounced, and when he got

¹⁰ home locked it up in the fireproof safe.

---

59) At no other time, even when he had lost heavily on the Stock Exchange: 한 번도 느껴보지 못했던, 심지어 주식 투기에서 거액을 날렸을 때에도 느껴보지 못했던

60) To avoid arousing unnecessary talk: 불필요한 말들이 떠돌지 않게 하려고

5

After Twenty Years

O. Henry[1]

1 The policeman on the beat[2] moved up the avenue impressively. The impressiveness was habitual and not for show, for spectators were few. The time was barely 10 o'clock at night, but chilly gusts of wind with a taste of[3] rain in them had well nigh[4] depeopled the streets.

5 Trying doors[5] as he went, twirling his club with many intricate and artful movements, turning now and then[6] to cast his watchful eye adown[7] the pacific thoroughfare,[8] the officer, with his stalwart form

---

1) 오 헨리(O. Henry, 1862-1910): 미국의 단편소설가로 본명은 윌리엄 시드니 포터(William Sydney Porter). 그는 유머 · 페이소스 · 위트로 가득 찬 교묘한 화술과 속어로 일반 미국인의 일상생활을 정확히 묘사한 작가로 유명하다. 우리에게는 「마지막 잎새」("The Last Leaf")의 작가로 잘 알려져 있다.

2) beat: 순찰구역

3) a taste of: 소량의

4) well nigh: 아주 거의

5) try doors: 문단속을 하다

6) now and then: 때때로

7) adown: = down. 아래로

8) thoroughfare: 가로, 주요 도로, 주요 거리

1 and slight swagger,⁹⁾ made a fine picture of a guardian of the peace. The vicinity was one that kept early hours.¹⁰⁾ Now and then you might see the lights of a cigar store or of an all–night lunch counter; but the majority of the doors belonged to business places that had long since¹¹⁾ 5 been closed.

When about midway of a certain block the policeman suddenly slowed his walk. In the doorway of a darkened hardware store a man leaned, with an unlighted cigar in his mouth. As the policeman walked up to him the man spoke up quickly.

10 "It's all right, officer," he said, reassuringly. "I'm just waiting for a friend. It's an appointment made twenty years ago. Sounds a little funny to you, doesn't it? Well, I'll explain if you'd like to make certain it's all straight. About that long ago there used to be a restaurant where this store stands — 'Big Joe' Brady's restaurant."

15 "Until five years ago," said the policeman. "It was torn down¹²⁾ then."

The man in the doorway struck a match and lit his cigar. The light showed a pale, square–jawed face with keen eyes, and a little white scar near his right eyebrow. His scarfpin was a large diamond, oddly set.¹³⁾

20 "Twenty years ago tonight," said the man, "I dined here at 'Big Joe' Brady's with Jimmy Wells, my best chum,¹⁴⁾ and the finest chap in the world. He and I were raised here in New York, just like two brothers,

---

9) swagger: 으스대며 걷기, 활보. 〈동사〉 거드름피우며 걷다
10) keep early hours: 일찍 자고 일찍 일어나다
11) long since: 훨씬 전(옛날)에
12) tear down: 부수다, 분해하다
13) oddly set: 기묘하게(어울리지 않게) 박혀 있는
14) chum: = best friend. 친구, 단짝

together. I was eighteen and Jimmy was twenty. The next morning I was
to start for the West to make my fortune.[15] You couldn't have dragged
Jimmy out of New York; he thought it was the only place on earth. Well,
we agreed that night that we would meet here again exactly twenty years
from that date and time, no matter what our conditions might be or
from what distance we might have to come. We figured that in twenty
years each of us ought to have our destiny worked out and our fortunes
made, whatever they were going to be."

"It sounds pretty interesting," said the policeman. "Rather a long
time between meets, though, it seems to me. Haven't you heard from
your friend since you left?"

"Well, yes, for a time we corresponded," said the other. "But after
a year or two we lost track of[16] each other. You see, the West is a pretty
big proposition,[17] and I kept hustling around over it pretty lively. But I
know Jimmy will meet me here if he's alive, for he always was the truest,
stanchest[18] old chap in the world. He'll never forget. I came a thousand
miles to stand in this door tonight, and it's worth it if my old partner
turns up."

The waiting man pulled out a handsome watch, the lids of it set with
small diamonds.

"Three minutes to ten," he announced. "It was exactly ten o'clock
when we parted here at the restaurant door."

---

15) make a fortune: 돈을 벌다, 재산을 만들다

16) lose track of: = lose touch with. ~와 연락이 끊어지다, ~을 놓치다

17) proposition: 일, 사물, 상대. the West is a pretty big proposition: 서부는 정말 큰 곳(상업이 활발한 곳)이죠

18) stanch: = staunch. 견실한, 신뢰할 만한, 충실한

"Did pretty well out West, didn't you?"[19)] asked the policeman.

"You bet![20)] I hope Jimmy has done half as well. He was a kind of plodder,[21)] though, good fellow as he was. I've had to compete with some of the sharpest wits going to get my pile.[22)] A man gets in a groove[23)] in
5 New York. It takes the West to put a razor–edge[24)] on him."

The policeman twirled his club and took a step or two.

"I'll be on my way. Hope your friend comes around all right. Going to call time on him sharp?"[25)]

"I should say not!" said the other. "I'll give him half an hour at least.
10 If Jimmy is alive on earth he'll be here by that time. So long, officer."

"Good–night, sir," said the policeman, passing on along his beat, trying doors as he went.

There was now a fine, cold drizzle falling, and the wind had risen from its uncertain puffs into a steady blow. The few foot passengers
15 astir[26)] in that quarter hurried dismally and silently along with coat collars turned high and pocketed hands. And in the door of the hardware store the man who had come a thousand miles to fill an appointment,

---

19) Did pretty well out West, didn't you?: 서부에서는 일이 잘 풀렸나보죠, 그렇죠? 이 문장은 밥이 서부에서 적어도 금전적으로는 성공했음을 의미한다. (= Bob apparently has done well, at least financially, out West.)

20) You bet!: = Of course! 물론이지

21) plodder: 터벅터벅 걷는 사람, 말없이 노력하는 사람, 꾸준히 일하는 사람

22) get a pile: 성공하다, 재산을 벌다. pile: = large amount of money. 큰 돈

23) get in a groove: (삶에서) 판에 박히다, 천편일률이 되다

24) razor–edge: 위기. '거친 서부'(Wild West)는 오 헨리의 단편소설 속의 무대 배경으로 자주 등장한다. 20세기 초 도시로서 자리 잡은 지 오래된 뉴욕과 같은 곳에서 억제되었던 불법 활동들이 서부에서는 쉽게 성행되었는데, 이것은 부분적으로는 충분한 법이 집행되지 않았고 사람들이 유동적이었기 때문이다. 따라서 밥이 연루되었던 것과 같은 불법 활동의 기회가 여전히 많이 존재했다.

25) Going to call time on him sharp?: = Are you going to leave if he isn't exactly on time? 그에게 칼같이 시간을 적용할 건가요? 그가 정확하게 제 시간에 나타나지 않으면 당신은 떠날 건가요?

26) astir: 움직여, 일어나

¹ uncertain almost to absurdity, with the friend of his youth, smoked his cigar and waited.

About twenty minutes he waited, and then a tall man in a long overcoat, with collar turned up to his ears, hurried across from the
⁵ opposite side of the street. He went directly to the waiting man.

"Is that you, Bob?" he asked, doubtfully.

"Is that you, Jimmy Wells?" cried the man in the door.

"Bless my heart!" exclaimed the new arrival, grasping both the other's hands with his own. "It's Bob, sure as fate. I was certain I'd find you here
¹⁰ if you were still in existence. Well, well, well! — twenty years is a long time. The old restaurant's gone, Bob; I wish it had lasted, so we could have had another dinner there. How has the West treated you, old man?"

"Bully; it has given me everything I asked it for. You've changed lots, Jimmy. I never thought you were so tall by two or three inches."

¹⁵ "Oh, I grew a bit after I was twenty."

"Doing well in New York, Jimmy?"

"Moderately. I have a position in one of the city departments. Come on, Bob; we'll go around to a place I know of, and have a good long talk about old times."

²⁰ The two men started up the street, arm in arm. The man from the West, his egotism enlarged by success, was beginning to outline the history of his career. The other, submerged in his overcoat, listened with interest.

At the corner stood a drug store, brilliant with electric lights. When
²⁵ they came into this glare each of them turned simultaneously to gaze upon the other's face.

The man from the West stopped suddenly and released his arm.

1   "You're not Jimmy Wells," he snapped. "Twenty years is a long time, but not long enough to change a man's nose from a Roman to a pug."[27]

"It sometimes changes a good man into a bad one," said the tall man. "You've been under arrest for ten minutes, 'Silky'[28] Bob. Chicago
5   thinks you may have dropped over our way and wires us she wants to have a chat with you. Going quietly, are you? That's sensible. Now, before we go on to the station here's a note I was asked to hand you. You may read it here at the window. It's from Patrolman Wells."

The man from the West unfolded the little piece of paper handed
10   him. His hand was steady when he began to read, but it trembled a little by the time he had finished. The note was rather short.

> "Bob: I was at the appointed place on time.
>
> When you struck the match to light your cigar
15 > I saw it was the face of the man wanted in Chicago.
>
> Somehow I couldn't do it myself,
>
> so I went around and got
>
> a plain clothes man[29] to do the job. JIMMY."

---

27) pug: = pug-nose. 사자코, 들창코
28) Silky: 서부에서의 밥(Bob)의 별명으로 여기서는 '요령 있게 요리조리 잘 피하는' 정도의 의미임.
29) a plain clothes man: 사복형사

6

The Gift of the Magi[1]

O. Henry

1

    One dollar and eighty–seven cents. That was all. And sixty cents of it was in pennies. Pennies saved one and two at a time by bulldozing[2] the grocer and the vegetable man and the butcher until one's cheeks burned
5 with the silent imputation[3] of parsimony[4] that such close dealing implied. Three times Della counted it. One dollar and eighty–seven cents. And the next day would be Christmas.

    There was clearly nothing to do but flop[5] down on the shabby little couch and howl. So Della did it. Which instigates[6] the moral
10 reflection that life is made up of sobs, sniffles, and smiles, with sniffles

---

1)   The Gift of the Magi: 1906년에 발표된 오 헨리의 단편소설로, 원제는 「세 동방 박사의 선물」이다. 가난한 서민의 애환을 유머와 페이소스로 그려낸 작품으로 작가 특유의 '반전 결말'(twist ending)이 잘 드러나 있다.

2)   bulldoze: 밀고 나가다, 강요하다

3)   imputation: 돌림, 전가, 비난

4)   parsimony: (돈에 지독히) 인색함

5)   flop: 털썩 주저앉다

6)   instigate: 부추기다, 선동하다

1 predominating.

While the mistress of the home is gradually subsiding from the first stage to the second, take a look at the home. A furnished flat[7] at $8 per week. It did not exactly beggar description, but it certainly had that word

5 on the lookout for the mendicancy squad.[8]

In the vestibule[9] below was a letter–box into which no letter would go, and an electric button from which no mortal finger could coax a ring. Also appertaining[10] thereunto was a card bearing the name "Mr. James Dillingham Young."

10 The "Dillingham" had been flung to the breeze during a former period of prosperity when its possessor was being paid $30 per week. Now, when the income was shrunk to $20, though, they were thinking seriously of contracting to a modest and unassuming[11] D. But whenever Mr. James Dillingham Young came home and reached his flat above he

15 was called "Jim" and greatly hugged by Mrs. James Dillingham Young, already introduced to you as Della. Which is all very good.

Della finished her cry and attended to her cheeks with the powder rag. She stood by the window and looked out dully at a gray cat walking a gray fence in a gray backyard. Tomorrow would be Christmas Day, and

20 she had only $1.87 with which to buy Jim a present. She had been saving every penny she could for months, with this result. Twenty dollars a week doesn't go far. Expenses had been greater than she had calculated.[12] They

---

7) A furnished flat: 가구가 딸려 있는 아파트

8) mendicancy squad: 거지들이나 집 없는 사람들을 체포하는 경찰. mendicancy: 거지, 구걸

9) vestibule: 현관

10) appertain: 속하다, 부속하다, 관계하다

11) unassuming: 잘난 체하지 않는

12) Expenses had been greater than she had calculated: 지출은 그녀가 계산한 것보다 컸다

¹ always are. Only $1.87 to buy a present for Jim. Her Jim. Many a happy hour she had spent planning for something nice for him. Something fine and rare and sterling¹³⁾ — something just a little bit near to being worthy of the honor of being owned by Jim.

⁵ There was a pier-glass¹⁴⁾ between the windows of the room. Perhaps you have seen a pier-glass in an $8 flat. A very thin and very agile¹⁵⁾ person may, by observing his reflection in a rapid sequence of longitudinal strips, obtain a fairly accurate conception of his looks. Della, being slender, had mastered the art.

¹⁰ Suddenly she whirled from the window and stood before the glass. Her eyes were shining brilliantly, but her face had lost its color within twenty seconds. Rapidly she pulled down her hair and let it fall to its full length.¹⁶⁾

Now, there were two possessions of the James Dillingham Youngs in ¹⁵ which they both took a mighty pride. One was Jim's gold watch that had been his father's and his grandfather's. The other was Della's hair. Had the queen of Sheba lived in the flat across the air shaft,¹⁷⁾ Della would have let her hair hang out the window some day to dry just to depreciate¹⁸⁾ Her Majesty's jewels and gifts. Had King Solomon been the janitor, with ²⁰ all his treasures piled up in the basement, Jim would have pulled out his watch every time he passed, just to see him pluck at his beard from envy.

So now Della's beautiful hair fell about her rippling and shining like

---

13) sterling: 훌륭한
14) pier–glass: (창문과 창문 사이 벽에 거는) 체경, 큰 거울
15) agile: 민첩한
16) to its full length: 끝까지
17) air shaft: (건물 등의) 통풍공간, 바람벽
18) depreciate: 가치가 떨어지다

1 a cascade[19] of brown waters. It reached below her knee and made itself almost a garment for her. And then she did it up again nervously and quickly. Once she faltered[20] for a minute and stood still while a tear or two splashed on the worn red carpet.

5 On went her old brown jacket; on went her old brown hat. With a whirl of skirts and with the brilliant sparkle still in her eyes, she fluttered out the door and down the stairs to the street.

Where she stopped the sign read: "Mme.[21] Sofronie. Hair Goods of All Kinds." One flight up Della ran, and collected herself, panting.
10 Madame, large, too white, chilly, hardly looked the "Sofronie."

"Will you buy my hair?" asked Della.

"I buy hair," said Madame. "Take yer hat off and let's have a sight at the looks of it."

Down rippled the brown cascade.

15 "Twenty dollars," said Madame, lifting the mass with a practised hand.[22]

"Give it to me quick," said Della.

Oh, and the next two hours tripped by on rosy wings. Forget the hashed metaphor. She was ransacking[23] the stores for Jim's present.

20 She found it at last. It surely had been made for Jim and no one else. There was no other like it in any of the stores, and she had turned all of

---

19) cascade: 작은 폭포
20) falter: 불안정해지다, 흔들리다
21) Mme.: = Madame
22) with a practised hand: 익숙한 솜씨로
23) ransack: 뒤지다

them inside out. It was a platinum fob chain[24] simple and chaste[25] in design, properly proclaiming[26] its value by substance alone and not by meretricious[27] ornamentation — as all good things should do. It was even worthy of The Watch. As soon as she saw it she knew that it must be Jim's. It was like him. Quietness and value — the description applied to both. Twenty–one dollars they took from her for it, and she hurried home with the 87 cents. With that chain on his watch Jim might be properly anxious about the time in any company. Grand as the watch was, he sometimes looked at it on the sly[28] on account of the old leather strap that he used in place of a chain.

When Della reached home her intoxication[29] gave way a little to prudence and reason. She got out her curling irons and lighted the gas and went to work repairing the ravages made by generosity added to love. Which is always a tremendous task, dear friends — a mammoth task.

Within forty minutes her head was covered with tiny, close–lying curls that made her look wonderfully like a truant[30] schoolboy. She looked at her reflection in the mirror long, carefully, and critically.

"If Jim doesn't kill me," she said to herself, "before he takes a second look at me, he'll say I look like a Coney Island chorus girl. But what could I do — oh! what could I do with a dollar and eighty–seven cents?"

At 7 o'clock the coffee was made and the frying–pan was on the back

---

24) a platinum fob chain: 백금으로 된 시곗줄
25) chaste: 간결한
26) proclaim: 분명히 보여주다
27) meretricious: 겉치레뿐인, 겉만 번지르르한
28) on the sly: 은밀히
29) intoxication: 황홀감, 극도의 흥분, 열중
30) truant: 장난꾸러기

¹ of the stove hot and ready to cook the chops.

Jim was never late. Della doubled the fob chain in her hand and sat on the corner of the table near the door that he always entered. Then she heard his step on the stair away down on the first flight, and she turned

⁵ white for just a moment. She had a habit for saying little silent prayer about the simplest everyday things, and now she whispered: "Please God, make him think I am still pretty."

The door opened and Jim stepped in and closed it. He looked thin and very serious. Poor fellow, he was only twenty–two — and to be

¹⁰ burdened with a family! He needed a new overcoat and he was without gloves.

Jim stopped inside the door, as immovable as a setter³¹⁾ at the scent of quail.³²⁾ His eyes were fixed upon Della, and there was an expression in them that she could not read, and it terrified her. It was not anger, nor

¹⁵ surprise, nor disapproval, nor horror, nor any of the sentiments that she had been prepared for. He simply stared at her fixedly with that peculiar expression on his face.

Della wriggled off the table and went for him.

"Jim, darling," she cried, "don't look at me that way. I had my hair

²⁰ cut off and sold because I couldn't have lived through Christmas without giving you a present. It'll grow out again — you won't mind, will you? I just had to do it. My hair grows awfully fast. Say 'Merry Christmas!' Jim, and let's be happy. You don't know what a nice — what a beautiful, nice gift I've got for you."

---

31) setter: 세터(사냥개로 쓰이기도 하는, 털이 길고 몸집이 큰 개)
32) quail: 메추라기, 메추라기 고기

"You've cut off your hair?" asked Jim, laboriously,[33] as if he had not arrived at that patent[34] fact yet even after the hardest mental labor.

"Cut it off and sold it," said Della. "Don't you like me just as well, anyhow? I'm me without my hair, ain't I?"

Jim looked about the room curiously.

"You say your hair is gone?" he said, with an air almost of idiocy.

"You needn't look for it," said Della. "It's sold, I tell you — sold and gone, too. It's Christmas Eve, boy. Be good to me, for it went for you. Maybe the hairs of my head were numbered," she went on with sudden serious sweetness, "but nobody could ever count my love for you. Shall I put the chops on, Jim?"

Out of his trance[35] Jim seemed quickly to wake. He enfolded his Della. For ten seconds let us regard with discreet[36] scrutiny[37] some inconsequential[38] object in the other direction. Eight dollars a week or a million a year — what is the difference? A mathematician or a wit would give you the wrong answer. The Magi brought valuable gifts, but that was not among them. This dark assertion[39] will be illuminated later on.

Jim drew a package from his overcoat pocket and threw it upon the table.

"Don't make any mistake, Dell," he said, "about me. I don't think there's anything in the way of a haircut or a shave or a shampoo that

---

33) laboriously: 힘들게, 열심히
34) patent: 명백한
35) Out of his trance: 가수 상태에서
36) discreet: 신중한
37) scrutiny: 정밀조사
38) inconsequential: 중요하지 않은, 하찮은
39) assertion: 주장

¹ could make me like my girl any less. But if you'll unwrap that package you may see why you had me going a while at first."

White fingers and nimble tore at the string and paper. And then an ecstatic scream of joy; and then, alas! a quick feminine change to
⁵ hysterical tears and wails, necessitating the immediate employment of all the comforting powers of the lord of the flat.

For there lay The Combs — the set of combs, side and back, that Della had worshipped long in a Broadway window. Beautiful combs, pure tortoise shell, with jewelled rims — just the shade to wear in the
¹⁰ beautiful vanished hair. They were expensive combs, she knew, and her heart had simply craved and yearned over them without the least hope of possession. And now, they were hers, but the tresses that should have adorned the coveted adornments were gone.

But she hugged them to her bosom, and at length she was able to
¹⁵ look up with dim eyes and a smile and say: "My hair grows so fast, Jim!"

And them Della leaped up like a little singed cat and cried, "Oh, oh!"

Jim had not yet seen his beautiful present. She held it out to him eagerly upon her open palm. The dull precious metal seemed to flash
²⁰ with a reflection of her bright and ardent spirit.

"Isn't it a dandy, Jim? I hunted all over town to find it. You'll have to look at the time a hundred times a day now. Give me your watch. I want to see how it looks on it."

Instead of obeying, Jim tumbled down on the couch and put his
²⁵ hands under the back of his head and smiled.

"Dell," said he, "let's put our Christmas presents away and keep 'em a while. They're too nice to use just at present. I sold the watch to get the

¹ money to buy your combs. And now suppose you put the chops on."

The Magi, as you know, were wise men — wonderfully wise men — who brought gifts to the Babe in the manger. They invented the art of giving Christmas presents. Being wise, their gifts were no doubt wise
⁵ ones, possibly bearing the privilege of exchange in case of duplication. And here I have lamely related to you the uneventful chronicle of two foolish children in a flat who most unwisely sacrificed for each other the greatest treasures of their house. But in a last word to the wise of these days let it be said that of all who give gifts these two were the wisest. Of
¹⁰ all who give and receive gifts, such as they are the wisest. Everywhere they are the wisest. They are the Magi.

7

The Last Leaf

O. Henry

1   In a little district west of Washington Square the streets have run crazy and broken themselves into small strips called "places."[1] These "places" make strange angles and curves. One Street crosses itself a time or two. An artist once discovered a valuable possibility in this street.
5   Suppose a collector with a bill for paints, paper and canvas should, in traversing this route, suddenly meet himself coming back, without a cent having been paid on account![2]

So, to quaint old Greenwich Village the art people soon came prowling,[3] hunting for north windows and eighteenth–century gables
10   and Dutch attics and low rents. Then they imported some pewter mugs and a chafing dish or two from Sixth Avenue, and became a "colony."[4]

At the top of a squatty, three–story brick Sue and Johnsy had their

---

1)   places: 거주지들
2)   on account: 신용 거래로, 할부로
3)   prowl: 몰려들다, 배회하다, 서성거리다
4)   colony: 점령지

studio. "Johnsy" was familiar for Joanna. One was from Maine;[5] the other from California. They had met at the table d'hte[6] of an Eighth Street "Delmonico's," and found their tastes in art, chicory salad and bishop sleeves so congenial[7] that the joint studio resulted.

That was in May. In November a cold, unseen stranger, whom the doctors called Pneumonia,[8] stalked about[9] the colony, touching one here and there with his icy fingers. Over on the east side this ravager[10] strode boldly, smiting[11] his victims by scores,[12] but his feet trod[13] slowly through the maze of the narrow and moss–grown[14] "places."

Mr. Pneumonia was not what you would call a chivalric old gentleman.[15] A mite of a little woman with blood thinned by California zephyrs[16] was hardly fair game for the red–fisted, short–breathed old duffer.[17] But Johnsy he smote;[18] and she lay, scarcely moving, on her painted iron bedstead, looking through the small Dutch window–panes at the blank side of the next brick house.

One morning the busy doctor invited Sue into the hallway with a

---

5) Maine: 메인주
6) a table d'hte: (요리) 테이블 도트
7) congenial: 마음이 맞는
8) Pneumonia: 폐렴
9) stalk about: 활보하다
10) ravager: 약탈자, 파괴자
11) smite: 강타하다, 고통을 주다
12) by scores: 수십 명
13) trod: tread의 과거형. 걷다, 걸어가다
14) moss – grown: 이끼가 낀, 이끼가 들어찬
15) chivalric old gentleman: 점잖은 늙은 신사
16) zephyr: 산들바람, 미풍
17) red – fisted, short – breathed old duffer: 손에 많은 피를 묻히고 숨을 고르고 있는 늙은이 얼간이. 본문에서는 폐렴을 지칭함.
18) smote: smite의 과거형. 세게 내리치다, 공격하다

1 shaggy, gray eyebrow.

"She has one chance in — let us say, ten," he said, as he shook down the mercury in his clinical thermometer. "And that chance is for her to want to live. This way people have of lining–u on the side of the

5 undertaker[19] makes the entire pharmacopoeia[20] look silly. Your little lady has made up her mind that she's not going to get well. Has she anything on her mind?"

"She — she wanted to go to Italy and paint the Bay of Naples some day." said Sue.

10 "Paint? — bosh! Has she anything on her mind worth thinking twice — a man for instance?"

"A man?" said Sue, with a jew's–harp twang in her voice. "Is a man worth — but, no, doctor; there is nothing of the kind."

"Well, it is the weakness, then," said the doctor. "I will do all that

15 science, so far as it may filter through my efforts, can accomplish. But whenever my patient begins to count the carriages in her funeral procession[21] I subtract 50 per cent from the curative power[22] of medicines. If you will get her to ask one question about the new winter styles in cloak sleeves I will promise you a one–in–five chance for her,

20 instead of one in ten."

After the doctor had gone Sue went into the workroom and cried a Japanese napkin to a pulp. Then she swaggered[23] into Johnsy's room with

---

19) undertaker: 장의사

20) pharmacopoeia: 약전, 약의 쓰임이 설명되어 있는 종합책

21) carriages in her funeral procession: 장례식에서 사용되는 운구마차

22) curative power: 치유능력

23) swagger: 으스대며 걷다

¹ her drawing board, whistling ragtime.

Johnsy lay, scarcely making a ripple under the bedclothes, with her face toward the window. Sue stopped whistling, thinking she was asleep.

She arranged her board and began a pen–and–ink drawing to illustrate a magazine story. Young artists must pave their way²⁴⁾ to Art by drawing pictures for magazine stories that young authors write to pave their way to Literature.

As Sue was sketching a pair of elegant horseshow riding trousers and a monocle of the figure of the hero, an Idaho cowboy, she heard a low sound, several times repeated. She went quickly to the bedside.

Johnsy's eyes were open wide. She was looking out the window and counting — counting backward.

"Twelve," she said, and little later "eleven"; and then "ten," and "nine"; and then "eight" and "seven", almost together.

Sue look solicitously²⁵⁾ out of the window. What was there to count? There was only a bare, dreary yard to be seen, and the blank side of the brick house twenty feet away. An old, old ivy vine, gnarled²⁶⁾ and decayed²⁷⁾ at the roots, climbed half way up the brick wall. The cold breath of autumn had stricken its leaves from the vine until its skeleton branches clung, almost bare, to the crumbling bricks.

"What is it, dear?" asked Sue.

"Six," said Johnsy, in almost a whisper. "They're falling faster now. Three days ago there were almost a hundred. It made my head ache to

---

24) pave one's way: ~의 기틀을 마련하다

25) solicitously: 걱정스럽게

26) gnarled: 울퉁불퉁하고 비틀린

27) decayed: 썩은

1 count them. But now it's easy. There goes another one. There are only five left now."

"Five what, dear? Tell your Sudie."

"Leaves. On the ivy vine. When the last one falls I must go, too. I've
5 known that for three days. Didn't the doctor tell you?"

"Oh, I never heard of such nonsense," complained Sue, with magnificent scorn.²⁸⁾ "What have old ivy leaves to do with your getting well? And you used to love that vine so, you naughty girl. Don't be a goosey.²⁹⁾ Why, the doctor told me this morning that your chances for
10 getting well real soon were — let's see exactly what he said — he said the chances were ten to one! Why, that's almost as good a chance as we have in New York when we ride on the street cars or walk past a new building. Try to take some broth³⁰⁾ now, and let Sudie go back to her drawing, so she can sell the editor man with it, and buy port wine for her sick child,
15 and pork chops for her greedy self."

"You needn't get any more wine," said Johnsy, keeping her eyes fixed out the window. "There goes another. No, I don't want any broth. That leaves just four. I want to see the last one fall before it gets dark. Then I'll go, too."

20 "Johnsy, dear," said Sue, bending over her, "will you promise me to keep your eyes closed, and not look out the window until I am done working? I must hand those drawings in by to–morrow. I need the light, or I would draw the shade down."

"Couldn't you draw in the other room?" asked Johnsy, coldly.

---

28) scorn: 경멸, 꾸짖음
29) goosey: 바보(어린 아이를 꾸짖는 말)
30) broth: 수프, 죽

1   "I'd rather be here by you," said Sue. "Beside, I don't want you to keep looking at those silly ivy leaves."

"Tell me as soon as you have finished," said Johnsy, closing her eyes, and lying white and still as a fallen statue, "because I want to see the last
5   one fall. I'm tired of waiting. I'm tired of thinking. I want to turn loose[31] my hold on everything, and go sailing down, down, just like one of those poor, tired leaves."

"Try to sleep," said Sue. "I must call Behrman up to be my model for the old hermit miner. I'll not be gone a minute. Don't try to move 'til
10   I come back."

Old Behrman was a painter who lived on the ground floor beneath them. He was past sixty and had a Michael Angelo's Moses beard curling down from the head of a satyr[32] along with the body of an imp.[33] Behrman was a failure in art. Forty years he had wielded[34] the brush
15   without getting near enough to touch the hem of his Mistress's robe. He had been always about to paint a masterpiece, but had never yet begun it. For several years he had painted nothing except now and then a daub[35] in the line of commerce or advertising. He earned a little by serving as a model to those young artists in the colony who could not pay the price
20   of a professional. He drank gin to excess,[36] and still talked of his coming

---

31) turn loose: 놓아주다
32) satyr: 사티로스(고대 그리스 신화에 나오는 숲의 신. 남자의 얼굴과 몸에 염소의 다리와 뿔을 가진 모습)
33) imp: 작은 도깨비
34) wield: (도구를) 들다
35) daub: 서투른 그림
36) to excess: 과도하게

masterpiece. For the rest he was a fierce little old man, who scoffed[37] terribly at softness in any one, and who regarded himself as especial mastiff–in–waiting[38] to protect the two young artists in the studio above.

Sue found Behrman smelling strongly of juniper berries in his dimly lighted den below. In one corner was a blank canvas on an easel that had been waiting there for twenty–five years to receive the first line of the masterpiece. She told him of Johnsy's fancy, and how she feared she would, indeed, light and fragile as a leaf herself, float away, when her slight hold upon the world grew weaker.

Old Behrman, with his red eyes plainly streaming, shouted his contempt and derision[39] for such idiotic imaginings.

"Vass!" he cried. "Is dere people in de world mit der foolishness to die because leafs dey drop off from a confounded vine? I haf not heard of such a thing. No, I will not bose[40] as a model for your fool hermit–dunderhead.[41] Vy do you allow dot[42] silly pusiness to come in der brain of her? Ach, dot poor leetle Miss Yohnsy."

"She is very ill and weak," said Sue, "and the fever has left her mind morbid and full of strange fancies. Very well, Mr. Behrman, if you do not care to pose for me, you needn't. But I think you are a horrid old — old flibbertigibbet."[43]

"You are just like a woman!" yelled Behrman. "Who said I will not

---

37) scoff: 조롱하다

38) especial mastiff – in – waiting: 특별 경호원

39) contempt and derision: 경멸과 조롱

40) bose: pose를 독일어 어투로 표현한 것.

41) hermit – dunderhead: hermit. 은둔자

42) Vy do you allow dot: Why do you allow that을 독일어 어투로 표현한 것.

43) flibbertigibbet: 경박한 사람

1 bose?[44] Go on. I come mit you. For half an hour I haf peen trying to say dot I am ready to bose. Gott! dis is not any blace in which one so goot as Miss Yohnsy shall lie sick. Some day I vill baint a masterpiece, and ve shall all go away. Gott! yes."

5 Johnsy was sleeping when they went upstairs. Sue pulled the shade down to the window–sill, and motioned Behrman into the other room. In there they peered out the window fearfully at the ivy vine. Then they looked at each other for a moment without speaking. A persistent, cold rain was falling, mingled with snow. Behrman, in his old blue shirt, took
10 his seat as the hermit miner on an upturned[45] kettle for a rock.

When Sue awoke from an hour's sleep the next morning she found Johnsy with dull, wide–open eyes staring at the drawn green shade.

"Pull it up; I want to see," she ordered, in a whisper.

Wearily Sue obeyed.

15 But, lo! after the beating rain and fierce gusts of wind that had endured through the livelong night, there yet stood out against the brick wall one ivy leaf. It was the last one on the vine. Still dark green near its stem, with its serrated[46] edges tinted with the yellow of dissolution and decay, it hung bravely from the branch some twenty feet above the
20 ground.

"It is the last one," said Johnsy. "I thought it would surely fall during the night. I heard the wind. It will fall to–day, and I shall die at the same time."

"Dear, dear!" said Sue, leaning her worn face down to the pillow,

---

44) hermit – dunderhead: hermit minder를 독일어 어투로 표현한 것

45) upturned: 뒤집어 놓은

46) serrated: 톱니 모양의

1 "think of me, if you won't think of yourself. What would I do?"

But Johnsy did not answer. The lonesomest[47] thing in all the world is a soul when it is making ready to go on its mysterious, far journey. The fancy seemed to possess her more strongly as one by one the ties that 5 bound her to friendship and to earth were loosed.

The day wore away, and even through the twilight they could see the lone ivy leaf clinging to its stem against the wall. And then, with the coming of the night the north wind was again loosed, while the rain still beat against the windows and pattered down from the low Dutch eaves.

10 When it was light enough Johnsy, the merciless, commanded that the shade be raised.

The ivy leaf was still there.

Johnsy lay for a long time looking at it. And then she called to Sue, who was stirring her chicken broth over the gas stove.

15 "I've been a bad girl, Sudie," said Johnsy. "Something has made that last leaf stay there to show me how wicked I was. It is a sin to want to die. You may bring a me a little broth now, and some milk with a little port in it, and — no; bring me a hand–mirror first, and then pack some pillows about me, and I will sit up and watch you cook."

20 And hour later she said:

"Sudie, some day I hope to paint the Bay of Naples."

The doctor came in the afternoon, and Sue had an excuse to go into the hallway as he left.

"Even chances,"[48] said the doctor, taking Sue's thin, shaking hand 25 in his. "With good nursing you'll win." And now I must see another case

---

47) lonesomest: 매우 외로운, 허전한
48) Even chances: 가능성이 절반이 되었군요

I have downstairs. Behrman, his name is — some kind of an artist, I believe. Pneumonia, too. He is an old, weak man, and the attack is acute. There is no hope for him; but he goes to the hospital to-day to be made more comfortable."

The next day the doctor said to Sue: "She's out of danger. You won. Nutrition and care now — that's all."

And that afternoon Sue came to the bed where Johnsy lay, contentedly[49] knitting a very blue and very useless woollen shoulder scarf, and put one arm around her, pillows and all.

"I have something to tell you, white mouse," she said. "Mr. Behrman died of pneumonia to-day in the hospital. He was ill only two days. The janitor found him the morning of the first day in his room downstairs helpless with pain. His shoes and clothing were wet through and icy cold. They couldn't imagine where he had been on such a dreadful night. And then they found a lantern, still lighted, and a ladder that had been dragged from its place, and some scattered brushes, and a palette with green and yellow colors mixed on it, and — look out the window, dear, at the last ivy leaf on the wall. Didn't you wonder why it never fluttered or moved when the wind blew? Ah, darling, it's Behrman's masterpiece — he painted it there the night that the last leaf fell."

---

49) contentedly: 만족스럽게

8

Witches' Loaves

O. Henry

1   Miss Martha Meacham kept the little bakery on the corner (the one where you go up three steps, and the bell tinkles when you open the door).

Miss Martha was forty, her bank–book[1] showed a credit of two thousand dollars, and she possessed two false teeth[2] and a sympathetic
5   heart.[3] Many people have married whose chances to do so were much inferior to Miss Martha's.

Two or three times a week a customer came in in whom she began to take an interest. He was a middle–aged man, wearing spectacles[4] and a brown beard trimmed to a careful point.

10   He spoke English with a strong German accent. His clothes were worn and darned[5] in places, and wrinkled and baggy in others. But he looked neat, and had very good manners.

---

1) bank – book: 통장
2) false teeth: 의치
3) a sympathetic heart: 동정심이 많은 마음
4) spectacles: 안경
5) darned: 꿰맨

He always bought two loaves of stale bread.[6] Fresh bread was five cents a loaf. Stale ones were two for five. Never did he call for anything but stale bread.

Once Miss Martha saw a red and brown stain on his fingers. She was sure then that he was an artist and very poor. No doubt he lived in a garret, where he painted pictures and ate stale bread and thought of the good things to eat in Miss Martha's bakery.

Often when Miss Martha sat down to her chops and light rolls and jam and tea she would sigh, and wish that the gentle–mannered artist might share her tasty meal instead of eating his dry crust in that draughty attic. Miss Martha's heart, as you have been told, was a sympathetic one.

In order to test her theory as to his occupation, she brought from her room one day a painting that she had bought at a sale, and set it against the shelves behind the bread counter.

It was a Venetian scene.[7] A splendid marble palazzo[8] (so it said on the picture) stood in the foreground — or rather forewater. For the rest there were gondolas (with the lady trailing her hand in the water), clouds, sky, and chiaro–oscuro[9] in plenty. No artist could fail to notice it.

Two days afterward the customer came in.

"Two loafs of stale bread, if you please.

"You haf[10] here a fine picture, madame," he said while she was wrapping up the bread.

---

6) stale bread: 묵은 빵
7) a Venetian scene: 베네치아 풍경화
8) palazzo: 궁전
9) chiaro – oscuro: 빛과 그림자, 명암의 배합
10) haf: have를 독일어의 어투를 가진 남자의 발음으로 표현한 것.

"Yes?" says Miss Martha, reveling in her own cunning.[11] "I do so admire art and" (no, it would not do to say "artists" thus early) "and paintings," she substituted.[12] "You think it is a good picture?"

"Der balance," said the customer, is not in good drawing. Der bairspective[13] of it is not true. Goot morning,[14] madame."

He took his bread, bowed, and hurried out.

Yes, he must be an artist. Miss Martha took the picture back to her room.

How gentle and kindly his eyes shone behind his spectacles! What a broad brow he had! To be able to judge perspective at a glance — and to live on stale bread! But genius often has to struggle before it is recognized.

What a thing it would be for art and perspective if genius were backed by two thousand dollars in bank, a bakery, and a sympathetic heart to — But these were day–dreams, Miss Martha.

Often now when he came he would chat for a while across the showcase. He seemed to crave[15] Miss Martha's cheerful words.

He kept on buying stale bread. Never a cake, never a pie, never one of her delicious Sally Lunns.

She thought he began to look thinner and discouraged. Her heart ached to add something good to eat to his meagre[16] purchase, but her courage failed at the act. She did not dare affront him. She knew the

---

11) reveling in her own cunning: 자기 자신의 잔꾀에 한껏 즐기며

12) substitute: 말을 바꾸다

13) Der bairspective: the perspective(균형감, 원근법)를 독일어 어투로 표현한 것.

14) Goot morning: Good morning을 독일어 어투로 표현한 것.

15) crave: ~을 갈망하다, 열망하다

16) meagre: 빈약한

1 pride of artists.

Miss Martha took to wearing her blue–dotted silk waist[17] behind the counter. In the back room she cooked a mysterious compound of quince seeds and borax.[18] Ever so many people use it for the complexion.[19]

5 One day the customer came in as usual, laid his nickel[20] on the showcase, and called for his stale loaves. While Miss Martha was reaching for them there was a great tooting and clanging,[21] and a fire–engine came lumbering past.

The customer hurried to the door to look, as any one will. Suddenly
10 inspired, Miss Martha seized the opportunity.

On the bottom shelf behind the counter was a pound of fresh butter that the dairyman had left ten minutes before. With a bread knife Miss Martha made a deep slash in each of the stale loaves, inserted a generous quantity of butter, and pressed the loaves tight again.

15 When the customer turned once more she was tying the paper around them.

When he had gone, after an unusually pleasant little chat, Miss Martha smiled to herself, but not without a slight fluttering of the heart.

Had she been too bold? Would he take offense?[22] But surely not.
20 There was no language of edibles. Butter was no emblem of unmaidenly forwardness.[23]

---

17) blue – dotted silk waist: 푸른 점이 있는 실크블라우스

18) quince seeds and borax: 모과 씨와 붕사(씻는 데 사용하는 하얀색 파우더)

19) complexion: 피부색

20) nickel: 5센트

21) tooting and clanging: 빵빵거리고 쨍그랑거리는 소리

22) take offense: 기분을 상해하다

23) unmaidenly forwardness: 숙녀답지 않은 나섬

For a long time that day her mind dwelt on the subject. She imagined the scene when he should discover her little deception.

He would lay down his brushes and palette. There would stand his easel with the picture he was painting in which the perspective was beyond criticism.

He would prepare for his luncheon of dry bread and water. He would slice into a loaf — ah!

Miss Martha blushed. Would he think of the hand that placed it there as he ate? Would he —

The front door bell jangled viciously.[24] Somebody was coming in, making a great deal of noise.

Miss Martha hurried to the front. Two men were there. One was a young man smoking a pipe — a man she had never seen before. The other was her artist.

His face was very red, his hat was on the back of his head, his hair was wildly rumpled. He clinched his two fists and shook them ferociously[25] at Miss Martha. At Miss Martha.

"Dummkopf!"[26] he shouted with extreme loudness; and then "Tausendonfer!" or something like it in German.

The young man tried to draw him away.

"I vill[27] not go," he said angrily, "else I shall told her."

He made a bass drum of Miss Martha's counter.

"You haf shpoilt[28] me," he cried, his blue eyes blazing behind his

---

24) viciously: 요란하게
25) ferociously: 사납게
26) Dummkopf: 이 멍청한 여자야!
27) vill: will을 독일어 발음으로 표기한 것.
28) haf shpoilt: have spoiled을 독일어 발음으로 표기한 것. 망쳐놓았다

spectacles. "I vill tell you. You vas von meddingsome old cat!"[29]

Miss Martha leaned weakly against the shelves and laid one hand on her blue–dotted silk waist. The young man took the other by the collar.

"Come on," he said, "you've said enough." He dragged the angry one out at the door to the sidewalk, and then came back.

"Guess you ought to be told, ma'am," he said, "what the row is about. That's Blumberger. He's an architectural draftsman.[30] I work in the same office with him.

"He's been working hard for three months drawing a plan for a new city hall. It was a prize competition. He finished inking the lines[31] yesterday. You know, a draftsman always makes his drawing in pencil first. When it's done he rubs out the pencil lines with handfuls of stale bread crumbs. That's better than India rubber.[32]

"Blumberger's been buying the bread here. Well, to–day — well, you know, ma'am, that butter isn't — well, Blumberger's plan isn't good for anything now except to cut up into railroad sandwiches."[33]

Miss Martha went into the back room. She took off the blue–dotted silk waist and put on the old brown serge[34] she used to wear. Then she poured the quince seed and borax mixture out of the window into the ash can.[35]

---

29) You vas von meddingsome old cat!: You are a meddlesome old cat!(당신은 참견하기 좋아하는 늙은 여편네라구!)를 독일어 어투로 표현한 것.

30) an architectural draftsman: 건축 제도사

31) inking the lines: 선들에 잉크를 먹이는 작업

32) India rubber: 인도산 지우개

33) railroad sandwiches: 철도역에서나 파는 샌드위치

34) serge: 울 셔츠

35) ash can: 쓰레기통

9

The Boarding House

James Joyce[1]

1   Mrs. Mooney was a butcher's daughter. She was a woman who was quite able to keep things to herself:[2] a determined woman. She had married her father's foreman and opened a butcher's shop near Spring Gardens.[3] But as soon as his father–in–law was dead Mr. Mooney began
5 to go to the devil.[4] He drank, plundered the till, ran headlong into debt. It was no use making him take the pledge:[5] he was sure to break out again a few days after. By fighting his wife in the presence of customers

---

1)   제임스 조이스(James Joyce, 1882-1941): 아일랜드의 더블린에서 태어났고, 캘트 신화나 아일랜드 민간 설화에 의존하는 아일랜드 문단의 편협성에 반발하고 유럽 문학 작품에 심취했다. 아일랜드 문예부흥 운동을 주도한 예이츠(Yeats), 싱(Synge) 등과 친분을 유지하기도 했다. 그는 기존의 전통적 소설 양식의 답습을 거부하면서 이를 혁신하고자 하는 새로운 실험을 시도한다. 작품으로는 『더블린 사람들』(*Dubliners*), 『젊은 예술가의 초상』(*A Portrait of the Artist As a Young Man*), 『율리시스』(*Ulysses*) 등이 있다.

2)   keep things to herself: 일을 혼자 알아서 처리하다

3)   Spring Gardens: 스프링 가든스. 영국의 런던에 있는 거리. 트릭분수가 특색인 이 장소의 이름을 본 따서 지어진 이름.

4)   go to the devil: 파멸의 길을 가다

5)   It was no use making him take the pledge: (잘못을 다시는 저지르지 않겠다는) 맹세를 시켜봤자 소용이 없었다

¹ and by buying bad meat he ruined his business. One night he went for his wife with the cleaver[6] and she had to sleep a neighbour's house.

After that they lived apart. She went to the priest and got a separation[7] from him with care of the children. She would give him
⁵ neither money nor food nor house–room; and so he was obliged to enlist himself as[8] a sheriff's man. He was a shabby stooped little drunkard with a white face and a white moustache and white eyebrows, pencilled above his little eyes, which were veined and raw; and all day long he sat in the bailiff's room, waiting to be put on a job. Mrs. Mooney, who had taken
¹⁰ what remained of her money out of the butcher business and set up a boarding house in Hardwicke Street, was a big imposing woman. Her house had a floating population[9] made up of tourists from Liverpool and the Isle of Man[10] and, occasionally, artistes from the music halls. Its resident population[11] was made up of clerks from the city. She governed
¹⁵ the house cunningly and firmly, knew when to give credit, when to be stern and when to let things pass.[12] All the resident young men spoke of her as The Madam.

Mrs. Mooney's young men paid fifteen shillings a week for board and lodgings[13] (beer or stout at dinner excluded). They shared in common tastes
²⁰ and occupations and for this reason they were very chummy with one

---

6)   he went for his wife with the cleaver: 식칼을 가지고 덤벼들었다

7)   a separation: 별거허가

8)   enlist himself as: ~로 취직하다

9)   a floating population: 뜨내기손님들

10) the Isle of Man: 맨섬. 영국 잉글랜드와 북아일랜드 사이의 아이리시해 중앙에 있는 섬

11) resident population: 고정 손님들

12) let things pass: 눈감아주다

13) for board and lodgings: 식대와 방값으로

1 another. They discussed with one another the chances of favourites and outsiders.[14] Jack Mooney, the Madam's son, who was clerk to a commission agent in Fleet Street, had the reputation of being a hard case.[15] He was fond of using soldiers' obscenities:[16] usually he came

5 home in the small hours.[17] When he met his friends he had always a good one to tell them and he was always sure to be on to a good thing — that is to say, a likely horse or a likely artiste. He was also handy with the mits[18] and sang comic songs. On Sunday nights there would often be a reunion in Mrs. Mooney's front drawing-room. The music-hall artistes

10 would oblige; and Sheridan played waltzes and polkas and vamped accompaniments. Polly Mooney, the Madam's daughter, would also sing. She sang:

I'm a... naughty girl.

You needn't sham:[19]

15 You know I am.

Polly was a slim girl of nineteen; she had light soft hair and a small full[20] mouth. Her eyes, which were grey with a shade of green through them, had a habit of glancing upwards when she spoke with anyone, which made her look like a little perverse madonna. Mrs. Mooney had

20 first sent her daughter to be a typist in a corn-factor's[21] office but, as

---

14) the chances of favourites and outsiders: (경마에서) 인기 있는 말과 인기 없는 말의 이길 확률

15) a hard case: 다루기 힘든 악당, 불한당

16) soldiers' obscenities: 군인들이 쓰는 욕설

17) in the small hours: 꼭두새벽에, (일반적으로) 새벽 1시나 2시경, 혹은 깊은 밤

18) handy with his mits: 주먹을 잘 쓰다

19) You needn't sham: 모르는 척할 필요가 없다

20) full: 통통한

21) corn – factor: 곡물도매상

a disreputable sheriff's man used to come every other day to the office, asking to be allowed to say a word to his daughter, she had taken her daughter home again and set her to do housework. As Polly was very lively the intention was to give her the run of the young men.[22] Besides
5 young men like to feel that there is a young woman not very far away. Polly, of course, flirted with the young men but Mrs. Mooney, who was a shrewd judge,[23] knew that the young men were only passing the time away: none of them meant business.[24] Things went on so for a long time and Mrs. Mooney began to think of sending Polly back to typewriting
10 when she noticed that something was going on between Polly and one of the young men. She watched the pair and kept her own counsel.[25]

Polly knew that she was being watched, but still her mother's persistent silence could not be misunderstood.[26] There had been no open complicity between mother and daughter,[27] no open understanding but,
15 though people in the house began to talk of the affair, still Mrs. Mooney did not intervene. Polly began to grow a little strange in her manner and the young man was evidently perturbed. At last, when she judged it to be the right moment, Mrs. Mooney intervened. She dealt with moral problems as a cleaver deals with meat: and in this case she had made up
20 her mind.

It was a bright Sunday morning of early summer, promising heat, but

---

22) give her the run of the young men: 젊은 하숙생들과 사귈 기회를 주다

23) a shrewd judge: 빈틈없는 판단력을 가진 사람

24) none of them meant business: 진지하게 생각하는 젊은이는 아무도 없었다

25) kept her own counsel: 그녀 혼자만 알아두고 있었다

26) her mother's persistent silence could not be misunderstood: 그녀의 엄마가 계속 침묵을 지키는 것이 무슨 뜻인지 잘 알고 있었다

27) open complicity between mother and daughter: 엄마와 딸 사이의 공공연한 공모

1 with a fresh breeze blowing. All the windows of the boarding house were open and the lace curtains ballooned gently towards the street beneath the raised sashes. The belfry of George's Church sent out constant peals and worshippers, singly or in groups, traversed the little circus before the

5 church, revealing their purpose by their self–contained demeanour no less than by the little volumes[28] in their gloved hands. Breakfast was over in the boarding house and the table of the breakfast–room was covered with plates on which lay yellow streaks of eggs with morsels of bacon–fat and bacon–rind. Mrs. Mooney sat in the straw arm–chair and watched

10 the servant Mary remove the breakfast things. She made Mary collect the crusts and pieces of broken bread to help to make Tuesday's bread–pudding. When the table was cleared, the broken bread collected, the sugar and butter safe under lock and key, she began to reconstruct the interview which she had had the night before with Polly. Things were

15 as she had suspected: she had been frank in her questions and Polly had been frank in her answers. Both had been somewhat awkward, of course. She had been made awkward by her not wishing to receive the news in too cavalier a fashion or to seem to have connived[29] and Polly had been made awkward not merely because allusions of that kind always made

20 her awkward but also because she did not wish it to be thought that in her wise innocence she had divined the intention behind her mother's tolerance.[30]

---

28) the little volumes: 성경이나 찬송가 따위의 책을 말함.

29) by her not wishing to receive the news in too cavalier a fashion or to seem to have connived: 딸이 남자와 관계를 가진 일을 너무 무신경하게 받아들이거나 묵인해주는 것처럼 보이기를 원치 않음으로 해서

30) She had divined the intention behind her mother's tolerance: 엄마의 관용 뒤에 숨어있는 의도를 알아차렸다

1   Mrs. Mooney glanced instinctively at the little gilt clock on the mantelpiece as soon as she had become aware through her revery[31] that the bells of George's Church had stopped ringing. It was seventeen minutes past eleven: she would have lots of time to have the matter

5   out with Mr. Doran[32] and then catch short twelve[33] at Marlborough Street. She was sure she would win. To begin with she had all the weight of social opinion on her side:[34] she was an outraged mother. She had allowed him to live beneath her roof, assuming that he was a man of honour and he had simply abused her hospitality.[35] He was thirty–

10 four or thirty–five years of age, so that youth could not be pleaded as his excuse;[36] nor could ignorance be his excuse since he was a man who had seen something of the world.[37] He had simply taken advantage of Polly's youth and inexperience: that was evident. The question was: What reparation would he make?

15   There must be reparation made in such case. It is all very well for the man:[38] he can go his ways as if nothing had happened, having had his moment of pleasure, but the girl has to bear the brunt.[39] Some mothers would be content to patch up such an affair for a sum of money;[40]

---

31) revery: 공상, 환상, 생각

32) have the matter out with Mr. Doran: 도란 씨와 담판을 짓다

33) catch short twelve: (미사 시간이) 짧은 정오미사에 참석하다

34) she had all the weight of social opinion on her side: 여론의 압력을 자기편으로 끌어들일 수 있었다

35) abused her hospitality: 그녀의 호의를 짓밟았다

36) youth could not be pleaded as his excuse: (나이가 서른이 넘은 사람이니) 나이가 어려 철없이 그런 일을 저질렀다는 변명을 할 수도 없었다

37) a man who had seen something of the world: 세상물정을 아는 사람

38) It is all very well for the man: 그런 일이 남자에게는 아무렇지도 않다

39) bear the brunt: (고통스러운 상황 따위를) 참다, 견디다

40) patch up such an affair for a sum of money: 일정한 돈을 받고 그런 문제를 수습하다

1 she had known cases of it. But she would not do so. For her only one
reparation could make up for the loss of her daughter's honour: marriage.

She counted all her cards[41] again before sending Mary up to Doran's
room to say that she wished to speak with him. She felt sure she would
5 win. He was a serious young man, not rakish[42] or loud–voiced like the
others. If it had been Mr. Sheridan or Mr. Meade or Bantam Lyons her
task would have been much harder. She did not think he would face
publicity.[43] All the lodgers in the house knew something of the affair;
details had been invented by some. Besides, he had been employed for
10 thirteen years in a great Catholic wine–merchant's office and publicity
would mean for him, perhaps, the loss of his job. Whereas if he agreed
all might be well. She knew he had a good screw for one thing[44] and she
suspected he had a bit of stuff put by.[45]

Nearly the half–hour! She stood up and surveyed herself in the
15 pier–glass.[46] The decisive expression[47] of her great florid face satisfied
her and she thought of some mothers she knew who could not get their
daughters off their hands.[48]

Mr. Doran was very anxious indeed this Sunday morning. He had
made two attempts to shave but his hand had been so unsteady that he
20 had been obliged to desist.[49] Three days' reddish beard fringed his jaws

---

41) counted all her cards: 모든 수를 계산해보았다
42) rakish: 난봉꾼 같은
43) face publicity: 세상에 알려져도 태연하다
44) he had a good screw for one thing: 그는 우선 봉급을 많이 받고 있었다. screw: = salary
45) he had a bit of stuff put by: 그는 얼마간의 돈을 저축하고 있었다. stuff: 현금
46) pier‑glass: (창문과 창문 사이 벽에 거는) 체경, 큰 거울
47) decisive expression: 결의에 찬 표정
48) get their daughters off their hands: 딸들을 품안에서 치워버리다, 즉 시집을 보내버리다
49) desist: 중단하다, 그만두다

1　and every two or three minutes a mist gathered on his glasses so that he
had to take them off and polish them with his pocket–handkerchief. The
recollection of his confession of the night before[50] was a cause of acute
pain to him; the priest had drawn out every ridiculous detail of the affair
5　and in the end had so magnified his sin that he was almost thankful at
being afforded a loophole of reparation.[51] The harm was done.[52] What
could he do now but marry her or run away? He could not brazen it
out.[53] The affair would be sure to be talked of[54] and his employer would
be certain to hear of it. Dublin is such a small city: everyone knows
10　everyone else's business. He felt his heart leap warmly in his throat as
he heard in his excited imagination old Mr. Leonard calling out in his
rasping voice: "Send Mr. Doran here, please."

　　All his long years of service gone for nothing! All his industry and
diligence thrown away! As a young man he had sown his wild oats,[55] of
15　course; he had boasted of his free–thinking and denied the existence of
God to his companions in public houses.[56] But that was all passed and
done with... nearly. He still bought a copy of Reynolds's Newspaper[57]
every week but he attended to his religious duties and for nine–tenths of
the year lived a regular life. He had money enough to settle down on; it

---

50) his confession of the night before: 전날 밤 (신부님 앞에서) 했던 (자기 죄의) 고백, 고해

51) had so magnified his sin that he was almost thankful at being afforded a loophole of reparation: 하도 자기 죄를 확대시켰기 때문에 그에 대한 보상이라는 탈출구가 있다면 고맙게 여길 지경이 되었다

52) The harm was done: 일은 이미 벌어지고 말았다

53) He could not brazen it out: 철면피처럼 뻔뻔하게 버틸 수 없었다

54) be talked of: 사람들의 입방아에 오르다

55) sow one's wild oats: 젊어서 방탕하다

56) public houses: 술집들

57) Reynolds's Newspaper: 스캔들 따위를 많이 실었던 신문

1 was not that.[58] But the family would look down on her. First of all there was her disreputable father and then her mother's boarding house was beginning to get a certain fame.[59] He had a notion that he was being had.[60] He could imagine his friends talking of the affair and laughing.

5 She was a little vulgar; some times she said "I seen" and "If I had've known."[61] But what would grammar matter if he really loved her? He could not make up his mind whether to like her or despise her for what she had done. Of course he had done it too. His instinct urged him to remain free, not to marry. Once you are married you are done for,[62] it

10 said.

While he was sitting helplessly on the side of the bed in shirt and trousers she tapped lightly at his door and entered. She told him all, that she had made a clean breast of[63] it to her mother and that her mother would speak with him that morning. She cried and threw her arms

15 round his neck, saying:

"O Bob! Bob! What am I to do? What am I to do at all?"

She would put an end to herself,[64] she said.

He comforted her feebly, telling her not to cry, that it would be all right, never fear. He felt against his shirt the agitation of her bosom.

20 It was not altogether his fault that it had happened. He remembered

---

58) it was not that: 문제는 그게 아니었다

59) get a certain fame: (좋지 못한) 어떤 평판을 얻다

60) He had a notion that he was being had: 그는 자신이 걸려들었다는 생각이 들었다. be had: 사기 당하다

61) she said "I seen" and "If I had've known": 무식하게 문법에 어긋나게 말한다는 것

62) Once you are married you are done for: 일단 결혼하면 끝장이다. do for: ~을 망치다

63) make a clean breast of something: (잘못을) 모두 다 털어놓다

64) put an end to herself: = kill herself

¹ well, with the curious patient memory of the celibate, the first casual caresses her dress, her breath, her fingers had given him. Then late one night as he was undressing for bed she had tapped at his door, timidly. She wanted to relight her candle at his for hers had been blown out
⁵ by a gust. It was her bath night.⁶⁵⁾ She wore a loose open combing-jacket⁶⁶⁾ of printed flannel. Her white instep shone in the opening of her furry slippers and the blood glowed warmly behind her perfumed skin. From her hands and wrists too as she lit and steadied her candle a faint perfume arose.

¹⁰   On nights when he came in very late it was she who warmed up his dinner. He scarcely knew what he was eating feeling her beside him alone, at night, in the sleeping house.⁶⁷⁾ And her thoughtfulness! If the night was anyway cold or wet or windy there was sure to be a little tumbler of punch ready for him. Perhaps they could be happy together...
¹⁵ They used to go upstairs together on tiptoe, each with a candle, and on the third landing⁶⁸⁾ exchange reluctant goodnights. They used to kiss. He remembered well her eyes, the touch of her hand and his delirium... But delirium passes.⁶⁹⁾ He echoed her phrase, applying it to himself: "What am I to do?" The instinct of the celibate warned him to hold back. But
²⁰ the sin was there;⁷⁰⁾ even his sense of honour told him that reparation must be made for such a sin. While he was sitting with her on the side of the bed Mary came to the door and said that the missus wanted to see

---

65) her bath night: 그녀가 목욕을 한 날 밤
66) combing‑jacket: 코밍 재킷(화장할 때 란제리 등의 위에 걸치는 침실용 상의)
67) in the sleeping house: 다른 모든 사람들이 잠든 집에서
68) the third landing: 3~4층 사이의 층계
69) delirium passes: 그런 꿈같은 상태는 사라지기 마련이다
70) But the sin was there: 그러나 저지른 죄는 피할 길 없었다

¹ him in the parlour. He stood up to put on his coat and waistcoat, more helpless than ever. When he was dressed he went over to her to comfort her. It would be all right, never fear. He left her crying on the bed and moaning softly: "O my God!" Going down the stairs his glasses became
⁵ so dimmed with moisture that he had to take them off and polish them. He longed to ascend through the roof and fly away to another country where he would never hear again of his trouble, and yet a force pushed him downstairs step by step. The implacable⁷¹⁾ faces of his employer and of the Madam stared upon his discomfiture.⁷²⁾ On the last flight of stairs
¹⁰ he passed Jack Mooney who was coming up from the pantry nursing two bottles of Bass.⁷³⁾ They saluted coldly; and the lover's eyes rested for a second or two on a thick bulldog face and a pair of thick short arms. When he reached the foot of the staircase he glanced up and saw Jack regarding him from the door of the return–room.⁷⁴⁾

¹⁵   Suddenly he remembered the night when one of the music–hall artistes, a little blond Londoner, had made a rather free allusion to Polly. The reunion had been almost broken up on account of Jack's violence. Everyone tried to quiet him. The music–hall artiste, a little paler than usual, kept smiling and saying that there was no harm meant: but Jack
²⁰ kept shouting at him that if any fellow tried that sort of a game on with his sister⁷⁵⁾ he'd bloody well put his teeth down his throat, so he would.⁷⁶⁾

---

71) impacable: 확고한, 달랠 수 없는

72) discomfiture: 쩔쩔맴, 당황

73) nursing two bottles of Bass: 배스 맥주 두 병을 안고

74) return – room: 모퉁이에 붙여 짓는 방

75) if any fellow tried that sort of a game on with his sister: 어떤 녀석이 자기 누이를 상대로 그런 수작을 부리려고 한다면

76) so he would: 능히 그럴 사람이었다

1 Polly sat for a little time on the side of the bed, crying. Then she dried her eyes and went over to the looking–glass. She dipped the end of the towel in the water–jug and refreshed her eyes with the cool water. She looked at herself in profile and readjusted a hairpin above her ear. Then she went

5 back to the bed again and sat at the foot. She regarded the pillows for a long time and the sight of them awakened in her mind secret, amiable memories. She rested the nape of her neck against the cool iron bed–rail and fell into a reverie.[77] There was no longer any perturbation[78] visible on her face. She waited on patiently, almost cheerfully, without alarm,

10 her memories gradually giving place to hopes and visions of the future.[79] Her hopes and visions were so intricate that she no longer saw the white pillows on which her gaze was fixed or remembered that she was waiting for anything. At last she heard her mother calling. She started to her feet[80] and ran to the banisters.

15   "Polly! Polly!"

"Yes, mamma?"

"Come down, dear. Mr. Doran wants to speak to you."

Then she remembered what she had been waiting for.

---

77) reverie: 환상, 공상, 몽상

78) perturbation: (심리적인) 동요, 작은 변화

79) her memories gradually giving place to hopes and visions of the future: 그녀의 기억은 점차 미래에 대한 희망과 꿈으로 바뀌었다

80) started to her feet: 벌떡 일어났다

10

Araby[1]

James Joyce

1   North Richmond Street,[2] being blind,[3] was a quiet street except
at the hour when the Christian Brothers' School[4] set the boys free.
An uninhabited house of two storeys stood at the blind end, detached
from its neighbours in a square ground. The other houses of the street,
5 conscious of decent lives within them, gazed at one another with brown
imperturbable[5] faces.

The former tenant of our house, a priest, had died in the back
drawing–room. Air, musty from having been long enclosed, hung in
all the rooms, and the waste room behind the kitchen was littered with
10 old useless papers. Among these I found a few paper–covered books,

---

1) Araby: 애러비 자선시장. 아라비아(Arabia)의 뜻으로, 1894년 5월 더블린에서 열린 동양적 풍물
   을 팔았던 자선바자회 이름. 실제로 1894년 5월 14일부터 19일 사이에 저비스가 병원(Jervis Street
   Hospital)을 돕기 위해 열렸다. Araby: = 〈고어〉 Arabia

2) North Richmond Street: 노스 리치몬드가. 더블린 북쪽 끝에 있는 거리 이름. 실제로 조이스가 소년
   시절에 이 골목 17호에 살았다고 한다.

3) blind: = with only one opening. 막다른

4) Christian Brothers' School: Christian Brothers 수도회에서 운영하는 초등학교

5) imperturbable: 침착한, 차분한

¹ the pages of which were curled and damp: *The Abbot*,⁶⁾ by Walter Scott, *The Devout Communicant*,⁷⁾ and *The Memoirs of Vidocq*.⁸⁾ I liked the last best because its leaves⁹⁾ were yellow. The wild garden behind the house contained a central apple–tree and a few straggling bushes, under one of ⁵ which I found the late tenant's rusty bicycle–pump. He had been a very charitable priest; in his will¹⁰⁾ he had left all his money to institutions and the furniture of his house to his sister.

When the short days of winter came, dusk fell before we had well eaten our dinners. When we met in the street the houses had grown ¹⁰ sombre. The space of sky above us was the colour of ever–changing violet and towards it the lamps of the street lifted their feeble lanterns. The cold air stung¹¹⁾ us and we played till our bodies glowed. Our shouts echoed in the silent street. The career¹²⁾ of our play brought us through the dark muddy lanes behind the houses, where we ran the gauntlet¹³⁾ ¹⁵ of the rough tribes¹⁴⁾ from the cottages, to the back doors of the dark dripping gardens where odours arose from the ashpits,¹⁵⁾ to the dark odorous stables where a coachman smoothed and combed the horse or

---

6) *The Abbot*: 『대수도원장』. 스코틀랜드의 소설가 · 시인인 월터 스콧(1771–1832)의 1820년 작품. 메리 여왕(Queen Mary)이 유폐당했던 시대를 다루었다.

7) *The Devout Communicant*: 『독실한 성체 배령자』(1813). 프란체스코 수도회의 수사인 파시피쿠스 베이커(Pacificus Baker, 1695–1774)가 저술한 종교 서적.

8) *The Memoirs of Vidocq*: 『비도크의 회고록』(1829). 비도크는 프랑스 탐정.

9) leaves: 책장. leaf: = a sheet of paper

10) will: = a legal statement of a person's wishes about what shall be done with his property after he is dead. 유언(장)

11) stung: (추위가) 살을 에는 듯했다

12) career: = course. 경로

13) ran the gauntlet: 태형을 당하다; 가혹한 공격을 받다. 양쪽으로 늘어선 아이들 사이를 통과하며 매를 맞았다는 뜻.

14) tribes: 패거리들

15) ashpits: 잿구멍, 재 떨어지는 구멍

shook music from the buckled harness.[16] When we returned to the street light from the kitchen windows had filled the areas. If my uncle was seen turning the corner, we hid in the shadow until we had seen him safely housed.[17] Or if Mangan's sister came out on the doorstep to call her brother in to his tea, we watched her from our shadow peer up and down the street.[18] We waited to see whether she would remain or go in and, if she remained, we left our shadow and walked up to Mangan's steps resignedly.[19] She was waiting for us, her figure defined by the light from the half–opened door.[20] Her brother always teased her before he obeyed, and I stood by the railings looking at her. Her dress swung as she moved her body, and the soft rope of her hair[21] tossed from side to side.

Every morning I lay on the floor in the front parlour watching her door. The blind was pulled down to within an inch of the sash so that I could not be seen. When she came out on the doorstep my heart leaped. I ran to the hall, seized my books and followed her. I kept her brown figure always in my eye and, when we came near the point at which our ways diverged, I quickened my pace and passed her. This happened morning after morning. I had never spoken to her, except for a few casual words, and yet her name was like a summons to all my foolish blood.[22]

Her image accompanied me even in places the most hostile to

---

16) shook music from the buckled harness: 죔쇠가 달린 마구를 흔들어 (음악) 소리를 내다

17) had seen him safely housed: 그가 확실히 집안에 들어간 것을 보았다

18) watched her from our shadow peer up and down the street: 그림자 속에 숨어 그녀가 거리 이곳저곳을 살피는 것을 지켜보았다

19) resignedly: 단념하고, 체념하고

20) her figure defined by the light from the half – opened door: 그녀의 윤곽은 반쯤 열린 문에서 새어 나오는 불빛으로 뚜렷해졌다

21) the soft rope of her hair: 그녀의 매끄럽게 땋아 늘인 머리

22) a summons to all my foolish blood: 어리석은 내 온 몸의 피를 불러 모으는 소환장

1　romance. On Saturday evenings when my aunt went marketing I had to
go to carry some of the parcels. We walked through the flaring streets,[23]
jostled by drunken men and bargaining women, amid the curses of
labourers, the shrill litanies[24] of shop–boys who stood on guard by the
5　barrels of pigs' cheeks,[25] the nasal chanting of street–singers, who sang a
come–all–you about O'Donovan Rossa,[26] or a ballad about the troubles
in our native land. These noises converged in a single sensation of life for
me: I imagined that I bore my chalice[27] safely through a throng of foes.
Her name sprang to my lips at moments in strange prayers and praises
10　which I myself did not understand. My eyes were often full of tears (I could
not tell why) and at times a flood from my heart seemed to pour itself out
into my bosom. I thought little of the future. I did not know whether I
would ever speak to her or not or, if I spoke to her, how I could tell her
of my confused adoration.[28] But my body was like a harp and her words
15　and gestures were like fingers running upon the wires.[29]

One evening I went into the back drawing–room in which the priest
had died. It was a dark rainy evening and there was no sound in the
house. Through one of the broken panes I heard the rain impinge[30] upon

---

23)　the flaring streets: 번지르르한 거리

24)　litanies: 원래는 가톨릭 신자들이 사제의 기도문에 화답하는 연도를 뜻하지만, 여기서는 '계속 외쳐
대는 소리'라는 뜻.

25)　by the barrels of pigs' cheeks: 수북한 돼지 엉덩잇살 옆에서. cheek: 〈속어〉 볼기짝, 엉덩이

26)　a *come‒all‒you* about O'Donovan Rossa: 오도노반 로사(1831‒1915)에 관한 '모두 모여라'로 시
작하는 어떤 노래. 오도노반 로사는 아일랜드의 독립 운동가이며, *come‒all‒you*는 "Come all you
gallant Irishmen, and listen to my song"으로 시작된다.

27)　chalice: 성배

28)　confused adoration: 혼란스러운 사랑(연모의 정)

29)　fingers running upon the wires: 하프의 줄을 튕기는 손가락

30)　impinge: hit, strike

¹ the earth, the fine incessant needles of water³¹⁾ playing in the sodden beds.³²⁾ Some distant lamp or lighted window gleamed below me. I was thankful that I could see so little. All my senses seemed to desire to veil themselves and, feeling that I was about to slip from them,³³⁾ I pressed
⁵ the palms of my hands together until they trembled, murmuring: '*O love! O love!*' many times.

At last she spoke to me. When she addressed the first words to me I was so confused that I did not know what to answer. She asked me was I going to *Araby*. I forgot whether I answered yes or no. It would be a
¹⁰ splendid bazaar; she said she would love to go.

"And why can't you?" I asked.

While she spoke she turned a silver bracelet round and round her wrist. She could not go, she said, because there would be a retreat³⁴⁾ that week in her convent.³⁵⁾ Her brother and two other boys were fighting
¹⁵ for their caps and I was alone at the railings. She held one of the spikes, bowing her head towards me. The light from the lamp opposite our door caught the white curve of her neck, lit up her hair that rested there and, falling, lit up the hand upon the railing. It fell over one side of her dress and caught the white border of a petticoat, just visible as she stood at
²⁰ ease.

"It's well for you," she said.

"If I go," I said, "I will bring you something."

---

31) fine incessant needles of water: 끊임없이 내리는 바늘과 같은 가는 비

32) sodden beds: 흠뻑 젖은 화단. bed: = piece of ground (for flowers, vegetable). 화단

33) feeling that I was about to slip from them: 내 자신이 그러한 감각에서 빠져나오려 하고 있다고 느끼면서

34) retreat: (가톨릭의) 피정, 묵상(시간)

35) convent: 수녀원에서 운영하는 학교

What innumerable follies[36] laid waste[37] my waking and sleeping thoughts after that evening! I wished to annihilate the tedious intervening days.[38] I chafed against the work of school.[39] At night in my bedroom and by day in the classroom her image came between me and the page I strove to read. The syllables of the word *Araby* were called to me through the silence in which my soul luxuriated[40] and cast an Eastern enchantment over me.[41] I asked for leave[42] to go to the bazaar on Saturday night. My aunt was surprised, and hoped it was not some Freemason[43] affair. I answered few questions in class. I watched my master's face pass from amiability to sternness;[44] he hoped I was not beginning to idle. I could not call my wandering thoughts together. I had hardly any patience with the serious work of life which, now that it stood between me and my desire, seemed to me child's play, ugly monotonous child's play.

On Saturday morning I reminded my uncle that I wished to go to the bazaar in the evening. He was fussing at the hallstand,[45] looking for the hat–brush, and answered me curtly:

---

36) innumerable follies: = very many foolish ideas. 수많은 어리석은 생각

37) lay waste: 황폐하게 하다, 폐허로 만들다

38) the tedious intervening days: 바자회까지의 (기다리기) 지루한 나날들

39) chafed against the work of school: 학교 공부가 짜증났다

40) through the silence in which my soul luxuriated: 내 영혼이 탐닉했던 침묵을 통해. luxuriate: = indulge. 탐닉하다

41) cast an Eastern enchantment over me: 동양적인 마법을 내게 걸었다

42) leave: = permission. 허락

43) Freemason: 프리메이슨 비밀결사조직. 1717년 런던에서 출범한 사교모임이다. 처음에는 친목 도모와 교육을 목적으로 출범하였으나 점차 직업 문제와 같은 현실적인 문제는 물론 윤리나 도덕 같은 철학적인 문제로까지 논의의 범위를 넓혔다. 세계시민주의와 세계단일정부를 모토로 하였으며 종교적 자유와 관용을 강조하면서 가톨릭 교회의 탄압을 받았다.

44) pass from amiability to sternness: 상냥한 표정이 냉혹하게 굳어지다

45) hallstand: 홀스탠드(옷걸이 · 모자걸이 · 우산꽂이 등이 있는 현관용 가구)

"Yes, boy, I know."

As he was in the hall I could not go into the front parlour and lie at the window. I left the house in bad humour[46] and walked slowly towards the school. The air was pitilessly raw[47] and already my heart misgave
5 me.[48]

When I came home to dinner my uncle had not yet been home. Still it was early. I sat staring at the clock for some time and, when its ticking began to irritate me, I left the room. I mounted the staircase and gained[49] the upper part of the house. The high, cold, empty, gloomy
10 rooms liberated me and I went from room to room singing. From the front window I saw my companions playing below in the street. Their cries reached me weakened and indistinct and, leaning my forehead against the cool glass, I looked over at the dark house where she lived. I may have stood there for an hour, seeing nothing but the brown–clad
15 figure cast by my imagination, touched discreetly by the lamplight at the curved neck, at the hand upon the railings and at the border[50] below the dress.

When I came downstairs again I found Mrs. Mercer sitting at the fire. She was an old, garrulous[51] woman, a pawnbroker's widow, who
20 collected used stamps for some pious purpose.[52] I had to endure the gossip of the tea–table. The meal was prolonged beyond an hour and still

---

46) in bad humour: 기분 나쁜 상태로

47) raw: 몹시 추운

48) my heart misgave me: 나는 마음이 불안해졌다. misgive: = cause to feel doubt, suspicion or anxiety

49) gain: = arrive at, get to. 여기서는 '힘들게 올라가다'의 뜻

50) border: = ornamental strip of woman's clothing

51) garrulous: 수다스러운

52) for some pious purpose: 무슨 종교적인 목적으로

1 my did not come. Mrs. Mercer stood up to go: she was sorry she couldn't wait any longer, but it was after eight o'clock and she did not like to be out late, as the night air was bad for her. When she had gone I began to walk up and down the room, clenching my fists. My aunt said:

5 "I'm afraid you may put off your bazaar for this night of Our Lord."[53]

At nine o'clock I heard my uncle's latchkey[54] in the hall door. I heard him talking to himself and heard the hallstand rocking when it had received the weight of his overcoat. I could interpret these signs. When 10 he was midway through his dinner[55] I asked him to give me the money to go to the bazaar. He had forgotten.

"The people are in bed and after their first sleep now," he said.

I did not smile. My aunt said to him energetically:

"Can't you give him the money and let him go? You've kept him late 15 enough as it is."[56]

My uncle said he was very sorry he had forgotten. He said he believed in the old saying: 'All work and no play makes Jack a dull boy.' He asked me where I was going and, when I had told him a second time, he asked me did I know *The Arab's Farewell to his Steed*.[57] When I left the 20 kitchen he was about to recite the opening lines of the piece to my aunt.

---

53) for this night of Our Lord: 오늘밤에는
54) latchkey: 바깥문 열쇠
55) midway through his dinner: 저녁 식사 도중에
56) late enough as it is: 이처럼 늦게
57) *The Arab's Farewell to his Steed*: 캐롤라인 엘리자베스 사라프 노턴(Caroline Elizabeth Saraph Norton, 1808-1877)의 시로, 아랍의 장수가 사랑하는 말을 팔고 읊은 석별의 시. 어떤 아랍인이 가난하여 자기 말을 팔아버렸으나 그 말을 잊지 못하여 돈을 써가며 말을 찾아다녔다. 그러나 찾지를 못해 그 말을 찾아주는 사람에게 그 말을 주겠다고 했다는 내용이다.

1   I held a florin[58] tightly in my hand as I strode down Buckingham Street towards the station. The sight of the streets thronged with buyers and glaring with gas recalled to me the purpose of my journey. I took my seat in a third–class carriage of a deserted train.[59] After an intolerable
5 delay the train moved out of the station slowly. It crept onward among ruinous houses and over the twinkling river. At Westland Row Station[60] a crowd of people pressed[61] to the carriage doors; but the porters moved them back, saying that it was a special train for the bazaar. I remained alone in the bare carriage.[62] In a few minutes the train drew up[63] beside
10 an improvised wooden platform. I passed out on to the road and saw by the lighted dial of a clock that it was ten minutes to ten. In front of me was a large building which displayed the magical name.

    I could not find any sixpenny entrance[64] and, fearing that the bazaar would be closed, I passed in quickly through a turnstile, handing
15 a shilling to a weary–looking man. I found myself in a big hall girded at half its height by a gallery. Nearly all the stalls[65] were closed and the greater part of the hall was in darkness. I recognized a silence like that which pervades a church after a service. I walked into the centre of the bazaar timidly. A few people were gathered about the stalls which were
20 still open. Before a curtain, over which the words *Cafe Chantant*[66] were

---

58) florin: 2실링짜리 은화. 소년의 용돈으로는 큰돈임.

59) deserted train: 텅 빈 기차

60) Westland Row Station: = railroad station near College Park in Dublin

61) pressed: 밀어닥쳤다

62) bare carriage: 텅 빈 열차 칸

63) drew up: = pulled up. 멈췄다, 정차했다

64) sixpenny entrance: 6펜스를 주고 들어가는 출입구

65) stall: 매점, 판매대

66) *Cafe Chantant*: 〈프랑스어〉 노래와 춤, 음악이 있는 카페

¹ written in coloured lamps, two men were counting money on a salver.[67] I listened to the fall of the coins.

Remembering with difficulty why I had come, I went over to one of the stalls and examined porcelain vases and flowered tea–sets.[68] At the
⁵ door of the stall a young lady was talking and laughing with two young gentlemen. I remarked their English accents and listened vaguely to their conversation.

"O, I never said such a thing!"

"O, but you did!"

¹⁰ "O, but I didn't!"

"Didn't she say that?"

"Yes. I heard her."

"O, there's a … fib!"[69]

Observing me, the young lady came over and asked me did I wish to
¹⁵ buy anything. The tone of her voice was not encouraging;[70] she seemed to have spoken to me out of a sense of duty.[71] I looked humbly at the great jars that stood like eastern guards at either side of the dark entrance to the stall and murmured:

"No, thank you."

²⁰ The young lady changed the position of one of the vases and went back to the two young men. They began to talk of the same subject. Once or twice the young lady glanced at me over her shoulder.

---

67) salver: = tray. 둥근 쟁반
68) flowered tea‑sets: 꽃무늬가 있는 찻잔 세트
69) fib: (사소한) 거짓말
70) encouraging: 물건 사기를 권하는
71) out of a sense of duty: 의무감에서

1   I lingered before her stall, though I knew my stay was useless, to make my interest in her wares[72] seem the more real. Then I turned away slowly and walked down the middle of the bazaar. I allowed the two pennies to fall against the sixpence in my pocket. I heard a voice call
5 from one end of the gallery that the light was out. The upper part of the hall was now completely dark.

    Gazing up into the darkness I saw myself as a creature driven and derided by vanity;[73] and my eyes burned with anguish and anger.

---

72) wares: 물품, 도자기
73) a creature driven and derided by vanity: 허영에 쫓기고 농락당한 인간

11

Adventure

Sherwood Anderson[1]

1   ALICE HINDMAN, a woman of twenty–seven when George Willard was a mere boy, had lived in Winesburg all her life. She clerked[2] in Winney's Dry Goods Store and lived with her mother, who had married a second husband.

5   Alice's step–father was a carriage painter,[3] and given to drink.[4] His story is an odd one. It will be worth telling some day.

    At twenty–seven Alice was tall and somewhat slight. Her head was

---

1) 셔우드 앤더슨(Sherwood Anderson, 1876-1941): 미국 소설에 모더니즘 기법을 도입한 작가. 모더니즘 기법은 일상의 구어에 매우 근접한 보다 단순한 문체를 포함하고 있으며, 내용보다는 형식을 더 강조한다. 또한 시간을 특수하게 사용하여, 과거와 현재, 미래가 혼재되어 나타나기도 한다. 헤밍웨이(Hemingway)도 그의 문체에 영향을 받았다. 윌리엄 포크너(William Faulkner)는 그를 "우리 세대 작가들의 아버지"라고 불렀으며, 토머스 울프(Thomas Wolfe)는 "나에게 모든 것을 가르쳐준 유일한 미국인"이라고 했다. 작품으로 『와인즈버그, 오하이오』(*Winesburg, Ohio*)(1919), 『이야기꾼의 이야기』(*A Story – Teller's Story*)(1924) 등이 있다.

2) clerk: 상점에서 일하다

3) carriage painter: 마차 페인트공

4) given to drink: 술에 빠져 지내는

1 large and overshadowed[5] her body. Her shoulders were a little stooped[6] and her hair and eyes brown. She was very quiet but beneath a placid exterior[7] a continual ferment went on.

When she was a girl of sixteen and before she began to work in the 5 store, Alice had an affair with a young man. The young man, named Ned Currie, was older than Alice. He, like George Willard, was employed on the *Winesburg Eagle* and for a long time he went to see Alice almost every evening. Together the two walked under the trees through the streets of the town and talked of what they would do with their lives. Alice was 10 then a very pretty girl and Ned Currie took her into his arms and kissed her. He became excited and said things he did not intend to say and Alice, betrayed by her desire to have something beautiful come into her rather narrow life,[8] also grew excited. She also talked. The outer crust of her life, all of her natural diffidence[9] and reserve,[10] was torn away[11] and 15 she gave herself over to the emotions of love. When, late in the fall of her sixteenth year, Ned Currie went away to Cleveland where he hoped to get a place on a city newspaper and rise in the world,[12] she wanted to go with him. With a trembling voice she told him what was in her mind. "I will work and you can work," she said. "I do not want to harness[13] 20 you to a needless expense that will prevent your making progress. Don't

---

5) overshadow: 가리다, 그림자를 드리우다

6) stoop: 구부정하다

7) a placid exterior: 차분한 외양, 겉모습

8) her rather narrow life: 그녀의 단조로운(옹졸한) 삶

9) diffidence: 수줍음

10) reserve: 내성적 성격

11) be torn away: 찢겨져 나가다

12) rise in the world: 출세하다

13) harness: 속박하다

marry me now. We will get along without that and we can be together. Even though we live in the same house no one will say anything. In the city we will be unknown and people will pay no attention to us."

Ned Currie was puzzled by the determination and abandon[14] of his sweetheart and was also deeply touched. He had wanted the girl to become his mistress[15] but changed his mind. He wanted to protect and care for her. "You don't know what you're talking about," he said sharply; "you may be sure I'll let you do no such thing. As soon as I get a good job I'll come back. For the present you'll have to stay here. It's the only thing we can do."

On the evening before he left Winesburg to take up his new life in the city, Ned Currie went to call on[16] Alice. They walked about through the streets for an hour and then got a rig[17] from Wesley Moyer's livery[18] and went for a drive in the country. The moon came up and they found themselves unable to talk. In his sadness the young man forgot the resolutions[19] he had made regarding his conduct with the girl.

They got out of the buggy[20] at a place where a long meadow ran down to the bank of Wine Creek and there in the dim light became lovers. When at midnight they returned to town they were both glad. It did not seem to them that anything that could happen in the future

---

14) abandon: 자유분방함
15) mistress: 부인
16) call on: 방문하다
17) rig: 트럭
18) Wesley Moyer's livery: 웨슬리 자동차 대여점
19) resolution: 결심
20) buggy: 차

¹ could blot out²¹⁾ the wonder and beauty of the thing that had happened. "Now we will have to stick to each other, whatever happens we will have to do that," Ned Currie said as he left the girl at her father's door.

The young newspaper man did not succeed in getting a place on
⁵ a Cleveland paper and went west to Chicago. For a time he was lonely and wrote to Alice almost every day. Then he was caught up by the life of the city; he began to make friends and found new interests in life. In Chicago he boarded²²⁾ at a house where there were several women. One of them attracted his attention and he forgot Alice in Winesburg. At
¹⁰ the end of a year he had stopped writing letters, and only once in a long time, when he was lonely or when he went into one of the city parks and saw the moon shining on the grass as it had shone that night on the meadow by Wine Creek, did he think of her at all.

In Winesburg the girl who had been loved grew to be a woman.
¹⁵ When she was twenty–two years old her father, who owned a harness repair shop,²³⁾ died suddenly. The harness maker was an old soldier, and after a few months his wife received a widow's pension.²⁴⁾ She used the first money she got to buy a loom²⁵⁾ and became a weaver of carpets,²⁶⁾ and Alice got a place in Winney's store. For a number of years nothing
²⁰ could have induced her to believe that Ned Currie would not in the end return to her.

She was glad to be employed because the daily round of toil in the

---

21) blot out: ~을 완전히 덮다, 가리다
22) board: 하숙하다
23) a harness repair shop: 마구 수리점
24) a widow's pension: 미망인 연금
25) loom: 베틀
26) a weaver of carpets: 카펫을 짜는 사람

¹ store made the time of waiting seem less long and uninteresting. She began to save money, thinking that when she had saved two or three hundred dollars she would follow her lover to the city and try if her presence would not win back his affections.

⁵   Alice did not blame Ned Currie for what had happened in the moonlight in the field, but felt that she could never marry another man. To her the thought of giving to another what she still felt could belong only to Ned seemed monstrous. When other young men tried to attract her attention she would have nothing to do with them. "I am his wife
¹⁰ and shall remain his wife whether he comes back or not," she whispered to herself, and for all of her willingness to support herself could not have understood the growing modern idea²⁷⁾ of a woman's owning herself and giving and taking for her own ends²⁸⁾ in life.

    Alice worked in the dry goods store²⁹⁾ from eight in the morning
¹⁵ until six at night and on three evenings a week went back to the store to stay from seven until nine. As time passed and she became more and more lonely she began to practice the devices common to lonely people. When at night she went upstairs into her own room she knelt on the floor to pray and in her prayers whispered things she wanted to say to
²⁰ her lover. She became attached to inanimate objects,³⁰⁾ and because it was her own, could not bear to have anyone touch the furniture of her room. The trick of saving money, begun for a purpose, was carried on after the scheme of going to the city to find Ned Currie had been given up. It

---

27) the growing modern idea: 점진적으로 증가하는 현대적인 사상

28) ends: 목적

29) dry goods store: 포목점

30) became attached to inanimate objects: 생명 없는 물건들에 애착심을 가졌다

1   became a fixed habit, and when she needed new clothes she did not get them. Sometimes on rainy afternoons in the store she got out her bank book and, letting it lie open before her, spent hours dreaming impossible dreams of saving money enough so that the interest would support both
5   herself and her future husband.

    "Ned always liked to travel about," she thought. "I'll give him the chance. Some day when we are married and I can save both his money and my own, we will be rich. Then we can travel together all over the world."

10   In the dry goods store weeks ran into months and months into years as Alice waited and dreamed of her lover's return. Her employer, a grey old man with false teeth and a thin grey mustache that drooped down[31] over his mouth, was not given to conversation, and sometimes, on rainy days and in the winter when a storm raged in Main Street, long hours
15   passed when no customers came in. Alice arranged and rearranged the stock. She stood near the front window where she could look down the deserted street and thought of the evenings when she had walked with Ned Currie and of what he had said. "We will have to stick to each other now." The words echoed and re–echoed through the mind
20   of the maturing woman. Tears came into her eyes. Sometimes when her employer had gone out and she was alone in the store she put her head on the counter and wept. "Oh, Ned, I am waiting," she whispered over and over, and all the time the creeping fear[32] that he would never come back grew stronger within her.

25   In the spring when the rains have passed and before the long hot

---

31) droop down: 늘어져있다

32) creeping fear: 엄습하는 공포

190   Reading Perspectives

days of summer have come, the country about Winesburg is delightful. The town lies in the midst of open fields, but beyond the fields are pleasant patches[33] of woodlands. In the wooded places are many little cloistered nooks,[34] quiet places where lovers go to sit on Sunday afternoons. Through the trees they look out across the fields and see farmers at work about the barns or people driving up and down on the roads. In the town bells ring and occasionally a train passes, looking like a toy thing in the distance.

For several years after Ned Currie went away Alice did not go into the wood with the other young people on Sunday, but one day after he had been gone for two or three years and when her loneliness seemed unbearable, she put on her best dress and set out. Finding a little sheltered place from which she could see the town and a long stretch of the fields, she sat down. Fear of age and ineffectuality[35] took possession of her. She could not sit still, and arose. As she stood looking out over the land something, perhaps the thought of never ceasing life as it expresses itself in the flow of the seasons, fixed her mind on the passing years. With a shiver of dread,[36] she realized that for her the beauty and freshness of youth had passed. For the first time she felt that she had been cheated. She did not blame Ned Currie and did not know what to blame. Sadness swept over her. Dropping to her knees, she tried to pray, but instead of prayers words of protest[37] came to her lips. "It is not going

---

33) patch: 지역
34) cloistered nook: 은신처
35) ineffectuality: 무력감
36) With a shiver of dread: 두려움으로 몸을 떨며
37) words of protest: 항의하는 말

¹ to come to me. I will never find happiness. Why do I tell myself lies?"
she cried, and an odd sense of relief came with this, her first bold attempt
to face the fear that had become a part of her everyday life.

In the year when Alice Hindman became twenty–five two things
⁵ happened to disturb the dull uneventfulness of her days.³⁸⁾ Her mother
married Bush Milton, the carriage painter of Winesburg, and she herself
became a member of the Winesburg Methodist Church. Alice joined
the church because she had become frightened by the loneliness of
her position in life. Her mother's second marriage had emphasized her
¹⁰ isolation. "I am becoming old and queer.³⁹⁾ If Ned comes he will not
want me. In the city where he is living men are perpetually young. There
is so much going on that they do not have time to grow old," she told
herself with a grim little smile,⁴⁰⁾ and went resolutely about the business
of becoming acquainted with people.⁴¹⁾ Every Thursday evening when
¹⁵ the store had closed she went to a prayer meeting in the basement of the
church and on Sunday evening attended a meeting of an organization
called The Epworth League.

When Will Hurley, a middle–aged man who clerked in a drug store
and who also belonged to the church, offered to walk home with her she
²⁰ did not protest. "Of course I will not let him make a practice of being
with me, but if he comes to see me once in a long time there can be no
harm in that," she told herself, still determined in her loyalty to Ned
Currie.

---

38) dull uneventfulness of her days: 무료하지만 평탄하지 않은 그녀의 삶
39) queer: 괴상한
40) with a grim little smile: 암울한 미소를 살짝 지으며
41) the business of becoming acquainted with people: 사람들과 알고 지내게 되는 일

Without realizing what was happening, Alice was trying feebly[42] at first, but with growing determination, to get a new hold upon life. Beside the drug clerk she walked in silence, but sometimes in the darkness as they went stolidly[43] along she put out her hand and touched softly the folds of his coat.[44] When he left her at the gate before her mother's house she did not go indoors, but stood for a moment by the door. She wanted to call to the drug clerk, to ask him to sit with her in the darkness on the porch before the house, but was afraid he would not understand. "It is not him that I want," she told herself; "I want to avoid being so much alone. If I am not careful I will grow unaccustomed to being with people."

During the early fall of her twenty–seventh year a passionate restlessness[45] took possession of Alice. She could not bear to be in the company of the drug clerk, and when, in the evening, he came to walk with her she sent him away. Her mind became intensely active and when, weary from the long hours of standing behind the counter in the store, she went home and crawled into bed, she could not sleep. With staring eyes she looked into the darkness. Her imagination, like a child awakened from long sleep, played about the room. Deep within her there was something that would not be cheated by phantasies and that demanded some definite answer from life.

Alice took a pillow into her arms and held it tightly against her breasts. Getting out of bed, she arranged a blanket so that in the darkness

---

42) feebly: 약하게, 힘없이
43) stolidly: 둔감하게, 무뚝뚝하게
44) the folds of his coat: 코트 섶
45) passionate restlessness: 격렬한 불안감

it looked like a form lying between the sheets and, kneeling beside the bed, she caressed[46] it, whispering words over and over, like a refrain.[47] "Why doesn't something happen? Why am I left here alone?" she muttered. Although she sometimes thought of Ned Currie, she no longer
5 depended on him. Her desire had grown vague. She did not want Ned Currie or any other man. She wanted to be loved, to have something answer the call that was growing louder and louder within her.

And then one night when it rained Alice had an adventure. It frightened and confused her. She had come home from the store at nine
10 and found the house empty. Bush Milton had gone off to town and her mother to the house of a neighbor. Alice went upstairs to her room and undressed in the darkness. For a moment she stood by the window hearing the rain beat against the glass and then a strange desire took possession of her. Without stopping to think of what she intended to do,
15 she ran downstairs through the dark house and out into the rain. As she stood on the little grass plot before the house and felt the cold rain on her body a mad desire to run naked through the streets took possession of her.

She thought that the rain would have some creative and wonderful
20 effect on her body. Not for years had she felt so full of youth and courage. She wanted to leap and run, to cry out, to find some other lonely human and embrace him. On the brick sidewalk before the house a man stumbled homeward. Alice started to run. A wild, desperate mood[48] took possession of her. "What do I care who it is. He is alone, and I will go to

---

46) caress: 어루만지다

47) like a refrain: 후렴구처럼

48) A wild, desperate mood: 야성적이고 필사적인 분위기

¹ him," she thought; and then without stopping to consider the possible result of her madness, called softly. "Wait!" she cried. "Don't go away. Whoever you are, you must wait."

The man on the sidewalk stopped and stood listening. He was an
⁵ old man and somewhat deaf. Putting his hand to his mouth, he shouted. "What? What say?" he called.

Alice dropped to the ground and lay trembling. She was so frightened at the thought of what she had done that when the man had gone on his way she did not dare get to her feet, but crawled on
¹⁰ hands and knees through the grass to the house. When she got to her own room she bolted the door and drew her dressing table across the doorway. Her body shook as with a chill and her hands trembled so that she had difficulty getting into her nightdress. When she got into bed she buried her face in the pillow and wept brokenheartedly.[49] "What is the
¹⁵ matter with me? I will do something dreadful if I am not careful," she thought, and turning her face to the wall, began trying to force herself to face bravely the fact that many people must live and die alone, even in Winesburg.

---

49) brokenheartedly: 비탄에 잠겨서

12

The Egg

Sherwood Anderson

1   My father was, I am sure, intended by nature[1] to be a cheerful, kindly man. Until he was thirty–four years old he worked as a farm–hand[2] for a man named Thomas Butterworth whose place lay near the town of Bidwell, Ohio. He had then a horse of his own and on Saturday

5   evenings drove into town to spend a few hours in social intercourse[3] with other farm–hands. In town he drank several glasses of beer and stood about in Ben Head's saloon[4] — crowded on Saturday evenings with visiting farm–hands. Songs were sung and glasses thumped on the bar. At ten o'clock father drove home along a lonely country road, made

10   his horse comfortable for the night and himself went to bed, quite happy in his position in life. He had at that time no notion of trying to rise in the world.[5]

---

1)   by nature: 천성적으로
2)   hand: 일꾼
3)   social intercourse: 사교
4)   saloon: 선술집
5)   rise in the world: = succeed; get up in the world. 출세하다

It was in the spring of his thirty–fifth year that father married my mother, then a country school–teacher, and in the following spring I came wriggling and crying into the world. Something happened to the two people. They became ambitious. The American passion for getting up in the world took possession of[6] them.

It may have been that mother was responsible. Being a school–teacher she had no doubt read books and magazines. She had, I presume, read of how Garfield,[7] Lincoln,[8] and other Americans rose from poverty to fame and greatness and as I lay beside her — in the days of her lying–in[9] — she may have dreamed that I would some day rule men and cities. At any rate she induced father to give up his place as a farm–hand, sell his horse and embark on[10] an independent enterprise of his own. She was a tall silent woman with a long nose and troubled grey eyes.[11] For herself she wanted nothing. For father and myself she was incurably ambitious.

The first venture into which the two people went[12] turned out badly. They rented ten acres of poor stony land on Griggs's Road, eight miles from Bidwell, and launched into chicken raising. I grew into boyhood on the place and got my first impressions of life there. From the beginning they were impressions of disaster and if, in my turn,[13] I am a gloomy man inclined to see the darker side of life, I attribute it to the fact that what should have been for me the happy joyous days of childhood were

---

6) took possession of: = possessed; took hold of. 사로잡았다
7) Garfield: 제임스 어브램(James Abram, 1831-1881), 제20대 미국 대통령.
8) Lincoln: 에이브러햄 링컨(Abraham Lincoln, 1809-1865), 제6대 미국 대통령.
9) lying – in: 산욕, 해산 자리에 눕기
10) embark on: = start, set out. 시작하다
11) troubled grey eyes: 수심에 찬 회색빛 두 눈
12) into which the two people went: went into: = began
13) in my turn: 나의 기질에 있어서

spent on a chicken farm.

One unversed in such matters[14] can have no notion of the many and tragic things that can happen to a chicken. It is born out of an egg, lives for a few weeks as a tiny fluffy thing such as you will see pictured on Easter cards, then becomes hideously naked, eats quantities of corn and meal bought by the sweat of your father's brow, gets diseases called pip,[15] cholera, and other names, stands looking with stupid eyes at the sun, becomes sick and dies. A few hens, and now and then a rooster, intended to serve God's mysterious ends, struggle through to maturity.[16] The hens lay eggs out of which come other chickens and the dreadful cycle is thus made complete. It is all unbelievably complex. Most philosophers must have been raised on chicken farms. One hopes for so much from a chicken and is so dreadfully disillusioned. Small chickens, just setting out on the journey of life,[17] look so bright and alert and they are in fact so dreadfully stupid. They are so much like people they mix one up in one's judgments of life. If disease does not kill them they wait until your expectations are thoroughly aroused and then walk under the wheels of a wagon — to go squashed and dead back to their maker.[18] Vermin infest[19] their youth, and fortunes[20] must be spent for curative powders. In later life I have seen how a literature[21] has been built up

---

14) one unversed in such matters: = one who is unexperienced [unpracticed, unskilled] in such things. 그런 일을 잘 알지 못하는 사람. unversed in: ~에 숙달하지 않은, ~에 밝지 않은

15) pip: (가금류의) 목구멍, 혀의 전염병

16) struggle through to maturity: 가까스로 성숙기(혹은 성계)에 이르다

17) just setting out on the journey of life: 인생 여정을 막 시작하는

18) their maker: their creator(= God), 조물주

19) infest: 들끓다, 우글거리다

20) fortunes: 큰돈

21) literature: = printed matter of any kind. (광고, 팸플릿 등의) 인쇄물, 광고

¹ on the subject of fortunes to be made out of the raising of chickens. It is intended to be read by the gods who have just eaten of the tree of the knowledge of good and evil. It is a hopeful literature and declares that much may be done by simple ambitious people who own a few hens. Do ⁵ not be led astray by it. It was not written for you. Go hunt[22] for gold on the frozen hills of Alaska, put your faith in the honesty of a politician, believe if you will[23] that the world is daily growing better and that good will triumph over evil, but do not read and believe the literature that is written concerning the hen. It was not written for you.

¹⁰   I, however, digress.[24] My tale does not primarily concern itself with the hen. If correctly told it will centre on the egg. For ten years my father and mother struggled to make our chicken farm pay[25] and then they gave up that struggle and began another. They moved into the town of Bidwell, Ohio and embarked in the restaurant business. After ten years ¹⁵ of worry with incubators that did not hatch, and with tiny — and in their own way[26] lovely — balls of fluff that passed on into semi–naked pullet–hood[27] and from that into dead hen–hood, we threw all aside and packing our belongings on a wagon drove down Griggs's Road toward Bidwell, a tiny caravan of hope looking for a new place from which to ²⁰ start on our upward journey through life.[28]

   We must have been a sad looking lot,[29] not, I fancy, unlike refugees

---

22) Go hunt: = Go and hunt

23) if you will: 굳이 원한다면, 그럴 뜻이 있다면

24) digress: 주제에서 벗어나다, 다른 말을 하기 시작하다, 얘기가 옆길로 새다

25) pay: = be profitable. 수지가 맞다

26) in their own way: 그들 나름대로

27) pullet – hood: state of being a young hen. pullet: (특히 1년 미만의) 어린 닭

28) to start on our upward journey through life: 위쪽으로의 우리의 삶의 여정을 시작할

29) lot: = group. 떼거리

1 fleeing from a battlefield. Mother and I walked in the road. The wagon
   that contained our goods had been borrowed for the day from Mr. Albert
   Griggs, a neighbor. Out of its sides stuck the legs of cheap chairs and at
   the back of the pile of beds, tables, and boxes filled with kitchen utensils
5 was a crate[30] of live chickens, and on top of that the baby carriage[31] in
   which I had been wheeled about in my infancy. Why we stuck to[32] the
   baby carriage I don't know. It was unlikely other children would be born
   and the wheels were broken. People who have few possessions cling tightly
   to those they have. That is one of the facts that make life so discouraging.

10   Father rode on top of the wagon. He was then a bald–headed man
   of forty–five, a little fat and from long association[33] with mother and the
   chickens he had become habitually silent and discouraged. All during our
   ten years on the chicken farm he had worked as a laborer on neighboring
   farms and most of the money he had earned had been spent for remedies
15 to cure chicken diseases, on Wilmer's White Wonder Cholera Cure[34]
   or Professor Bidlow's Egg Producer[35] or some other preparations[36] that
   mother found advertised in the poultry papers.[37] There were two little
   patches of hair on father's head just above his ears. I remember that as a
   child I used to sit looking at him when he had gone to sleep in a chair
20 before the stove on Sunday afternoons in the winter. I had at that time

---

30) crate: = a large box used to pack furniture. (물품 운송용 대형 나무) 상자
31) baby carriage: 유모차
32) stuck to: stick to(집착하다, 고수하다)의 과거형
33) from long association: 오래 같이 지내다 보니
34) Wilmer's White Wonder Cholera Cure: 윌머 씨의 백색의 경이로운 콜레라 치료제
35) Professor Bidlow's Egg Producer: 비들로 교수의 산란약
36) preparations: 조제약, (약 · 화장품 등으로 사용하기 위한) 조제용 물질
37) papers: 잡지

already begun to read books and have notions of my own and the bald path that led over the top of his head was, I fancied, something like a broad road, such a road as Caesar might have made on which to lead his legions out of Rome and into the wonders of an unknown world. The tufts[38] of hair that grew above father's ears were, I thought, like forests. I fell into a half–sleeping, half–waking state and dreamed I was a tiny thing going along the road into a far beautiful place where there were no chicken farms and where life was a happy eggless affair.

One might write a book concerning our flight from the chicken farm into town. Mother and I walked the entire eight miles — she to be sure that nothing fell from the wagon and I to see the wonders of the world. On the seat of the wagon beside father was his greatest treasure. I will tell you of that. On a chicken farm where hundreds and even thousands of chickens come out of eggs surprising things sometimes happen. Grotesques[39] are born out of eggs as out of people. The accident does not often occur — perhaps once in a thousand births. A chicken is, you see, born that has four legs, two pairs of wings, two heads or what not.[40] The things do not live. They go quickly back to the hand of their maker that has for a moment trembled. The fact that the poor little things could not live was one of the tragedies of life to father. He had some sort of notion that if he could but[41] bring into hen–hood or rooster–hood a five–legged hen or a two–headed rooster[42] his fortune would be made. He

---

38) tufts: 다발
39) Grotesques: 괴이한 것들
40) or what not: = all kinds of other things. 기타 등등, ~따위
41) but: = only
42) bring into hen–hood or rooster–hood a five–legged hen or a two–headed rooster: 다리가 다섯 달린 암탉이나 머리가 둘 달린 수탉을 성계로 기르다

¹ dreamed of taking the wonder about to county fairs and of growing rich by exhibiting it to other farm–hands.

At any rate he saved all the little monstrous things that had been born on our chicken farm. They were preserved in alcohol and put each
⁵ in its own glass bottle. These he had carefully put into a box and on our journey into town it was carried on the wagon seat beside him. He drove the horses with one hand and with the other clung to the box. When we got to our destination the box was taken down at once and the bottles removed. All during our days as keepers of a restaurant in the town of
¹⁰ Bidwell, Ohio, the grotesques in their little glass bottles sat on a shelf back of the counter.⁴³⁾ Mother sometimes protested but father was a rock⁴⁴⁾ on the subject of his treasure. The grotesques were, he declared, valuable. People, he said, liked to look at strange and wonderful things.

Did I say that we embarked in the restaurant business in the town
¹⁵ of Bidwell, Ohio? I exaggerated a little. The town itself lay at the foot of a low hill and on the shore of a small river. The railroad did not run through the town and the station was a mile away to the north at a place called Pickleville. There had been a cider mill⁴⁵⁾ and pickle factory at the station, but before the time of our coming they had both gone out of
²⁰ business.⁴⁶⁾ In the morning and in the evening busses came down to the station along a road called Turner's Pike⁴⁷⁾ from the hotel on the main street of Bidwell. Our going to the out–of–the–way place⁴⁸⁾ to embark in

---

43) a shelf back of the counter: 카운터 뒤의 선반
44) a rock: 요지부동
45) cider mill: 사과주 공장
46) go out of business: 파산하다, 폐업하다
47) Turner's Pike: pike는 turnpike road. 통행료를 받는 고속도로
48) out–of–the–way place: 구석진 곳

¹ the restaurant business was mother's idea. She talked of it for a year and then one day went off and rented an empty store building opposite the railroad station. It was her idea that the restaurant would be profitable. Travelling men, she said, would be always waiting around to take
⁵ trains out of town and town people would come to the station to await incoming trains. They would come to the restaurant to buy pieces of pie and drink coffee. Now that I am older I know that she had another motive in going. She was ambitious for me. She wanted me to rise in the world, to get into a town school and become a man of the towns.

¹⁰   At Pickleville father and mother worked hard as they always had done. At first there was the necessity of putting our place into shape⁴⁹⁾ to be a restaurant. That took a month. Father built a shelf on which he put tins⁵⁰⁾ of vegetables. He painted a sign on which he put his name in large red letters. Below his name was the sharp command — "EAT HERE"
¹⁵ — that was so seldom obeyed. A showcase was bought and filled with cigars and tobacco. Mother scrubbed the floor and the walls of the room. I went to school in the town and was glad to be away from the farm and from the presence of the discouraged, sad–looking chickens. Still I was not very joyous. In the evening I walked home from school along Turner's
²⁰ Pike and remembered the children I had seen playing in the town school yard. A troop of little girls had gone hopping about and singing. I tried that. Down along the frozen road I went hopping solemnly on one leg. "Hippity Hop To The Barber Shop,"⁵¹⁾ I sang shrilly.⁵²⁾ Then I stopped

---

49) putting our place into shape: = arranging. 꾸미다

50) tins: 깡통

51) Hippity Hop To The Barber Shop: 이발소까지 깡충깡충 뛰다. 동요의 일종.

52) shrilly: 쩌렁쩌렁 울리게

1   and looked doubtfully about. I was afraid of being seen in my gay mood. It must have seemed to me that I was doing a thing that should not be done by one who, like myself, had been raised on a chicken farm where death was a daily visitor.

5   Mother decided that our restaurant should remain open at night. At ten in the evening a passenger train went north past our door followed by a local freight.[53] The freight crew had switching[54] to do in Pickleville and when the work was done they came to our restaurant for hot coffee and food. Sometimes one of them ordered a fried egg. In the morning
10 at four they returned north–bound[55] and again visited us. A little trade began to grow up. Mother slept at night and during the day tended the restaurant and fed our boarders while father slept. He slept in the same bed mother had occupied during the night and I went off to the town of Bidwell and to school. During the long nights, while mother and I
15 slept, father cooked meats that were to go into sandwiches for the lunch baskets of our boarders. Then an idea in regard to getting up in the world came into his head. The American spirit took hold of him. He also became ambitious.

    In the long nights when there was little to do father had time to
20 think. That was his undoing.[56] He decided that he had in the past been an unsuccessful man because he had not been cheerful enough and that in the future he would adopt a cheerful outlook on life. In the early morning he came upstairs and got into bed with mother. She woke and

---

53) followed by a local freight: 그 뒤를 이어 지역의 화물열차가 지나갔다
54) switching: = shifting a train from one track to another. (철도의) 선로 바꾸기
55) north–bound: = bound for north. 북행
56) undoing: = case of destruction or ruin. 실패(파멸)의 원인

the two talked. From my bed in the corner I listened.

It was father's idea that both he and mother should try to entertain the people who came to eat at our restaurant. I cannot now remember his words, but he gave the impression of one about to become[57] in some obscure way a kind of public entertainer.[58] When people, particularly young people from the town of Bidwell, came into our place, as on very rare occasions they did, bright entertaining conversation was to be made. From father's words I gathered that something of the jolly inn–keeper effect was to be sought. Mother must have been doubtful from the first, but she said nothing discouraging. It was father's notion that a passion for the company[59] of himself and mother would spring up in the breasts of the younger people of the town of Bidwell. In the evening bright happy groups would come singing down Turner's Pike. They would troop shouting with joy and laughter into our place. There would be song and festivity. I do not mean to give the impression that father spoke so elaborately[60] of the matter. He was as I have said an uncommunicative[61] man. "They want some place to go. I tell you they want some place to go," he said over and over. That was as far as he got.[62] My own imagination has filled in the blanks.

For two or three weeks this notion of father's invaded our house. We did not talk much, but in our daily lives tried earnestly to make smiles take the place of glum looks. Mother smiled at the boarders

---

57) about to become: = who was about to become

58) public entertainer: 공공 예능인

59) a passion for the company: 사귀어보겠다는 정열, 친교를 향한 열정

60) elaborately: 공들여, 상세히

61) uncommunicative: 말을 잘 안 하는, 말이 별로 없는

62) That was as far as he got: 그게 그가 말할 수 있는 전부였다

¹ and I, catching the infection,⁶³⁾ smiled at our cat. Father became a little feverish⁶⁴⁾ in his anxiety to please. There was no doubt, lurking somewhere in him, a touch of⁶⁵⁾ the spirit of the showman. He did not waste much of his ammunition⁶⁶⁾ on the railroad men he served at night

⁵ but seemed to be waiting for a young man or woman from Bidwell to come in to show what he could do. On the counter in the restaurant there was a wire basket kept always filled with eggs, and it must have been before his eyes when the idea of being entertaining⁶⁷⁾ was born in his brain. There was something pre–natal⁶⁸⁾ about the way eggs kept

¹⁰ themselves connected with the development of his idea. At any rate an egg ruined his new impulse in life. Late one night I was awakened by a roar of anger coming from father's throat. Both mother and I sat upright in our beds. With trembling hands she lighted a lamp that stood on a table by her head. Downstairs the front door of our restaurant went shut

¹⁵ with a bang and in a few minutes father tramped up the stairs. He held an egg in his hand and his hand trembled as though he were having a chill. There was a half insane light in his eyes. As he stood glaring at us I was sure he intended throwing the egg at either mother or me. Then he laid it gently on the table beside the lamp and dropped on his knees⁶⁹⁾

²⁰ beside mother's bed. He began to cry like a boy and I, carried away by

---

63) catching the infection: = infecting. 감염되어
64) feverish: 과열된, 몹시 흥분한
65) a touch of~: ~의 기미, 흔적
66) his ammunition: 그의 실력(재간)
67) the idea of being entertaining: 환대해야겠다는 생각
68) pre – natal: = previous to birth. 태어나기 전의, 선천적인
69) drop on his knees: 무릎을 털썩 꿇다

his grief,[70] cried with him. The two of us filled the little upstairs room with our wailing voices. It is ridiculous, but of the picture we made I can remember only the fact that mother's hand continually stroked the bald path that ran across the top of his head. I have forgotten what mother said to him and how she induced him to tell her of what had happened downstairs. His explanation also has gone out of my mind. I remember only my own grief and fright and the shiny path over father's head glowing in the lamp light as he knelt by the bed.

As to what happened downstairs.[71] For some unexplainable reason I know the story as well as though I had been a witness to my father's discomfiture.[72] One in time[73] gets to know many unexplainable things. On that evening young Joe Kane, son of a merchant of Bidwell, came to Pickleville to meet his father, who was expected on the ten o'clock evening train from the South. The train was three hours late and Joe came into our place to loaf about[74] and to wait for its arrival. The local freight train came in and the freight crew were fed. Joe was left alone in the restaurant with father.

From the moment he came into our place the Bidwell young man must have been puzzled by my father's actions. It was his notion that father was angry at him for hanging around.[75] He noticed that the restaurant keeper was apparently disturbed by his presence and he thought of going out. However, it began to rain and he did not fancy the

---

70) carried away by his grief: 아버지의 슬픔에 감염되어. carry away: ~의 넋을 잃게 하다
71) As to what happened downstairs: 아래층에서 일어난 일에 관해서 (말하자면 다음과 같다)
72) discomfiture: = defeat of plans or hopes. 당황, 실패
73) in time: = sooner or later. 때가 되면
74) loaf about: = idle away; hang around. 빈둥거리다, 어슬렁거리다
75) hang around: 배회하다, 어정거리다

1 long walk to town and back. He bought a five–cent cigar and ordered a cup of coffee. He had a newspaper in his pocket and took it out and began to read. "I'm waiting for the evening train. It's late," he said apologetically.

5 For a long time father, whom Joe Kane had never seen before, remained silently gazing at his visitor. He was no doubt suffering from an attack of stage fright.[76] As so often happens in life he had thought so much and so often of the situation that now confronted him that he was somewhat nervous in its presence.[77]

10 For one thing, he did not know what to do with his hands. He thrust one of them nervously over the counter and shook hands with Joe Kane. "How– de–do,"[78] he said. Joe Kane put his newspaper down and stared at him. Father's eye lighted on[79] the basket of eggs that sat on the counter and he began to talk. "Well," he began hesitatingly, "well, you have heard of Christopher Columbus, eh?" He seemed to be angry. "That Christopher Columbus was a cheat,"[80] he declared emphatically. "He talked of making an egg stand on its end. He talked, he did, and then he went and broke the end of the egg."

My father seemed to his visitor to be beside himself[81] at the duplicity of Christopher Columbus. He muttered and swore. He declared it was wrong to teach children that Christopher Columbus was a great man when, after all, he cheated at the critical moment. He had declared he

---

76) stage fright: 무대공포증

77) in its presence: 그것(상황)이 현실적으로 나타나자

78) How – de – do: = How do you do?

79) light on: ~을 우연히 보다

80) cheat: 사기꾼

81) be beside himself: = be very much excited; be somewhat crazy. 제정신을 잃고 있다

1 would make an egg stand on end and then when his bluff had been called[82] he had done a trick.[83] Still grumbling at Columbus, father took an egg from the basket on the counter and began to walk up and down. He rolled the egg between the palms of his hands. He smiled genially.

5 He began to mumble words regarding the effect to be produced on an egg by the electricity that comes out of the human body. He declared that without breaking its shell and by virtue of[84] rolling it back and forth in his hands he could stand the egg on its end. He explained that the warmth of his hands and the gentle rolling movement he gave the egg

10 created a new centre of gravity, and Joe Kane was mildly interested. "I have handled thousands of eggs," father said. "No one knows more about eggs than I do."

He stood the egg on the counter and it fell on its side. He tried the trick again and again, each time rolling the egg between the palms of his

15 hands and saying the words regarding the wonders of electricity and the laws of gravity. When after a half hour's effort he did succeed in making the egg stand for a moment he looked up to find that his visitor was no longer watching. By the time he had succeeded in calling Joe Kane's attention to the success of his effort the egg had again rolled over and lay

20 on its side.

Afire with[85] the showman's passion and at the same time a good deal disconcerted[86] by the failure of his first effort, father now took the

---

82) when his bluff had been called: 그 장담을 실천해보도록 요청을 받자. bluff: 허풍

83) do a trick: 속임수를 쓰다

84) by virtue of: ~에 의하여, ~의 덕분에

85) afire with: = enthused by. ~에 불타서

86) disconcerted: = disturbed; confused. disconcert: 당황하게 하다, 불안하게 하다

1 bottles containing the poultry monstrosities down from their place on the shelf and began to show them to his visitor. "How would you like to have seven legs and two heads like this fellow?" he asked, exhibiting the most remarkable of his treasures. A cheerful smile played over his face.

5 He reached over the counter and tried to slap Joe Kane on the shoulder as he had seen men do in Ben Head's saloon when he was a young farm-hand and drove to town on Saturday evenings. His visitor was made a little ill[87] by the sight of the body of the terribly deformed bird floating in the alcohol in the bottle and got up to go. Coming from behind the

10 counter father took hold of the young man's arm and led him back to his seat. He grew a little angry and for a moment had to turn his face away and force himself to smile. Then he put the bottles back on the shelf. In an outburst of generosity he fairly compelled Joe Kane to have a fresh cup of coffee and another cigar at his expense.[88] Then he took a

15 pan and filling it with vinegar, taken from a jug[89] that sat beneath the counter, he declared himself about to do a new trick. "I will heat this egg in this pan of vinegar," he said. "Then I will put it through the neck of a bottle without breaking the shell. When the egg is inside the bottle it will resume its normal shape[90] and the shell will become hard again. Then I

20 will give the bottle with the egg in it to you. You can take it about[91] with you wherever you go. People will want to know how you got the egg in the bottle. Don't tell them. Keep them guessing. That is the way to have

---

87) was made a little ill: 다소 기분이 언짢아졌다

88) at his expense: 그(아버지)의 비용으로, 무료로

89) jug: (액체를 담아 부을 수 있게 주둥이가 있고 손잡이가 달린) 주전자

90) resume its normal shape: 평상시의 모양을 되찾다

91) take it about: 이리저리 가지고 다니다

¹ fun with this trick."

Father grinned and winked at his visitor. Joe Kane decided that the man who confronted him was mildly insane but harmless. He drank the cup of coffee that had been given him and began to read his paper again.

⁵ When the egg had been heated in vinegar father carried it on a spoon to the counter and going into a back room got an empty bottle. He was angry because his visitor did not watch him as he began to do his trick, but nevertheless went cheerfully to work. For a long time he struggled, trying to get the egg to go through the neck of the bottle. He put the pan

¹⁰ of vinegar back on the stove, intending to reheat the egg, then picked it up and burned his fingers. After a second bath in the hot vinegar the shell of the egg had been softened a little but not enough for his purpose. He worked and worked and a spirit of desperate determination took possession of him. When he thought that at last the trick was about to

¹⁵ be consummated[92] the delayed train came in at the station and Joe Kane started to go nonchalantly[93] out at the door. Father made a last desperate effort to conquer the egg and make it do the thing that would establish his reputation as one who knew how to entertain guests who came into his restaurant. He worried the egg.[94] He attempted to be somewhat

²⁰ rough with it. He swore and the sweat stood out on his forehead. The egg broke under his hand. When the contents spurted over his clothes, Joe Kane, who had stopped at the door, turned and laughed.

A roar of anger rose from my father's throat. He danced[95] and

---

92) consummate: 완벽하게 하다, 완성하다

93) nonchalantly: 무심하게, 무관심하게

94) worry the egg: 달걀을 움켜쥐고 집요하게 애를 쓰다. worry: 성가시게 하다

95) dance: (흥분으로) 뛰어 돌아다니다

1 shouted a string of[96] inarticulate[97] words. Grabbing another egg from the basket on the counter, he threw it, just missing the head of the young man as he dodged through the door and escaped.

Father came upstairs to mother and me with an egg in his hand.
5 I do not know what he intended to do. I imagine he had some idea of destroying it, of destroying all eggs, and that he intended to let mother and me see him begin. When, however, he got into the presence of mother something happened to him. He laid the egg gently on the table and dropped on his knees by the bed as I have already explained. He later
10 decided to close the restaurant for the night and to come upstairs and get into bed. When he did so he blew out the light and after much muttered conversation[98] both he and mother went to sleep. I suppose I went to sleep also, but my sleep was troubled.

I awoke at dawn and for a long time looked at the egg that lay on
15 the table. I wondered why eggs had to be and why from the egg came the hen who again laid the egg. The question got into my blood. It has stayed there, I imagine, because I am the son of my father. At any rate, the problem remains unsolved in my mind. And that, I conclude, is but[99] another evidence of the complete and final triumph of the egg —
20 at least as far as my family is concerned.[100]

---

96) a string of: 여러 개의

97) inarticulate: 표현을 제대로 하지 못하는, 음성이 불분명한, 알아들을 수 없는

98) after much muttered conversation: 소리를 죽여 대화를 많이 한 뒤에

99) but: = only

100) as far as my family is concerned: 내 가족에 관한 한

13

The Fly

Katherine Mansfield[1]

1   "Y'are[2] very snug[3] in here," piped old Mr. Woodifield, and he peered out of the great, green leather armchair by his friend the boss's desk as a baby peers out of its pram.[4] His talk was over; it was time for him to be off. But he did not want to go. Since he had retired, since

5 his...stroke,[5] the wife and the girls kept him boxed up in the house[6] every day of the week except Tuesday. On Tuesday he was dressed and brushed and allowed to cut back[7] to the City for the day. Though what he did there the wife and girls couldn't imagine. Made a nuisance of

---

1) 캐서린 맨스필드(Katherine Mansfield, 1888-1923): 뉴질랜드의 저명한 단편소설 작가. 19세에 뉴질랜드를 떠나 영국에 정착했다. 로렌스(D. H. Lawrence), 버지니아 울프(Virginia Woolf)와 같은 세계적으로 유명한 작가들과 교류를 했다. 폐결핵으로 34세라는 이른 나이에 사망했다. 「파리」 ("The Fly")는 1922년에 발표된 단편소설로 『네이션 & 아테나이움』(*The Nation & Athenaeum*)에 실렸다.

2) Y'are: = You are

3) snug: 안락하게 있는, 아늑한

4) pram: 유모차

5) stroke: 뇌졸중

6) kept him boxed up in the house: 그를 집 안에 틀어박혀 있게 했다. box up: 가두다

7) cut back: = hurry back. 급히 되돌아오다, 곧 다시 오다

1 himself[8] to his friends, they supposed....Well, perhaps so. All the same, we cling to[9] our last pleasures as the tree clings to its last leaves. So there sat old Woodifield, smoking a cigar and staring almost greedily at the boss, who rolled in his office chair, stout, rosy, five years older than he,
5 and still going strong, still at the helm.[10] It did one good to see him.[11]

Wistfully, admiringly, the old voice added, "It's snug in here, upon my word!"[12]

"Yes, it's comfortable enough," agreed the boss, and he flipped the *Financial Times* with a paper–knife. As a matter of fact he was proud of
10 his room; he liked to have it admired, especially by old Woodifield. It gave him a feeling of deep, solid satisfaction to be planted there[13] in the midst of it in full view of that frail old figure in the muffler.

"I've had it done up lately,"[14] he explained, as he had explained for the past — how many? — weeks.[15] "New carpet," and he pointed to the
15 bright red carpet with a pattern of large white rings. "New furniture," and he nodded towards the massive bookcase and the table with legs like twisted treacle.[16] "Electric heating!" He waved almost exultantly[17] towards the five transparent, pearly sausages[18] glowing so softly in the

---

8) make a nuisance of oneself: 성가신 일을 저지르다, 다른 사람들을 귀찮게 하다

9) cling to: ~을 고수하다, ~에 매달리다

10) at the helm: (조직, 사업 등을) 책임지고 있는, 키를 잡고 있는, 실권을 쥐고 있는

11) It did one good to see him: 그를 보는 것이 기분이 좋았다

12) upon my word: 정말로, 확실히

13) to be planted there: 거기 뿌리를 박고 있는 것이

14) I've had it done up lately: 최근에 이 방을 새로 꾸미도록 했다

15) explained for the past — how many? — weeks: 이때까지 몇 주간이나 될까? 매우 많이 설명했다는 뜻.

16) like twisted treacle: 당밀이나 엿가락을 꼬아 놓은 것 같은 의자 다리. treacle: 당밀

17) exultantly: 의기양양하게

18) transparent, pearly sausages: 진줏빛이 나는 소시지 모양의 전열봉

1   tilted copper pan.[19]

But he did not draw old Woodifield's attention to the photograph over the table of a grave–looking boy in uniform standing in one of those spectral photographers' parks with photographers' storm–clouds[20] behind him. It was not new. It had been there for over six years.

"There was something I wanted to tell you," said old Woodifield, and his eyes grew dim remembering. "Now what was it? I had it in my mind when I started out this morning." His hands began to tremble, and patches of red[21] showed above his beard.

Poor old chap, he's on his last pins,[22] thought the boss. And, feeling kindly, he winked at the old man, and said jokingly, "I tell you what.[23] I've got a little drop of something[24] here that'll do you good before you go out into the cold again. It's beautiful stuff. It wouldn't hurt a child." He took a key off his watch–chain, unlocked a cupboard below his desk, and drew forth a dark, squat bottle. "That's the medicine," said he. "And the man from whom I got it told me on the strict Q.T.[25] it came from the cellars at Windsor Cassel."[26]

Old Woodifield's mouth fell open at the sight. He couldn't have looked more surprised if the boss had produced a rabbit.

"It's whisky, ain't it?" he piped, feebly.

---

19)   in the tilted copper pan: 위쪽으로 기울어진 구리 원반 속에서 (전기히터의 껍데기를 말함)

20)   those spectral photographers' parks ... storm – clouds: 실제로는 있을 것 같지 않은 환상적인 사진사들이 배경으로 쓰는 공원과, 그 위에 내려 낀 비구름

21)   patches of red: 빨간 점

22)   on his last pins: = to be approaching the end of life. 죽을 때가 다가오고 있는. pins: 〈속어〉 legs

23)   I tell you what: = The truth is

24)   drop of something: 약간의 술

25)   on the strict Q.T.: 비밀스럽게 혹은 절대 비밀로. Q.T.: = quiet

26)   Windsor Cassel: 윈저궁. cassel은 castle을 잘못 발음한 것.

1   The boss turned the bottle and lovingly showed him the label.
Whisky it was.

"D'you know," said he, peering up at the boss wonderingly, "they
won't let me touch it at home." And he looked as though he was going to
5 cry.[27)]

"Ah, that's where we know a bit more than the ladies," cried the
boss, swooping across for two tumblers[28)] that stood on the table with the
water–bottle, and pouring a generous finger[29)] into each. "Drink it down.
It'll do you good. And don't put any water with it. It's sacrilege to tamper
10 with[30)] stuff like this. Ah!" He tossed off his, pulled out his handkerchief,
hastily wiped his moustaches, and cocked an eye at[31)] old Woodifield,
who was rolling his in his chaps.[32)]

The old man swallowed, was silent a moment, and then said faintly,
"It's nutty!"[33)]

15   But it warmed him; it crept into his chill old brain — he
remembered.

"That was it," he said, heaving[34)] himself out of his chair. "I thought
you'd like to know. The girls[35)] were in Belgium last week having a look
at poor Reggie's grave, and they happened to come across your boy's.[36)]

---

27) was going to cry: 울상을 짓고 있었다

28) swooping across for two tumblers: 손을 뻗어서 술잔 두 개를 집어 들면서

29) a generous finger: 넉넉하게 손가락 폭만큼

30) sacrilege to tamper with: (이런 좋은 술에 물을 타는 등의 행동으로) 손을 대는 것은 신성모독.
   tamper with: 손대다, 조작하다

31) cock an eye at: ~에게 눈짓하다

32) was rolling his in his chaps: 그의 술을 입안에서 굴리고 있었다. 입안에서 술을 음미하는 행동.

33) It's nuty: 맛이 구수하군

34) heave: 들어 올리다

35) The girls: 내 딸년들이 (Mr. Woodifield의 딸들을 가리키는 말)

36) your boy's: = your boy's grave

¹ They're quite near each other, it seems."

Old Woodifield paused, but the boss made no reply. Only a quiver in his eyelids showed that he heard.

"The girls were delighted with the way the place is kept,"³⁷⁾ piped
⁵ the old voice. "Beautifully looked after. Couldn't be better if they were at home.³⁸⁾ You've not been across, have yer?"³⁹⁾

"No, no!" For various reasons the boss had not been across.⁴⁰⁾

"There's miles of it,"⁴¹⁾ quavered old Woodifield, "and it's all as neat as a garden. Flowers growing on all the graves. Nice broad paths." It was
¹⁰ plain from his voice how much he liked a nice broad path.

The pause came again. Then the old man brightened wonderfully.

"D'you know what the hotel made the girls pay for a pot of jam?" he piped. "Ten francs! *Robbery*, I call it. It was a little pot, so Gertrude⁴²⁾ says, no bigger than a half–crown. And she hadn't taken more than a
¹⁵ spoonful when they charged her ten francs. Gertrude brought the pot away with her to teach 'em a lesson.⁴³⁾ Quite right, too; it's trading on our feelings.⁴⁴⁾ They think because we're over there having a look round⁴⁵⁾ we're ready to pay anything. That's what it is."⁴⁶⁾ And he turned towards the door.

---

37) the way the place is kept: 묘지를 잘 관리하고 있는 방법. the place: = the grave

38) if they were at home: 그들의 묘소가 국내에 있더라도

39) You've not been across, have yer: 자넨 아직 가본 적이 없지? have yer: = have you

40) across: 묘지가 있는 곳은 유럽 대륙이니까 바다를 건너간다는 뜻

41) There's miles of it: 묘지가 넓어서 여러 마일이나 된다

42) Gertrude: Mr. Woodfield의 딸 이름

43) to teach 'em a lesson: 그들에게 본때를 보여주려고. 'em: = them

44) it's trading on our feelings: 그것은 우리의 감정을 이용하는 짓이다. trade on: ~을 이용하다

45) have a look round: 둘러보다

46) That's what it is.: 바로 그래

1　"Quite right, quite right!" cried the boss, though what was quite right he hadn't the least idea. He came round by his desk, followed the shuffling[47] footsteps to the door, and saw the old fellow out. Woodifield was gone.

5　For a long moment the boss stayed, staring at nothing, while the grey–haired office messenger, watching him, dodged in and out of his cubby–hole[48] like a dog that expects to be taken for a run. Then: "I'll see nobody for half an hour, Macey," said the boss. "Understand? Nobody at all."

10　"Very good, sir."

The door shut, the firm heavy steps recrossed the bright carpet, the fat body plumped down[49] in the spring chair, and leaning forward, the boss covered his face with his hands. He wanted, he intended, he had arranged to weep....

15　It had been a terrible shock to him when old Woodifield sprang that remark upon him about the boy's grave. It was exactly as though the earth had opened and he had seen the boy lying there with Woodifield's girls staring down at him. For it was strange. Although over six years had passed away, the boss never thought of the boy except as lying
20　unchanged, unblemished in his uniform, asleep for ever. "My son!" groaned the boss. But no tears came yet. In the past, in the first few months and even years after the boy's death, he had only to say those words to be overcome by such grief that nothing short of[50] a violent fit

---

47)　shuffle: 발을 질질 끌며 걷다

48)　dodged in and out of his cubby – hole: 비좁고 갑갑한 방을 들락날락했다

49)　plumped down: 털썩 주저앉았다

50)　short of ~: ~외에

1 of weeping could relieve him. Time, he had declared then, he had told everybody, could make no difference. Other men perhaps might recover, might live their loss down, but not he. How was it possible? His boy was an only son. Ever since his birth the boss had worked at building up this

5 business for him; it had no other meaning if it was not for the boy. Life itself had come to have no other meaning. How on earth[51] could he have slaved, denied himself, kept going all those years without the promise for ever before him of the boy's stepping into his shoes[52] and carrying on where he left off?

10 And that promise had been so near being fulfilled. The boy had been in the office learning the ropes[53] for a year before the war. Every morning they had started off[54] together; they had come back by the same train. And what congratulations he had received as the boy's father! No wonder; he had taken to it marvelously. As to his popularity with the staff, every

15 man jack[55] of them down to old Macey couldn't make enough of[56] the boy. And he wasn't the least spoilt. No, he was just his bright natural self, with the right word for everybody, with that boyish look and his habit of saying, "Simply splendid!"

But all that was over and done with[57] as though it never had been.

20 The day had come when Macey had handed him the telegram that brought the whole place crashing about his head. "Deeply regret to

---

51) on earth: 도대체

52) step into one's shoes: ~이 시작한 일을 계속하다, ~의 사업을 이어받다

53) learn the ropes: 요령을 익히다

54) start off together: 함께 출근하다

55) every man jack: = each and every person. 누구나 다

56) make enough of: 충분히 좋아하다

57) all that was over and done with: = all that was finished. 모든 일이 다 끝장이 나버렸다

¹ inform you..." And he had left the office a broken man, with his life in ruins.

Six years ago, six years.... How quickly time passed! It might have happened yesterday. The boss took his hands from his face; he was
⁵ puzzled. Something seemed to be wrong with him.[58] He wasn't feeling as he wanted to feel. He decided to get up and have a look at the boy's photograph. But it wasn't a favorite photograph of his; the expression was unnatural. It was cold, even stern–looking. The boy had never looked like that.

¹⁰ At that moment the boss noticed that a fly had fallen into his broad inkpot, and was trying feebly but desperately to clamber[59] out again. Help! help! said those struggling legs. But the sides of the inkpot were wet and slippery; it fell back again and began to swim. The boss took up a pen, picked the fly out of the ink, and shook it on to a piece of
¹⁵ blotting–paper.[60] For a fraction of a second it lay still on the dark patch that oozed round it. Then the front legs waved, took hold, and, pulling its small, sodden body up, it began the immense task of cleaning the ink from its wings. Over and under,[61] over and under, went a leg along a wing, as the stone goes over and under the scythe.[62] Then there was
²⁰ a pause, while the fly, seeming to stand on the tips of its toes, tried to expand first one wing and then the other. It succeeded at last, and,

---

58) Something seemed to be wrong with him: 무언가 잘못된 것 같았다. 울고 싶어져야 마땅한데 울음이 나오지 않는 것을 말한다.

59) clamber: 기어오르다

60) blotting – paper: 압지(잉크 글씨를 눌러서 덜 마른 부분을 닦아내는 종이)

61) over and under: 위로 아래로. 파리의 다리가 움직이는 모습을 말한다.

62) scythe: 큰 낫, 숫돌

1 sitting down, it began, like a minute[63] cat, to clean its face. No one could imagine that the little front legs rubbed against each other lightly, joyfully. The horrible danger was over; it had escaped; 1t was ready for life again.

5   But just then the boss had an idea. He plunged his pen back into the ink, leaned his thick wrist on the blotting–paper, and as the fly tried its wings down came a great heavy blot. What would it make of that?[64] What indeed! The little beggar seemed absolutely cowed,[65] stunned,[66] and afraid to move because of what would happen next. But then, as if
10 painfully, it dragged itself forward. The front legs waved, caught hold, and, more slowly this time, the task began from the beginning.

      He's a plucky[67] little devil, thought the boss, and he felt a real admiration for the fly's courage. That was the way to tackle things; that was the right spirit. Never say die;[68] it was only a question of... But
15 the fly had again finished its laborious task, and the boss had just time to refill his pen, to shake fair and square[69] on the new–cleaned body yet another dark drop. What about it this time? A painful moment of suspense followed. But behold, the front legs were again waving; the boss felt a rush of relief. He leaned over the fly and said to it tenderly, "You
20 artful little b..."[70] And he actually had the brilliant notion of breathing

---

63) minute: 매우 작은
64) What would it make of that?: 파리 놈이 뭐라고 생각할까? it은 파리를, that은 펜촉에 가득 떠서 파리 위에 떨어뜨린 잉크 방울을 가리킨다.
65) cow: 위협하다
66) stun: 기절시키다
67) plucky: 용기 있는
68) Never say die: 절대 희망을 버리지 마라
69) fair and square: 공명정대하게, 정정당당하게, 정확히
70) You artful little b...: 요 교활한 놈. b...는 beggar라고 말하려 한 것.

1 on it to help the drying process. All the same, there was something timid
and weak about its efforts now, and the boss decided that this time
should be the last, as he dipped the pen deep into the inkpot.

It was.[71] The last blot fell on the soaked blotting–paper, and the
5 draggled[72] fly lay in it and did not stir. The back legs were stuck[73] to the
body; the front legs were not to be seen.

"Come on," said the boss. "Look sharp!"[74] And he stirred it with his
pen — in vain. Nothing happened or was likely to happen. The fly was
dead.

10 The boss lifted the corpse on the end of the paper–knife and
flung it into the waste–paper basket. But such a grinding feeling[75] of
wretchedness[76] seized him that he felt positively frightened. He started
forward and pressed the bell for Macey.

"Bring me some fresh blotting–paper," he said sternly, "and look
15 sharp about it." And while the old dog[77] padded away he fell to
wondering what it was he had been thinking about before. What was it?
It was... He took out his handkerchief and passed it inside his collar. For
the life of him[78] he could not remember.

---

71) It was: It was the last

72) draggled: 물이 흠뻑 젖어서 더러워진

73) were stuck: 딱 달라붙어 있었다

74) Look sharp: 빨리 해라, 서둘러라

75) grinding feeling: 쑤시고 아픈 느낌. 여기서는 끝도 없이 반복되는 느낌.

76) wretchedness: 가엾음. 여기서는 불쾌감, 무엇인지 모를 불쾌감을 뜻한다.

77) the old dog: 늙은이. dog은 사람을 경멸적으로 말한 것.

78) for the life of him: 그가 아무리 애를 써도 (생각이 나지 않았다는 것)

14

A Cup of Tea

Katherine Mansfield

1   Rosemary Fell was not exactly beautiful. No, you couldn't have called her beautiful. Pretty? Well, if you took her to pieces... But why be so cruel as to take anyone to pieces? She was young, brilliant, extremely modern, exquisitely well dressed, amazingly well read in the newest of the 5 new books, and her parties were the most delicious mixture of the really important people and... artists — quaint creatures,[1] discoveries of hers,[2] some of them too terrifying for words, but others quite presentable and amusing.

Rosemary had been married two years. She had a duck of a boy.[3] 10 No, not Peter — Michael.[4] And her husband absolutely adored her. They were rich, really rich, not just comfortably well off, which is odious and stuffy and sounds like one's grandparents. But if Rosemary wanted to

---

1) quaint creatures: 진기한 인물들
2) discoveries of hers: 그녀가 발굴한 신인들
3) a duck of a boy: 떡두꺼비 같은 아들
4) No, not Peter – Michael: 이름은 (그 흔한) 피터가 아니라 마이클이다

shop she would go to Paris as you and I would go to Bond Street. If she wanted to buy flowers, the car pulled up at that perfect shop in Regent Street, and Rosemary inside the shop just gazed in her dazzled, rather exotic way,[5] and said: "I want those and those and those. Give me four bunches of those. And that jar of roses. Yes, I'll have all the roses in the jar.

No, no lilac. I hate lilac. It's got no shape." The attendant bowed and put the lilac out of sight, as though this was only too true; lilac was dreadfully shapeless. "Give me those stumpy[6] little tulips. Those red and white ones." And she was followed to the car by a thin shop–girl staggering[7] under an immense white paper armful that looked like a baby in long clothes....

One winter afternoon she had been buying something in a little antique shop in Curzon Street. It was a shop she liked. For one thing, one usually had it to oneself. And then the man who kept it[8] was ridiculously fond of serving her. He beamed[9] whenever she came in. He clasped his hands; he was so gratified he could scarcely speak. Flattery, of course. All the same, there was something...

"You see, madam," he would explain in his low respectful tones, "I love my things. I would rather not part with them[10] than sell them to someone who does not appreciate them, who has not that fine[11] feeling

---

5) in her dazzled, rather exotic way: 현혹적이고 다소 이국적인 스타일로

6) stumpy: 뭉툭한

7) stagger: 비틀거리다, 휘청거리다

8) the man who kept it: 가게를 운영하는 남자, 가게 주인

9) beam: 활짝 웃다

10) I would rather not part with them: 차라리 그대로 두겠습니다

11) fine: 예민한

1 which is so rare…" And, breathing deeply, he unrolled a tiny square of
blue velvet and pressed it on the glass counter with his pale finger–tips.

To–day it was a little box. He had been keeping it for her. He
had shown it to nobody as yet. An exquisite little enamel box with a
5 glaze[12] so fine it looked as though it had been baked in cream. On the
lid a minute creature[13] stood under a flowery tree, and a more minute
creature still had her arms round his neck. Her hat, really no bigger than
a geranium petal,[14] hung from a branch; it had green ribbons.

And there was a pink cloud like a watchful cherub[15] floating above
10 their heads. Rosemary took her hands out of her long gloves. She always
took off her gloves to examine such things. Yes, she liked it very much.
She loved it; it was a great duck.[16] She must have it. And, turning the
creamy box, opening and shutting it, she couldn't help noticing how
charming her hands were against the blue velvet. The shopman, in some
15 dim cavern[17] of his mind, may have dared to think so too. For he took
a pencil, leant over the counter, and his pale, bloodless fingers crept[18]
timidly towards those rosy, flashing ones, as he murmured gently: "If
I may venture to point out to madam, the flowers on the little lady's
bodice."[19]

20 "Charming!" Rosemary admired the flowers. But what was the

---

12) glaze: 유약, 광택제

13) minute creature: 작은 사람

14) geranium petal: 제라늄 꽃잎

15) cherub: 천사, 아기천사

16) a great duck: 대단히 진귀한 것

17) dim cavern: 어두침침한 동굴

18) crept: creep의 과거형. 슬며시 다가가다

19) bodice: 보디스(드레스의 상체 부분)

price? For a moment the shopman did not seem to hear. Then a murmur reached her. "Twenty–eight guineas, madam."

"Twenty–eight guineas." Rosemary gave no sign. She laid the little box down; she buttoned her gloves again. Twenty–eight guineas. Even if one is rich...

She looked vague. She stared at a plump tea–kettle like a plump[20] hen above the shopman's head, and her voice was dreamy as she answered: "Well, keep it for me — will you? I'll..."

But the shopman had already bowed as though keeping it for her was all any human being could ask. He would be willing, of course, to keep it for her for ever.

The discreet door shut with a click. She was outside on the step, gazing at the winter afternoon. Rain was falling, and with the rain it seemed the dark came too, spinning down like ashes. There was a cold bitter taste in the air, and the newlighted[21] lamps looked sad. Sad were the lights in the houses opposite. Dimly they burned as if regretting something. And people hurried by, hidden under their hateful[22] umbrellas. Rosemary felt a strange pang.[23] She pressed her muff against her breast; she wished she had the little box, too, to cling to. Of course the car was there. She'd only to cross the pavement. But still she waited. There are moments, horrible moments in life, when one emerges from shelter and looks out, and it's awful. One oughtn't to give way to them.[24]

---

20) plump: 포동포동한, 살찐

21) newlighted: 새로 켜진

22) hateful: 밉살스러운

23) pang: (갑자기 격렬하게 일어나는 육체적·정신적) 아픔, 고통

24) One oughtn't to give way to them: 사람들은 그런 것들에게 자신의 마음을 점령당하도록 내버려 두어서는 안 된다

¹ One ought to go home and have an extraspecial tea. But at the very instant of thinking that, a young girl, thin, dark, shadowy — where had she come from? — was standing at Rosemary's elbow and a voice like a sigh, almost like a sob,²⁵⁾ breathed: "Madam, may I speak to you a ⁵ moment?"

"Speak to me?" Rosemary turned. She saw a little battered creature²⁶⁾ with enormous eyes, someone quite young, no older than herself, who clutched at her coat–collar with reddened hands, and shivered as though she had just come out of the water.

¹⁰ "M–madam, stammered²⁷⁾ the voice. Would you let me have the price of a cup of tea?"

"A cup of tea?" There was something simple, sincere in that voice; it wasn't in the least the voice of a beggar. "Then have you no money at all?" asked Rosemary.

¹⁵ "None, madam," came the answer.

"How extraordinary!"²⁸⁾ Rosemary peered through the dusk and the girl gazed back at her. How more than extraordinary! And suddenly it seemed to Rosemary such an adventure. It was like something out of a novel by Dostoevsky,²⁹⁾ this meeting in the dusk. Supposing³⁰⁾ she took ²⁰ the girl home? Supposing she did do one of those things she was always reading about or seeing on the stage, what would happen? It would be thrilling. And she heard herself saying afterwards to the amazement of

---

25) almost like a sob: 거의 흐느낌에 가까운

26) battered creature: 힘이 빠진 사람

27) stammer: 더듬거리며 말하다

28) How extraordinary: 어쩜 이렇게도 놀라운 일이

29) Dostoevsky: 도스토예프스키. 러시아의 소설가.

30) Supposing S + V: 만약 ~라면

1 her friends: "I simply took her home with me," as she stepped forward and said to that dim person beside her: "Come home to tea with me."

The girl drew back startled.[31] She even stopped shivering for a moment.

5 Rosemary put out a hand and touched her arm. "I mean it," she said, smiling. And she felt how simple and kind her smile was. "Why won't you? Do. Come home with me now in my car and have tea."

"You — you don't mean it, madam," said the girl, and there was pain in her voice.

10 "But I do," cried Rosemary. "I want you to. To please me. Come along."

The girl put her fingers to her lips and her eyes devoured Rosemary. "You're — you're not taking me to the police station?" she stammered.

"The police station!" Rosemary laughed out. "Why should I be so 15 cruel? No, I only want to make you warm and to hear — anything you care to tell me."

Hungry people are easily led. The footman[32] held the door of the car open, and a moment later they were skimming[33] through the dusk.

"There!" said Rosemary. She had a feeling of triumph as she slipped 20 her hand through the velvet strap. She could have said, "Now I've got you," as she gazed at the little captive she had netted.[34] But of course she meant it kindly. Oh, more than kindly. She was going to prove to this girl that — wonderful things did happen in life, that — fairy

---

31) draw back startled: 깜짝 놀라서 뒤로 물러서다

32) footman: 하인

33) skim: 스치듯이 지나가다

34) net: 그물을 치다

1 godmothers[35] were real, that — rich people had hearts, and that women were sisters. She turned impulsively, saying, "Don't be frightened. After all, why shouldn't you come back with me? We're both women. If I'm the more fortunate, you ought to expect..."

5 But happily at that moment, for she didn't know how the sentence was going to end, the car stopped. The bell was rung, the door opened, and with a charming, protecting, almost embracing movement,[36] Rosemary drew the other into the hall.

Warmth, softness, light, a sweet scent, all those things so familiar to 10 her she never even thought about them, she watched that other receive. It was fascinating. She was like the rich little girl in her nursery with all the cupboards to open, all the boxes to unpack.

"Come, come upstairs," said Rosemary, longing to[37] begin to be generous.

15 "Come up to my room." And, besides, she wanted to spare this poor little thing from being stared at by the servants; she decided as they mounted the stairs she would not even ring to Jeanne, but take off her things by herself. The great things were to be natural!

And "There!" cried Rosemary again, as they reached her beautiful 20 big bedroom with the curtains drawn, the fire leaping on her wonderful lacquer furniture, her gold cushions and the primrose and blue rugs.

The girl stood just inside the door; she seemed dazed.[38] But Rosemary didn't mind that.

---

35) fairy godmothers: 도움이 간절히 필요할 때 도와주는 사람(대모)

36) almost embracing movement: 거의 껴안는 듯한 동작으로

37) longing to~: ~하고 싶은 생각이 간절하다

38) dazed: 멍한, 아찔한

1   "Come and sit down," she cried, dragging her big chair up to the
fire, "in this comfy chair. Come and get warm. You look so dreadfully
cold."

"I daren't, madam," said the girl, and she edged backwards.[39]

5   "Oh, please," — Rosemary ran forward — "you mustn't be
frightened, you mustn't, really. Sit down, when I've taken off my things
we shall go into the next room and have tea and be cozy. Why are you
afraid?" And gently she half pushed the thin figure into its deep cradle.

But there was no answer. The girl stayed just as she had been put,
10   with her hands by her sides and her mouth slightly open. To be quite
sincere, she looked rather stupid. But Rosemary wouldn't acknowledge
it. She leant over her, saying: "Won't you take off your hat? Your pretty
hair is all wet. And one is so much more comfortable without a hat, isn't
one?"

15   There was a whisper that sounded like "Very good, madam," and the
crushed hat was taken off.

"And let me help you off with your coat, too," said Rosemary.

The girl stood up. But she held on to the chair with one hand and
let Rosemary pull. It was quite an effort. The other scarcely helped her
20   at all. She seemed to stagger like a child, and the thought came and
went through Rosemary's mind, that if people wanted helping they must
respond a little, just a little, otherwise it became very difficult indeed.
And what was she to do with the coat now? She left it on the floor, and
the hat too. She was just going to take a cigarette off the mantelpiece[40]
25   when the girl said quickly, but so lightly and strangely: "I'm very sorry,

---

39) edge backwards: 슬금슬금 뒤로 물러서다
40) mantelpiece: 벽난로 위의 선반

madam, but I'm going to faint. I shall go off,[41] madam, if I don't have something."

"Good heavens,[42] how thoughtless I am!" Rosemary rushed to the bell.

"Tea! Tea at once! And some brandy immediately!"

The maid was gone again, but the girl almost cried out: "No, I don't want no brandy. I never drink brandy. It's a cup of tea I want, madam." And she burst into tears. It was a terrible and fascinating moment. Rosemary knelt beside her chair.

"Don't cry, poor little thing," she said. "Don't cry." And she gave the other her lace handkerchief. She really was touched beyond words.[43] She put her arm round those thin, bird–like shoulders.

Now at last the other forgot to be shy, forgot everything except that they were both women, and gasped out: "I can't go on no longer like this. I can't bear it. I can't bear it. I shall do away with myself.[44] I can't bear no more."

"You shan't have to.[45] I'll look after you. Don't cry any more. Don't you see what a good thing it was that you met me? We'll have tea and you'll tell me everything. And I shall arrange something. I promise. Do stop crying. It's so exhausting. Please!"

The other did stop just in time for Rosemary to get up before the tea came. She had the table placed between them. She plied the poor little

---

41) go off: 실신하다

42) Good heavens: 맙소사

43) beyond words: 말할 수 없을 정도로

44) do away with myself: 자살하다

45) You shan't have to: 그렇게 해서는 안 돼요. shan't는 shall not의 축약형.

1 creature with everything, all the sandwiches, all the bread and butter, and every time her cup was empty she filled it with tea, cream and sugar. People always said sugar was so nourishing. As for herself she didn't eat; she smoked and looked away tactfully so that the other should not be

5 shy.

And really the effect of that slight meal was marvelous. When the tea–table was carried away a new being, a light, frail[46] creature with tangled hair, dark lips, deep, lighted eyes, lay back in the big chair in a kind of sweet languor,[47] looking at the blaze.[48] Rosemary lit a fresh

10 cigarette; it was time to begin. "And when did you have your last meal?" she asked softly.

But at that moment the door–handle turned.

"Rosemary, may I come in?" It was Philip.

"Of course."

15 He came in. "Oh, I'm so sorry," he said, and stopped and stared.

"It's quite all right," said Rosemary, smiling. "This is my friend, Miss

—"

"Smith, madam," said the languid figure, who was strangely still and unafraid.

20 "Smith," said Rosemary. "We are going to have a little talk."

"Oh yes," said Philip. "Quite," and his eye caught sight of the coat and hat on the floor. He came over to the fire and turned his back to it. "It's a beastly[49] afternoon," he said curiously, still looking at that listless

---

46) frail: 약한, 부서지기 쉬운

47) sweet languor: 즐거운 나른함

48) blaze: (난로의) 활활 타는 불꽃

49) beastly: 끔찍한

1 figure, looking at its hands and boots, and then at Rosemary again.

"Yes, isn't it?" said Rosemary enthusiastically. "Vile."[50]

Philip smiled his charming smile. "As a matter of fact," said he, "I wanted you to come into the library for a moment. Would you? Will Miss Smith excuse us?"

The big eyes were raised to him, but Rosemary answered for her: "Of course she will." And they went out of the room together.

"I say," said Philip, when they were alone. "Explain. Who is she? What does it all mean?"

Rosemary, laughing, leaned against the door and said: "I picked her up in Curzon Street. Really. She's a real pick–up. She asked me for the price of a cup of tea, and I brought her home with me."

"But what on earth are you going to do with her?" cried Philip.

"Be nice to her," said Rosemary quickly. "Be frightfully nice to her. Look after her. I don't know how. We haven't talked yet. But show her — treat her — make her feel —"

"My darling girl," said Philip, "you're quite mad, you know. It simply can't be done."

"I knew you'd say that," retorted[51] Rosemary. Why not? I want to. Isn't that a reason? And besides, one's always reading about these things. I decided —"

"But," said Philip slowly, and he cut the end of a cigar, "she's so astonishingly pretty."

"Pretty?" Rosemary was so surprised that she blushed. "Do you think so? I — I hadn't thought about it."

---

50) Vile: (날씨가) 몹시 나쁜, 불쾌한
51) retort: 쏘아붙이다, 대꾸하다

1   "Good Lord!" Philip struck a match. "She's absolutely lovely. Look again, my child. I was bowled over[52] when I came into your room just now. However... I think you're making a ghastly[53] mistake. Sorry, darling, if I'm crude and all that. But let me know if Miss Smith is going
5   to dine with us in time for me to look up The Milliner's Gazette."[54]

"You absurd creature!"[55] said Rosemary, and she went out of the library, but not back to her bedroom. She went to her writing–room and sat down at her desk.

Pretty! Absolutely lovely! Bowled over! Her heart beat like a heavy
10   bell. Pretty! Lovely! She drew her check–book towards her. But no, checks would be no use, of course. She opened a drawer and took out five pound notes, looked at them, put two back, and holding the three squeezed in her hand, she went back to her bedroom.

Half an hour later Philip was still in the library, when Rosemary
15   came in.

"I only wanted to tell you," said she, and she leaned against the door again and looked at him with her dazzled exotic gaze,[56] "Miss Smith won't dine with us tonight."

Philip put down the paper. "Oh, what's happened? Previous
20   engagement?"

Rosemary came over and sat down on his knee. "She insisted on going," said she, "so I gave the poor little thing a present of money. I

---

52) be bowled over: 어안이 벙벙하다
53) ghastly: 무시무시한
54) The Milliner's Gazette: 밀리너 여성지(잡지)
55) You absurd creature: 당신은 터무니없는 사람이군요!
56) with her dazzled exotic gaze: 현혹적이고 이국적인 그녀의 특유의 시선으로

couldn't keep her against her will, could I?" she added softly.

Rosemary had just done her hair, darkened her eyes a little and put on her pearls. She put up her hands and touched Philip's cheeks.

"Do you like me?" said she, and her tone, sweet, husky, troubled him.

"I like you awfully," he said, and he held her tighter. "Kiss me."

There was a pause.

Then Rosemary said dreamily:[57] "I saw a fascinating little box to–day. It cost twenty–eight guineas. May I have it?"

Philip jumped her on his knee. "You may, little wasteful one," said he.

But that was not really what Rosemary wanted to say.

"Philip," she whispered, and she pressed his head against her bosom, "am I pretty?"

---

57) dreamily: 꿈을 꾸듯이

15

Indian Camp[1]

Ernest Hemingway[2]

1   At the lake shore there was another rowboat drawn up. The two Indians stood waiting. Nick and his father[3] got in the stern of the boat and the Indians shoved it off[4] and one of them got in to row. Uncle George sat in the stern of the camp rowboat. The young Indian shoved

---

1) 「인디언 캠프」("Indian Camp")는 전형적인 성장소설(initiation story)이다. 성장소설의 주인공은 이전에는 몰랐던 생각, 경험, 의식, 지식과 접하게 된다. 헤밍웨이는 많은 성장소설을 썼는데, 가끔씩은 "통과의례"(rite of passage) 소설로 언급되기도 한다. 이 소설들의 주인공은 대부분 닉 아담스(Nick Adams)라는 이름으로 불린다.

2) 어니스트 헤밍웨이(Ernest Hemingway, 1899-1961): 미국의 대소설가. 윌리엄 포크너(William Faulkner)와 함께 현대 미국문학을 세계문학으로 끌어올린 공로자이다. 그는 『노인과 바다』(1952)로 1953년 퓰리처상과 노벨문학상을 수상했으며, 그 외에도 『무기여 잘 있거라』, 『누구를 위하여 종은 울리나』와 같은 명작을 남겼다. 그는 문명의 세계를 속임수로 보고, 인간의 비극적인 모습을 간결한 문체로 묘사한 20세기의 대표적 작가이다.

3) 이 소설의 주인공은 닉 아담스이며 그의 아버지는 닥터 아담스(Dr. Adams)인데, 헤밍웨이 자신의 아버지도 의사였다. 헤밍웨이의 아버지는 아들 헤밍웨이와 미시간(Michigan)의 북부 숲에서 많은 시간을 보낸 것으로 알려져 있다. 따라서 많은 비평가들은 이 소설을 어느 정도는 자서전적 소설로 읽는다. 이 작품에서 어린 닉은 헤밍웨이의 작품 전반에서 가장 중요하게 남아 있는 것들인 삶과 죽음, 고통과 인내, 그리고 자살에 대한 개념을 배운다.

4) shove off: = to move from the shore in a boat, depart. 밀고 나아가다

the camp boat off and got in to row Uncle George. The two boats started off in the dark. Nick heard the oarlocks of the other boat quite a way[5] ahead of them in the mist. The Indians rowed with quick choppy[6] strokes. Nick lay back with his father's arm around him. It was cold on the water. The Indian who was rowing them was working very hard, but the other boat moved further ahead in the mist all the time.

"Where are we going, Dad?" Nick asked.

"Over to the Indian camp. There is an Indian lady very sick."

"Oh," said Nick.

Across the bay they found the other boat beached.[7] Uncle George was smoking a cigar in the dark. The young Indian pulled the boat way up on the beach. Uncle George gave both the Indians cigars.

They walked up from the beach through a meadow that was soaking wet with dew, following the young Indian who carried a lantern. Then they went into the woods and followed a trail that led to the logging road[8] that ran back into the hills. It was much lighter on the logging road as the timber was cut away on both sides. The young Indian stopped and blew out his lantern and they all walked on along the road.

They came around a bend and a dog came out barking. Ahead were the lights of the shanties[9] where the Indian bark–peelers lived. More dogs rushed out at them. The two Indians sent them back to the shanties. In the shanty nearest the road there was a light in the window. An old

---

5) quite a way: 멀찌감치, 꽤 멀리
6) choppy: 파도가 일렁이는
7) beach: (배를) 바닷가에 끌어올리다
8) the logging road: 벌목용 도로
9) shanty: = crudely built cabins, or shacks. 오두막

¹ woman stood in the doorway holding a lamp.

Inside on a wooden bunk lay a young Indian woman. She had been trying to have her baby for two days. All the old women in the camp had been helping her. The men had moved off up the road to sit in the

⁵ dark and smoke out of range of the noise she made. She screamed just as Nick and the two Indians followed his father and Uncle George into the shanty. She lay in the lower bunk, very big under a quilt. Her head was turned to one side. In the upper bunk was her husband. He had cut his foot very badly with an ax three days before. He was smoking a pipe. The

¹⁰ room smelled very bad.

Nick's father ordered some water to be put on the stove, and while it was heating he spoke to Nick.

"This lady is going to have a baby, Nick," he said. "I know," said Nick. "You don't know," said his father. "Listen to me. What she is going

¹⁵ through is called being in labor.¹⁰⁾ The baby wants to be born and she wants it to be born. All her muscles are trying to get the baby born. That is what is happening when she screams."

"I see," Nick said. Just then the woman cried out. "Oh, Daddy, can't you give her something to make her stop screaming?" asked Nick.

²⁰ "No. I haven't any anaesthetic,"¹¹⁾ his father said. "But her screams are not important. I don't hear them because they are not important." The husband in the upper bunk rolled over against the wall. The woman in the kitchen motioned to the doctor that the water was hot. Nick's father went into the kitchen and poured about half of the water out of

²⁵ the big kettle into a basin. Into the water left in the kettle he put several

---

10) being in labor: 해산(분만) 중, 산고를 겪는 중

11) anaesthetic: 마취약

1 things he unwrapped from a handkerchief.

"Those must boil," he said, and began to scrub his hands in the basin of hot water with a cake of soap he had brought from the camp. Nick watched his father's hands scrubbing each other with the soap. While his
5 father washed his hands very carefully and thoroughly, he talked. "You see, Nick, babies are supposed to be born head first but sometimes they're not. When they're not they make a lot of trouble for everybody. Maybe I'll have to operate on this lady. We'll know in a little while." When he was satisfied with his hands he went in and went to work. "Pull back that
10 quilt, will you, George?" he said. "I'd rather not touch it."

Later when he started to operate Uncle George and three Indian men held the woman still. She bit Uncle George on the arm and Uncle George said, "Damn squaw bitch!"[12] and the young Indian who had rowed Uncle George over laughed at him. Nick held the basin for his
15 father. It all took a long time. His father picked the baby up and slapped it to make it breathe and handed it to the old woman. "See, it's a boy, Nick," he said. "How do you like being an interne?"

Nick said. "All right." He was looking away so as not to see what his father was doing. "There. That gets it."[13] said his father and put
20 something into the basin. Nick didn't look at it. "Now," his father said, "there's some stitches to put in.[14] You can watch this or not, Nick, just as you like. I'm going to sew up the incision[15] I made." Nick did not watch. His curiosity had been gone for a long time. His father finished

---

12) Damn squaw bitch!: 경을 칠 인디언 계집년! squaw: 북미 원주민 여자

13) There. That gets it: 됐어. 이젠 다 끝났어. 여기서 gets는 finishes라는 의미이며 it은 막연하게 일반적인 일을 말한다.

14) there's some stitches to put in: 몇 바늘 꿰매야 할 일이 남았다

15) incision: 절개

1 and stood up. Uncle George and the three Indian men stood up. Nick
put the basin out in the kitchen. Uncle George looked at his arm. The
young Indian smiled reminiscently.[16] "I'll put some peroxide[17] on that,
George," the doctor said. He bent over the Indian woman. She was quiet
5 now and her eyes were closed. She looked very pale. She did not know
what had become of the baby or anything. "I'll be back in the morning."
the doctor said, standing up. "The nurse should be here from St. Ignace[18]
by noon and she'll bring everything we need."

He was feeling exalted and talkative as football players are in the
10 dressing room after a game. "That's one for the medical journal, George,"
he said. "Doing a Caesarian with a jack–knife[19] and sewing it up with
nine–foot, tapered gut leaders."[20] Uncle George was standing against
the wall, looking at his arm. "Oh, you're a great man, all right," he said.
"Ought to have a look at the proud father. They're usually the worst
15 sufferers in these little[21] affairs," the doctor said. "I must say he took it all
pretty quietly."

He pulled back the blanket from the Indian's head. His hand came
away wet. He mounted on the edge of the lower bunk with the lamp in
one hand and looked in. The Indian lay with his face toward the wall.
20 His throat had been cut from ear to ear. The blood had flowed down
into a pool where his body sagged the bunk. His head rested on his left

---

16) reminiscently: 회상에 잠겨

17) peroxide: = a substance such as sodium peroxide that cleanses a wound. 과산화수소

18) St. Ignace: 세인트 이그네이스, 미국 미시건주 매키넉 카운티에 있는 도시.

· 19) Doing a Caesarian with a jack – knife: 잭나이프로 제왕절개 수술을 하다니. Caesarian: = Caesarean

20) tapered gut leaders: 가는 낚싯줄. leader: 본 낚싯줄 끝에 바늘을 달기 위해 사용하는 가느다란 보조
낚싯줄

21) little: 여기서는 반어적 의미로 쓰임.

arm. The open razor lay, edge up, in the blankets. "Take Nick out of the shanty, George." the doctor said. There was no need of that. Nick, standing in the door of the kitchen, had a good view of the upper bunk when his father, the lamp in one hand, tipped the Indian's head back.[22]

It was just beginning to be daylight when they walked along the logging road back toward the lake.

"I'm terribly sorry I brought you along, Nickie." said his father, all his post–operative exhilaration gone. "It was an awful mess to put you through."

"Do ladies always have such a hard time having babies?" Nick asked.

"No, that was very, very exceptional."

"Why did he kill himself, Daddy?"

"I don't know, Nick. He couldn't stand things,[23] I guess."

"Do many men kill themselves, Daddy?"

"Not very many, Nick."

"Do many women?"

"Hardly ever."

"Don't they ever?"

"Oh, yes. They do sometimes."

"Daddy?"

"Yes."

"Where did Uncle George go?"

"He'll turn up all right."

"Is dying hard, Daddy?"

"No, I think it's pretty easy, Nick. It all depends."

---

22) tip~back: ~을 뒤집다, 바로 눕히다
23) stand things: 만사를 참고 견디다

1   They were seated in the boat. Nick in the stern, his father rowing.[24] The sun was coming up over the hills. A bass jumped, making a circle in the water. Nick trailed his hand in the water. It felt warm in the sharp chill of the morning.

5   In the early morning on the lake sitting in the stern of the boat with his father rowing; he felt quite sure that he would never die.

---

24) 삶과 죽음의 목격 후 닉이 겪는 성장과정이 드러난 부분. 이 작품 도입부에서 닉은 아버지의 팔에 안겨서 왔지만, 돌아가는 길에는 아버지와 떨어져서 배의 선미에 혼자 앉는다.

16

The Pearl of Love

Herbert George Wells[1]

1　　The pearl is lovelier than the most brilliant of crystalline stones, the moralist declares, because it is made through the suffering of a living creature.[2] About that I can say nothing because I feel none of the fascination of pearls. Their cloudy lustre[3] moves me not at all. Nor can

5　I decide for myself upon that age–long dispute[4] whether 'The Pearl of Love' is the cruellest of stories or only a gracious fable of the immortality of beauty.

　　Both the story and the controversy will be familiar to students of mediaeval Persian prose. The story is a short one, though the

---

1)　허버트 조지 웰스(Herbert George Wells, 1866-1946): 14세의 어린 나이부터 포목상 점원, 약국의 조수, 학교의 수위 등을 거치며 어려운 환경에서 자란 그는 독학으로 대학을 졸업했다. 정치, 사회 문제에 관심을 가졌고, 진화론 및 기타 생물학 이론에 기초한 점진적 사회주의를 지향했다. 만년에 는 1, 2차 세계대전의 비극적 현실에 절망한 나머지 비관주의적인 성향도 보였다. 영국소설사에서 는 공상과학소설의 선구자로 꼽히기도 한다. 작품으로 『타임머신』(*The Time Machine*)(1895), 『보 이지 않는 인간』(*The Invisible Man*)(1897) 등이 있다.

2)　a living creature: 조개를 의미함.

3)　lustre: 윤기, 광택

4)　age – long dispute: 아주 오래된 논쟁

¹ commentary⁵⁾ upon it is a respectable part⁶⁾ of the literature of that period. They have treated it as a poetic invention and they have treated it as an allegory meaning this, that, or the other thing. Theologians have had their copious⁷⁾ way with it, dealing with it particularly as concerning ⁵ the restoration of the body after death, and it has been greatly used as a parable by those who write about aesthetics.⁸⁾ And many have held it to be the statement of a fact, simply and baldly true.

The story is laid in⁹⁾ North India, which is the most fruitful soil for sublime love stories of all the lands in the world. It was in a country of ¹⁰ sunshine and lakes and rich forests and hills and fertile valleys; and far away the great mountains hung in the sky, peaks, crests, and ridges of inaccessible and eternal snow. There was a young prince, lord of all the land; and he found a maiden of indescribable beauty and delightfulness and he made her his queen and laid his heart at her feet.¹⁰⁾ Love was ¹⁵ theirs, full of joys and sweetness, full of hope, exquisite, brave and marvellous love, beyond anything you have ever dreamt of love. It was theirs for a year and a part of a year;¹¹⁾ and then suddenly, because of some venomous sting that came to her in a thicket,¹²⁾ she died.

She died and for a while the prince was utterly prostrated.¹³⁾ He ²⁰ was silent and motionless with grief. They feared he might kill himself,

---

5) commentary: 해설, 주석

6) a respectable part: 상당한 양

7) copious: 엄청난, 방대한

8) aesthetics: 미학

9) is laid in: ~을 배경으로 하고 있다

10) laid his heart at her feet: 헌신적으로 사랑했다, 구애했다

11) for a year and a part of a year: 일 년 그리고 몇 달 동안

12) thicket: 덤불

13) prostrate: (충격 등으로) 몸[정신]을 가누지 못하게 하다

1 and he had neither sons nor brothers to succeed him. For two days and nights he lay upon his face, fasting, across the foot of the couch which bore her calm and lovely body. Then he arose and ate, and went about very quietly like one who has taken a great resolution. He caused her

5 body to be put in a coffin of lead mixed with silver, and for that he had an outer coffin made of the most precious and scented woods wrought with gold,[14] and about that there was to be a sarcophagus of alabaster,[15] inlaid[16] with precious stones. And while these things were being done he spent his time for the most part by the pools and in the garden–houses

10 and pavilions and groves and in those chambers in the palace where they two had been most together, brooding upon[17] her loveliness. He did not rend his garments[18] nor defile[19] himself with ashes and sackcloth as the custom[20] was, for his love was too great for such extravagances. At last he came forth again among his councillors[21] and before the people, and told

15 them what he had a mind to do.

He said he could never more touch woman, he could never more think of them, and so he would find a seemly youth to adopt for his heir and train him to his task,[22] and that he would do his princely duties as became him; but that for the rest of it, he would give himself with

---

14) of the most precious and scented woods wrought with gold: 금으로 문양을 새겨 넣은 대단히 귀하고 향기로운 나무로

15) a sarcophagus of alabaster: 설화석고로 만든 석관

16) inlaid: (나무 · 금속 등으로) 무늬를 새긴, 상감 세공을 한

17) brood upon: ~에 대해 곰곰이 생각하다

18) rend his garments: 의관을 찢다

19) defile: (신성하거나 중요한 것을) 더럽히다

20) as the custom: 관습대로

21) councillors: 신하들

22) train him to his task: 그가 할 일을 가르치다

1 all his power and all his strength and all his wealth, all that he could
command,[23] to make a monument worthy of his incomparable,[24] dear,
lost mistress. A building it should be of perfect grace and beauty, more
marvellous than any other building had ever been or could ever be, so
5 that to the end of time[25] it should be a wonder, and men would treasure
it and speak of it and desire to see it and come from all the lands of the
earth to visit and recall the name and the memory of his queen. And this
building he said was to be called the Pearl of Love.

And this his councillors and people permitted him to do, and so he
10 did.

Year followed year[26] and all the years he devoted himself to building
and adorning the Pearl of Love. A great foundation was hewn[27] out
of the living rock[28] in a place whence one seemed to be looking at the
snowy wilderness of the great mountain across the valley of the world.
15 Villages and hills there were, a winding river, and very far away three
great cities. Here they put the sarcophagus of alabaster beneath a pavilion
of cunning workmanship;[29] and about it there were set pillars of strange
and lovely stone and wrought and fretted[30] walls, and a great casket of
masonry bearing a dome and pinnacles and cupolas,[31] as exquisite as a

---

23) all that he could command: 자기의 능력이 미치는 모든 것

24) incomparable: 비할 데가 없는

25) to the end of time: 시간이 끝날 때까지

26) Year followed year: 세월이 흘러흘러갔고

27) hewn: hew(자르다)의 과거분사

28) the living rock: 자연 그대로의 바위(파서 옮겨 놓은 것이 아니라 땅에 박혀 있는)

29) of cunning workmanship: 정교한 솜씨로 꾸며진

30) fretted: 무늬가 새겨진

31) a great casket of masonry bearing a dome and pinnacles and cupolas: 둥근 지붕과 뾰족한 봉우리와
둥근 천정이 있는 커다란 석조로 된 관

jewel. At first the design of the Pearl of Love was less bold and subtle than it became later. At first it was smaller and more wrought and encrusted;[32] there were many pierced screens and delicate clusters of rosy hued pillars, and the sarcophagus lay like a child that sleeps among flowers. The first dome was covered with green tiles, framed and held together by silver, but this was taken away again because it seemed close,[33] because it did not soar grandly enough for the broadening imagination of the prince.

For by this time he was no longer the graceful youth who had loved the girl queen. He was now a man, grave and intent, wholly set upon the building of the Pearl of Love. With every year of effort he had learnt new possibilities in arch and wall and buttress;[34] he had acquired greater power over the material he had to use and he had learnt of a hundred stones and hues and effects that he could never have thought of in the beginning. His sense of colour had grown finer and colder;[35] he cared no more for the enamelled gold–lined brightness that had pleased him first, the brightness of an illuminated missal;[36] he sought now for blue colourings like the sky and for the subtle hues of great distances, for recondite[37] shadows and sudden broad floods of purple opalescence[38] and for grandeur and space. He wearied altogether of[39] carvings and pictures and inlaid ornamentation and all the little careful work of

---

32) more wrought and encrusted: (나중의 것보다) 더 가공이 많고 장식적인

33) close: 답답한, 비좁은

34) buttress: 버팀목, (벽의) 지지대, 부벽

35) had grown finer and colder: 더 섬세하고 냉철해졌다

36) an illuminated missal: 밝게 빛나는 [화려한 색채를 넣은] 기도서

37) recondite: 많이 알려지지 않은, 잘 이해받지 못하는

38) opalescence: 유백광

39) weary of: ~에 진절머리가 나다. wearied altogether of: ~을 전적으로 싫어하게 되었다

1 men. "Those were pretty things," he said of his earlier decorations; and
had them put aside into subordinate buildings where they would not
hamper his main design. Greater and greater grew his artistry. With
awe and amazement people saw the Pearl of Love sweeping up from its
5 first beginnings to a superhuman breadth and height and magnificence.
They did not know clearly what they had expected, but never had they
expected so sublime a thing as this. "Wonderful are the miracles," they
whispered, "that love can do," and all the women in the world, whatever
other loves they had,[40] loved the prince for the splendour of his devotion.
10   Through the middle of the building ran a great aisle, a vista, that the
prince came to care for more and more. From the inner entrance of the
building he looked along the length of an immense pillared gallery and
across the central area from which the rose–hued columns had long since
vanished, over the top of the pavilion under which lay the sarcophagus,
15 through a marvellously designed opening, to the snowy wildernesses of
the great mountain, the lord of all mountains, two hundred miles away.
The pillars and arches and buttresses and galleries soared and floated on
either side, perfect yet unobtrusive,[41] like great archangels[42] waiting in
the shadows about the presence of God. When men saw that austere[43]
20 beauty for the first time they were exalted, and then they shivered and
their hearts bowed down. Very often would the prince come to stand
there and look at that vista, deeply moved and not yet fully satisfied. The
Pearl of Love had still something for him to do, he felt, before his task

---

40) whatever other loves they had: 그들이 사랑하는 바가 각각 다르겠지만
41) unobtrusive: 불필요하게 관심을 끌지 않는, 지나치게 야단스럽지 않은
42) archangel: 대천사, 천사장
43) austere: 경건한, 근엄한

¹ was done. Always he would order some little alteration to be made or some recent alterations to be put back again. And one day he said that the sarcophagus would be clearer and simpler without the pavilion; and after regarding it very steadfastly for a long time, he had the pavilion

⁵ dismantled and removed.

The next day he came and said nothing, and the next day and the next. Then for two days he stayed away altogether. Then he returned, bringing with him an architect and two master craftsmen and a small retinue.⁴⁴⁾

¹⁰ All looked, standing together silently in a little group, amidst the serene vastness of their achievement. No trace of toil remained in its perfection. It was as if the God of nature's beauty had taken over their offspring to himself.⁴⁵⁾

Only one thing there was to mar the absolute harmony. There was

¹⁵ a certain disproportion⁴⁶⁾ about the sarcophagus. It had never been enlarged, and indeed how could it have been enlarged since the early days. It challenged the eye;⁴⁷⁾ it nicked⁴⁸⁾ the streaming lines. In that sarcophagus was the casket of lead and silver, and in the casket of lead and silver was the queen, the dear immortal cause of all this beauty. But

²⁰ now that sarcophagus seemed no more than a little dark oblong⁴⁹⁾ that

---

44) retinue: 수행원들

45) It was as if the God of nature's beauty had taken over their offspring to himself: 그것은 마치 자연의 아름다움을 만든 신이 그들의 자손(인간)의 일을 스스로(신이) 떠맡은 것처럼 보였다

46) disproportion: 불균형

47) It challenged the eye: 그것은 눈에 거슬렸다

48) nick: 흠집을 내다, 자국을 내다

49) a little dark oblong: 새카만 작은 타원형의 물건

1 lay incongruously[50] in the great vista of the Pearl of Love. It was as if someone had dropped a small valise[51] upon the crystal sea of heaven.

    Long the prince mused, but no one knew the thoughts that passed through his mind.

5   At last he spoke. He pointed.

    "Take that thing away," he said.

---

50) incongruously: 조화되지 않게
51) valise: (옷을 넣어 다니는) 작은 여행 가방

17

Shooting an Elephant

George Orwell[1]

1   In Moulmein,[2] in Lower Burma, I was hated by large numbers of people — the only time in my life that I have been important enough for this to happen to me. I was sub–divisional police officer of the town, and in an aimless, petty kind of way anti–European feeling was very
5 bitter. No one had the guts to raise a riot, but if a European woman went through the bazaars alone somebody would probably spit betel juice over her dress. As a police officer I was an obvious target and was baited whenever it seemed safe to do so. When a nimble Burman tripped me up on the football field[3] and the referee (another Burman) looked the other
10 way, the crowd yelled with hideous laughter. This happened more than

---

1) 조지 오웰(George Orwell, 1903-1950): 에릭 블레어(Eric Blair)가 본명이고 조지 오웰은 필명이다. 인도 식민지 관료로 있던 부모 때문에 인도에서 태어났으나 영국에서 교육받았다. 21세에 버마(오늘날의 미얀마)에서 5년 동안 경찰관으로 복무했다. 「코끼리를 쏘다」("Shooting an Elephant")는 이때의 경험을 바탕으로 쓴 에세이다. 조지 오웰의 가장 잘 알려진 작품으로는 풍자소설인 『동물농장』(*Animal Farm*)(1945), 『1984』(*Nineteen Eighty – Four*)(1949) 등이 있다.

2) Moulmein: 몰멘(버마 남부, 쌀윈강 하구의 항구 도시)

3) trip me up on the football field: 나를 축구장에 엎어뜨리다. football은 영국이 그들의 식민지에서 시행한 자신들의 문화를 상징한다. 근대 축구는 19세기에 영국에서 개발되었다.

1 once. In the end the sneering yellow faces of young men that met me everywhere, the insults hooted after me when I was at a safe distance, got badly on my nerves.[4] The young Buddhist priests were the worst of all. There were several thousands of them in the town and none of them
5 seemed to have anything to do except stand on street corners and jeer at Europeans.

All this was perplexing and upsetting. For at that time I had already made up my mind that imperialism was an evil thing and the sooner I chucked up my job[5] and got out of it the better. Theoretically —
10 and secretly, of course — I was all for the Burmese and all against their oppressors, the British. As for the job I was doing, I hated it more bitterly than I can perhaps make clear. In a job like that you see the dirty work of Empire at close quarters.[6] The wretched prisoners huddling in the stinking cages of the lock–ups,[7] the grey, cowed faces[8] of the long–term
15 convicts, the scarred buttocks of the men who had been flogged with bamboos — all these oppressed me with an intolerable sense of guilt. But I could get nothing into perspective.[9] I was young and ill–educated and I had had to think out my problems[10] in the utter silence that is imposed on every Englishman in the East. I did not even know that the British
20 Empire is dying, still less did I know that it is a great deal better than the younger empires that are going to supplant[11] it. All I knew was that I

---

4) get on one's nerves: ~의 신경을 거스르다

5) chuck up my job: = chuck up: resign. 나의 일을 그만둬버리다

6) at close quarters: = in close proximity; near by

7) the lock – ups: = jail

8) cowed faces: = frightened faces

9) could get nothing into perspective: 어떤 것도 바른 견해라고 볼 수 없었다

10) think out my problems: 나의 고민을 풀 방도를 어떻게든 생각해내다

11) to supplant: = to take the place of; supersede or oust

1 was stuck between my hatred of the empire I served and my rage against the evil–spirited little beasts who tried to make my job impossible. With one part of my mind I thought of the British Raj[12] as an unbreakable tyranny, as something clamped down,[13] in *saecula saeculorum*,[14] upon
5 the will of prostrate peoples; with another part I thought that the greatest joy in the world would be to drive a bayonet into a Buddhist priest's guts. Feelings like these are the normal by–products of imperialism; ask any Anglo–Indian[15] official, if you can catch him off duty.

　　One day something happened which in a roundabout way[16] was
10 enlightening. It was a tiny incident in itself, but it gave me a better glimpse[17] than I had had before of the real nature of imperialism — the real motives for which despotic[18] governments act. Early one morning the sub–inspector at a police station the other end of the town rang me up on the phone and said that an elephant was ravaging the bazaar. Would I
15 please come and do something about it? I did not know what I could do, but I wanted to see what was happening and I got on to a pony and started out. I took my rifle, an old .44 Winchester[19] and much too small to kill an elephant, but I thought the noise might be useful *in terrorem*.[20] Various Burmans stopped me on the way and told me about the elephant's

---

12) Raj: (주로 인도에서) 지배, 통치, 주권

13) as something clamped down: 강요, 강제된 것으로

14) in *saecula saeculorum*: 〈라틴어〉 in this age and for all ages: 영원히, 세상 끝날 때까지

15) Anglo – Indian: = of British birth but living of having lived long in India

16) roundabout: = indirect

17) glimpse: = understanding

18) despotic: 전제적인, 횡포한

19) an old .44 Winchester: 구경 0.44인치의 구식 원체스터 연발총 (.44는 (point) forty – four라고 읽는다.)

20) *in terrorem*: 〈라틴어〉 = as a warning. 경고로서, 협박으로

1 doings. It was not, of course, a wild elephant, but a tame one which had gone "must."[21] It had been chained up, as tame elephants always are when their attack of "must" is due,[22] but on the previous night it had broken its chain and escaped. Its mahout,[23] the only person who
5 could manage it when it was in that state, had set out in pursuit, but had taken the wrong direction and was now twelve hours' journey away, and in the morning the elephant had suddenly reappeared in the town. The Burmese population had no weapons and were quite helpless against it. It had already destroyed somebody's bamboo hut, killed a cow and raided
10 some fruit–stalls and devoured the stock; also it had met the municipal rubbish van and, when the driver jumped out and took to his heels,[24] had turned the van over and inflicted violences upon it.

The Burmese sub–inspector and some Indian constables were waiting for me in the quarter where the elephant had been seen. It was
15 a very poor quarter, a labyrinth[25] of squalid bamboo huts, thatched with palm–leaf, winding all over a steep hillside.[26] I remember that it was a cloudy, stuffy morning at the beginning of the rains.[27] We began questioning the people as to where the elephant had gone and, as usual, failed to get any definite information. That is invariably the case[28] in the
20 East; a story always sounds clear enough at a distance, but the nearer you

---

21) must: = into sexual heat. 발정한
22) due: calculated; foreseen
23) mahout: (인도, 버마에서) 코끼리 부리는 사람
24) take to one's heels: 도망치다
25) labyrinth: 미로, 미궁
26) winding all over a steep hillside: 가파른 산허리를 온통 둘러 감싸고 위치한
27) at the beginning of the rains: 열대지방의 우기 초기에
28) That is invariably the case: 항상 그렇다

get to the scene of events the vaguer it becomes. Some of the people said that the elephant had gone in one direction, some said that he had gone in another, some professed not even to have heard of any elephant. I had almost made up my mind that the whole story was a pack of lies,[29] when we heard yells a little distance away. There was a loud, scandalized[30] cry of "Go away, child! Go away this instant!"[31] and an old woman with a switch in her hand came round the corner of a hut, violently shooing away a crowd of naked children. Some more women followed, clicking their tongues and exclaiming; evidently there was something that the children ought not to have seen. I rounded[32] the hut and saw a man's dead body sprawling in the mud.[33] He was an Indian, a black Dravidian coolie,[34] almost naked, and he could not have been dead many minutes. The people said that the elephant had come suddenly upon him round the corner of the hut, caught him with its trunk, put its foot on his back and ground him into the earth. This was the rainy season and the ground was soft, and his face had scored a trench a foot deep and a couple of yards long.[35] He was lying on his belly[36] with arms crucified[37] and head sharply twisted to one side. His face was coated with[38] mud,

---

29) a pack of lies: a lot of lies. 새빨간 거짓말

30) scandalize: 분개하게 만들다

31) this instant: = at once

32) rounded: went round

33) mud: 진흙은 영국의 통치하에서 버마인들이 살아야 하는 불결함을 상징한다. 그것은 또한 영국인들이 인도와 버마를 식민지화했을 때 자신들 스스로를 위해 만들었던 정치적 수렁을 상징하기도 한다.

34) Dravidian coolie: 드라비다어족 하층 노동자

35) his face had scored a trench a foot deep and a couple of yards long: 얼굴로 도랑에 30cm 깊이로 약 2m 길이의 자국을 냈다. 사망한 버마 원주민(dead coolie)은 탄압받은 버마인들의 상징으로 보인다.

36) on his belly: 엎드려

37) with arms crucified: 양팔을 대자로 뻗치고

38) was coated with: = was covered with

¹ the eyes wide open, the teeth bared and grinning with an expression of unendurable agony. (Never tell me, by the way, that the dead look peaceful. Most of the corpses I have seen looked devilish.) The friction of the great beast's foot had stripped the skin from his back as neatly as one skins a rabbit. As soon as I saw

⁵ the dead man I sent an orderly³⁹⁾ to a friend's house nearby to borrow an elephant rifle. I had already sent back the pony, not wanting it to go mad with fright and throw me if it smelt the elephant.

The orderly came back in a few minutes with a rifle and five cartridges, and meanwhile some Burmans had arrived and told us that

¹⁰ the elephant was in the paddy fields below, only a few hundred yards away. As I started forward practically the whole population of the quarter flocked out of the houses and followed me. They had seen the rifle and were all shouting excitedly that I was going to shoot the elephant. They had not shown much interest in the elephant when he was merely

¹⁵ ravaging their homes, but it was different now that he was going to be shot. It was a bit of fun to them, as it would be to an English crowd; besides they wanted the meat. It made me vaguely uneasy. I had no intention of shooting the elephant — I had merely sent for the rifle to defend myself if necessary — and it is always unnerving⁴⁰⁾ to have

²⁰ a crowd following you. I marched down the hill, looking and feeling a fool, with the rifle over my shoulder and an ever–growing army of people jostling at my heels.⁴¹⁾ At the bottom, when you got away from the huts, there was a metalled road⁴²⁾ and beyond that a miry waste of paddy fields

---

39) orderly: 연락원

40) unnerving: = depriving of firmness of courage; disconcerting

41) at my heels: = just behind me

42) a metalled road: 포장된 길

a thousand yards across, not yet ploughed[43] but soggy from the first rains and dotted with coarse grass. The elephant was standing eight yards from the road, his left side towards us. He took not the slightest notice of the crowd's approach. He was tearing up bunches of grass, beating them against his knees to clean them and stuffing them into his mouth.

I had halted on the road. As soon as I saw the elephant I knew with perfect certainty that I ought not to shoot him. It is a serious matter to shoot a working elephant — it is comparable to destroying a huge and costly piece of machinery — and obviously one ought not to do it if it can possibly be avoided. And at that distance, peacefully eating, the elephant looked no more dangerous than a cow. I thought then and I think now that his attack of "must" was already passing off; in which case he would merely wander harmlessly about until the mahout came back and caught him. Moreover, I did not in the least want to shoot him. I decided that I would watch him for a little while to make sure that he did not turn savage again, and then go home.

But at that moment I glanced round at the crowd that had followed me. It was an immense crowd, two thousand at the least and growing every minute. It blocked the road for a long distance on either side. I looked at the sea of yellow faces above the garish clothes — faces all happy and excited over this bit of fun, all certain that the elephant was going to be shot. They were watching me as they would watch a conjurer[44] about to perform a trick. They did not like me, but with the magical rifle in my hands I was momentarily worth watching. And suddenly I realized that I should have to shoot the elephant after all.

---

43) not yet ploughed: 아직 쟁기질이 되지 않은
44) conjurer: 마술사

The people expected it of me and I had got to do it; I could feel their two thousand wills pressing me forward, irresistibly. And it was at this moment, as I stood there with the rifle in my hands, that I first grasped the hollowness, the futility[45] of the white man's dominion in the East. Here was I, the white man with his gun, standing in front of the unarmed native crowd — seemingly the leading actor of the piece; but in reality I was only an absurd puppet pushed to and fro by the will of those yellow faces behind. I perceived in this moment that when the white man turns tyrant it is his own freedom that he destroys. He becomes a sort of hollow, posing dummy, the conventionalized figure of a sahib.[46] For it is the condition of his rule that he shall spend his life in trying to impress the "natives," and so in every crisis he has got to do what the "natives" expect of him. He wears a mask, and his face grows to fit it. I had got to shoot the elephant. I had committed myself to doing it when I sent for the rifle. A sahib has got to act like a sahib; he has got to appear resolute, to know his own mind[47] and do definite things. To come all that way, rifle in hand, with two thousand people marching at my heels, and then to trail feebly away,[48] having done nothing — no, that was impossible. The crowd would laugh at me. And my whole life, every white man's life in the East, was one long struggle not to be laughed at.

But I did not want to shoot the elephant. I watched him beating his bunch of grass against his knees, with that preoccupied grandmotherly air that elephants have. It seemed to me that it would be murder to shoot

---

45) futility: 무익함, 헛됨

46) sahib: (식민지 시대) 인도, 버마인들이 유럽 남성 이름 뒤에 붙이는 존칭(= Master, Sir)

47) know his own mind: = be resolute

48) trail away: 물러서다

him. At that age I was not squeamish[49] about killing animals, but I had never shot an elephant and never wanted to. (Somehow it always seems worse to kill a large animal.) Besides, there was the beast's owner to be considered. Alive, the elephant was worth at least a hundred pounds; dead, he would only be worth the value of his tusks, five pounds, possibly. But I had got to act quickly. I turned to some experienced–looking Burmans who had been there when we arrived, and asked them how the elephant had been behaving. They all said the same thing: he took no notice of you if you left him alone, but he might charge if you went too close to him.

It was perfectly clear to me what I ought to do. I ought to walk up to within, say, twenty–five yards of the elephant and test his behavior. If he charged, I could shoot; if he took no notice of me, it would be safe to leave him until the mahout came back. But also I knew that I was going to do no such thing. I was a poor shot with a rifle and the ground was soft mud into which one would sink at every step. If the elephant charged and I missed him, I should have about as much chance as a toad under a steam–roller. But even then I was not thinking particularly of my own skin, only of the watchful yellow faces behind. For at that moment, with the crowd watching me, I was not afraid in the ordinary sense, as I would have been if I had been alone. A white man mustn't be frightened in front of "natives"; and so, in general, he isn't frightened. The sole thought in my mind was that if anything went wrong those two thousand Burmans would see me pursued, caught, trampled on and reduced to a grinning corpse like that Indian up the hill. And if that happened it was quite probable that some of them would laugh. That

---

49) squeamish: 비위가 약한

1 would never do.

There was only one alternative.[50] I shoved[51] the cartridges into the magazine[52] and lay down on the road to get a better aim. The crowd grew very still, and a deep, low, happy sigh, as of people who see the theatre

5 curtain go up at last, breathed from innumerable throats. They were going to have their bit of fun after all. The rifle was a beautiful German thing with cross–hair sights.[53] I did not then know that in shooting an elephant one would shoot to cut an imaginary bar running from ear–hole to ear–hole. I ought, therefore, as the elephant was sideways on,

10 to have aimed straight at his ear–hole, actually I aimed several inches in front of this, thinking the brain would be further forward.

When I pulled the trigger I did not hear the bang or feel the kick[54] — one never does when a shot goes home[55] — but I heard the devilish roar of glee that went up from the crowd. In that instant, in

15 too short a time, one would have thought, even for the bullet to get there, a mysterious, terrible change had come over the elephant. He neither stirred nor fell, but every line of his body had altered. He looked suddenly stricken,[56] shrunken, immensely old, as though the frightful impact of the bullet had paralysed him without knocking him down. At

20 last, after what seemed a long time — it might have been five seconds, I dare say — he sagged flabbily[57] to his knees. His mouth slobbered.

---

50) one alternative: = one other way

51) shoved: = put

52) magazine: (연발총의) 탄창

53) cross – hair sights: 조준용 십자선, 열십자의 조준기

54) kick: (총의) 반동

55) go home: 명중하다

56) stricken: = deeply affected, as with horror, fear

57) flabbily: 힘없이

1 An enormous senility[58] seemed to have settled upon him. One could have imagined him thousands of years old. I fired again into the same spot. At the second shot he did not collapse but climbed with desperate slowness to his feet and stood weakly upright, with legs sagging and
5 head drooping. I fired a third time. That was the shot that did for him.[59] You could see the agony of it jolt[60] his whole body and knock the last remnant of strength from his legs. But in falling he seemed for a moment to rise, for as his hind legs collapsed beneath him he seemed to tower upward like a huge rock toppling,[61] his trunk reaching skyward like a
10 tree. He trumpeted, for the first and only time. And then down he came, his belly towards me, with a crash that seemed to shake the ground even where I lay.

I got up. The Burmans were already racing past me across the mud. It was obvious that the elephant would never rise again, but he was not
15 dead. He was breathing very rhythmically with long rattling gasps, his great mound of a side painfully rising and falling. His mouth was wide open — I could see far down into caverns of pale pink throat. I waited a long time for him to die, but his breathing did not weaken. Finally I fired my two remaining shots into the spot where I thought his heart
20 must be. The thick blood welled out[62] of him like red velvet, but still he did not die. His body did not even jerk when the shots hit him, the tortured breathing continued without a pause. He was dying, very slowly and in great agony, but in some world remote from me where not even

---

58) senility: 노령, 노쇠
59) did for him: = killed him; finished off him
60) jolt: 충격을 주다
61) topple: 넘어지다, 넘어뜨리다
62) welled out: 솟아 나왔다

a bullet could damage him further. I felt that I had got to put an end to that dreadful noise. It seemed dreadful to see the great beast lying there, powerless to move and yet powerless to die, and not even to be able to finish him. I sent back for my small rifle and poured shot after shot[63] into his heart and down his throat. They seemed to make no impression. The tortured gasps continued as steadily as the ticking of a clock.

In the end I could not stand it any longer and went away. I heard later that it took him half an hour to die. Burmans were bringing dahs[64] and baskets even before I left, and I was told they had stripped his body almost to the bones by the afternoon.

Afterwards, of course, there were endless discussions about the shooting of the elephant. The owner was furious, but he was only an Indian and could do nothing. Besides, legally I had done the right thing, for a mad elephant has to be killed, like a mad dog, if its owner fails to control it. Among the Europeans opinion was divided. The older men said I was right, the younger men said it was a damn shame to shoot an elephant for killing a coolie, because an elephant was worth more than any damn Coringhee[65] coolie. And afterwards I was very glad that the coolie had been killed; it put me legally in the right and it gave me a sufficient pretext[66] for shooting the elephant. I often wondered whether any of the others grasped that I had done it solely to avoid looking a fool.

---

63) poured shot after shot: 계속 퍼부었다
64) dahs: 미얀마 사람의 작은 검(칼)
65) Coringhee: 인도 동남부 도시(Coringha) 출신의
66) pretext: 구실, 핑계

Part **IV**

Poem

1

—

Shall I Compare Thee to a Summer's Day?[1]

William Shakespeare[2]

1　Shall I compare thee[3] to a summer's day?

　　Thou art[4] more lovely and more temperate.[5]

　　Rough winds do shake the darling buds of May,

　　And summer's lease hath all too short a date:[6]

5　Sometime too hot the eye of heaven shines,

　　And often is his gold complexion[7] dimmed;

---

1)　총 154편으로 이루어진 셰익스피어의 『소네트』(*The Sonnets*) 중 18번 소네트이다. 대부분 1590년
　　에서 1609년 사이에 완성된 『소네트』는 2부로 이루어지는데 제1부(1~126)는 주로 젊은 친구에게
　　찬사와 충고를 주는 내용이며, 제2부(127~154)는 여인의 아름다움을 찬양하는 내용으로 이루어져
　　있다.

2)　윌리엄 셰익스피어(William Shakespeare, 1564-1616): 윌리엄 셰익스피어. 영국이 낳은 세계 최고
　　의 극작가로서, 희·비극을 포함한 37편의 희곡과 여러 권의 시집 및 소네트집이 있다. 주요 작품으
　　로는 『로미오와 줄리엣』, 『베니스의 상인』, 『햄릿』, 『맥베스』 등이 있다.

3)　thee: 당신을. 2인칭 인칭대명사 you의 목적격.

4)　Thou art: = You are

5)　temperate: 온화한

6)　date: duration

7)　complexion: 안색

1 And every fair from fair sometimes declines,

   By chance, or nature's changing course, untrimmed;

   But thy eternal summer shall not fade

   Nor lose possession of that fair thou ow'st,[8]

5 Nor shall death brag[9] thou wander'st in his shade,

   When in eternal lines[10] to Time thou grow'st;

    So long as men can breathe, or eyes can see,

    So long lives this, and this gives life to thee.[11]

---

8) that fair thou ow'st: 그대가 지닌 아름다움. ow'st: = ownest

9) brag: 자랑하다

10) lines: 시행

11) So lone as... to thee: 자기 시의 불멸성을 자랑하는 것으로, 이는 르네상스시대 시의 관습이다.

2

The Chimney Sweeper

William Blake[1]

1   When my mother died I was very young,
     And my father sold me while yet my tongue
     Could scarcely cry "'weep! 'weep! 'weep!"[2]

5   So your chimneys I sweep & in soot I sleep.

     There's little Tom Dacre, who cried when his head
     That curl'd like a lamb's back, was shav'd, so I said,
     "Hush, Tom! never mind it, for when your head's bare,
10   You know that the soot cannot spoil your white hair."

---

1) 윌리엄 블레이크(William Blake, 1757-1827): 영국 시인. 조각, 그림에 조예가 깊었고, 신비주의 철학서를 집필하기도 했다. 18세기의 기계적, 유물론적 합리주의에 의해 억압된 인간의 순수한 감정과 자유로운 정신을 회복시켜 자연의 세계에서 생명의 신비와 경이를 찾으려 노력했다. 대표작으로 『시 스케치』(*Poetical Sketches*), 『순수의 노래』(*The Songs of Innocence*), 『경험의 노래』(*The Songs of Experience*) 등이 있다.

2) "'weep! 'weep! 'weep!": "sweep! sweep! sweep!"

1   And so he was quiet, & that very night,
     As Tom was a-sleeping he had such a sight!
     That thousands of sweepers, Dick, Joe, Ned, & Jack,
     Were all of them lock'd up in coffins of black;

5   And by came an Angel who had a bright key,
     And he open'd the coffins & set them all free;
     Then down a green plain, leaping, laughing they run,
     And wash in a river and shine in the Sun.

10   Then naked & white, all their bags left behind,
     They rise upon clouds, and sport in the wind.
     And the Angel told Tom, if he'd be a good boy,
     He'd have God for his father & never want joy.

15   And so Tom awoke; and we rose in the dark
     And got with our bags & our brushes to work.
     Tho' the morning was cold, Tom was happy & warm;
     So if all do their duty, they need not fear harm.

3

How Do I Love Thee?[1]

Elizabeth Barrett Browning[2]

1   How do I love thee? Let me count the ways.

     I love thee to the depth and breadth[3] and height

     My soul can reach, when feeling out of sight

     For the ends of being and ideal grace.

5   I love thee to the level of every day's

     Most quiet need, by sun and candle–light.

     I love thee freely, as men strive for right.

---

1) 1850년에 출판된 『포르투갈어에서 옮긴 소네트』(*Sonnets from the Portuguese*)에 수록된 43번 소네트. 이 시는 남편인 시인 로버트 브라우닝(Robert Browning, 1812-1889)에게 쓴 시로, 역시를 가장하여 남편에 대한 애정을 솔직하게 노래한 작품이다. 1845~46년까지 2년 동안 두 사람은 많은 편지를 교환했고, 그 편지에는 두 사람이 서로를 얼마나 많이 사랑했는지가 여실히 드러난다. 이 시는 셰익스피어의 소네트와 더불어 영시에서 가장 아름다운 사랑의 시 가운데 하나로 알려져 있다.

2) 엘리자베스 배릿 브라우닝(Elizabeth Barrett Browning, 1806-1861): 영국 빅토리아 시대의 대표 여류 시인. 8살부터 시작했던 시 창작은 그녀에게 유일한 즐거움이었으며 낙마사고로 시한부 인생을 살아야 했음에도 불구하고 꾸준히 정기간행물에 시를 기고하였고 마침내 계관시인으로 지목되기까지 했다. 그녀의 작품은 에드거 앨런 포와 에밀리 디킨슨(Emily Dickinson)을 포함한 당대의 저명한 작가들에게 영향을 미쳤다.

3) breadth: 폭, 너비

1   I love thee purely, as they turn from praise.

       I love thee with the passion put to use

       In my old griefs, and with my childhood's faith.

       I love thee with a love I seemed to lose

5   With my lost saints. I love thee with the breath,

       Smiles, tears, of all my life; and, if God choose,

       I shall but love thee better after death.

4

Annabel Lee[1)]

Edgar Allan Poe

1   It was many and many a year ago,

In a kingdom by the sea,

That a maiden there lived whom you may know

By the name of Annabel Lee;

5   And this maiden she lived with no other thought

Than to love and be loved by me.

I was a child and *she* was a child,

In this kingdom by the sea:

10   But we loved with a love that was more than love —

I and my Annabel Lee —

---

1) 자전적 시로 평가받는 「애너벨 리」("Annabel Lee")는 포의 1849년 발표작이다. 1842년부터 지병
으로 투병생활을 하던 그의 아내가 1847년에 결핵으로 사망하자, 포는 충격으로 우울증에 시달리
다가 아편을 복용하거나 자살을 시도하기도 했다. 버지니아 클렘에 있는 아내의 무덤을 배회하는
등 피폐한 생활을 이어가던 끝에 사별한 아내를 추모하는 내용의 마지막 시를 발표하는데, 그것이
바로 「애너벨 리」이다.

1　　With a love that the wingèd seraphs²⁾ of Heaven
Coveted³⁾ her and me.

And this was the reason that, long ago,
5　　In this kingdom by the sea,
A wind blew out of a cloud, chilling
My beautiful Annabel Lee;
So that her highborn⁴⁾ kinsman⁵⁾ came
And bore her away from me,
10　　To shut her up in a sepulchre⁶⁾
In this kingdom by the sea.

The angels, not half so happy in Heaven,
Went envying her and me —
15　　Yes! — that was the reason (as all men know,
In this kingdom by the sea)
That the wind came out of the cloud by night,
Chilling and killing my Annabel Lee.

20　　But our love it was stronger by far⁷⁾ than the love
Of those who were older than we —

---

2)　seraphs: 천사(구품 천사 가운데 가장 높은 천사)
3)　covet: 탐내다
4)　highborn: 상류 가문 태생의
5)　kinsman: 친척, 일가
6)　sepulchre: 무덤
7)　by far: 훨씬

1   Of many far[8] wiser than we —
And neither the angels in Heaven above,
Nor the demons down under the sea,
Can ever dissever[9] my soul from the soul
5   Of the beautiful Annabel Lee;

For the moon never beams, without bringing me dreams
Of the beautiful Annabel Lee;
And the stars never rise, but I feel the bright eyes
10   Of the beautiful Annabel Lee;
And so, all the night–tide, I lie down by the side
Of my darling — my darling — my life and my bride,
In her sepulchre there by the sea —
In her tomb by the sounding sea.

---

8)   far: 훨씬
9)   dissever: 분리하다, 떼어 놓다

5

A Broken Appointment

Thomas Hardy[1]

1   You did not come,
    And marching Time drew on, and wore me numb,[2] —
    Yet less for loss of your dear presence there
    Than that I thus found lacking in your make[3]
5   That high compassion[4] which can overbear[5]
    Reluctance[6] for pure lovingkindness' sake
    Grieved I, when, as the hope–hour stroked its sum,
    You did not come.

---

1) 토머스 하디(Thomas Hardy, 1840-1928): 영국의 소설가이자 시인. 『더버빌 가의 테스』(*Tess of the d'Urbervilles*), 『이름 없는 주드』(*Jude the Obscure*) 등의 소설로 유명하다. 「깨어진 약속」("A Broken Appointment")에서는 토머스 하디 시의 전형적인 특징인 실망, 좌절된 사랑과 염세주의를 엿볼 수 있다. 이 시는 플로렌스 헤니커(Florence Henniker)라는 여성과의 좌절된 우정이 모티브인 것으로 알려져 있다.

2) numb: 감각이 없는

3) make: 성격, 기질

4) compassion: 연민, 동정심

5) overbear: 제압하다, 압도하다

6) reluctance: 거리낌, 꺼려함

1   You love not me,
     And love alone can lend you loyalty;
       — I know and knew it. But, unto the store
     Of human deeds divine in all but name,[7]
5   Was it not worth a little hour or more
     To add yet this: Once you, a woman, came
     To soothe a time–torn man;[8] even though it be
     You love not me.

---

7) in all but name: 명목상으로는 아니지만 실질적으로는
8) a time – torn man: 기다림에 지친 남자

6

He Wishes for the Cloths of Heaven[1]

William Butler Yeats[2]

1   HAD I the heavens' embroidered[3] cloths,

       Enwrought[4] with golden and silver light,

       The blue and the dim and the dark cloths

       Of night and light and the half–light,

5   I would spread the cloths under your feet:

       But I, being poor, have only my dreams;

---

1) 시인이 누군가를 향해 가지는 강렬한 사랑의 시. 이 시는 시인 에이츠가 거의 평생 동안 사랑한 여인인 모드 곤(Maud Gonne)을 위해 쓴 것으로 알려져 있다. 영화 〈이퀼리브리엄〉(Equilibrium, 84 Charing CrossRoad)과 한국 영화인 〈다세포 소녀〉의 한 장면에 인용된 시이기도 하다. 이 시의 화자는 아데(Aedhe)라는 인물인데, 그는 에이츠 시의 신화에 나오는 전형적인 두 인물(Michael Robartes와 Red Hanrahan)과 더불어 에이츠의 작품에 등장하는 인물이다. 아데는 창백하고 사랑에 우는 캐릭터이다.

2) 윌리엄 버틀러 에이츠(William Butler Yeats, 1865–1939): 아일랜드의 시인이자 극작가. 1923년 아일랜드 최초로 노벨 문학상을 수상했다. 독자적 신화로써 자연(자아)의 세계와 자연 부정(예술)의 세계의 상극을 극복하려 노력했다.

3) embroidered: 수놓아진

4) enwrought: = inwrought. 짜여진

1   I have spread my dreams under your feet;

Tread[5] softly because you tread on my dreams.

---

5)   tread: 밟다

7

The Road Not Taken[1]

Robert Frost[2]

1   Two roads diverged[3] in a yellow wood,
     And sorry I could not travel both
     And be one traveler, long I stood
     And looked down one as far as I could
5   To where it bent in the undergrowth;[4]

     Then took the other, as just as fair,
     And having perhaps the better claim,

---

1) 이 시는 1916년 『마운틴 인터벌』(*Mountain Interval*)에 수록된 시로 소박한 전원의 정서를 인생의 문제로 승화시킨 서정시이다. 제재는 숲속에 난 두 갈래의 길이며, 주제는 삶에 대한 희구와 인생행로에 대한 회고이다. 「가지 않은 길」은 자신이 걸어온 길보다는 걷지 않았던 길에 대한 미련을 표현한다. 외면적 자연풍광을 통해 인생에 대한 관조적 자세를 엿볼 수 있다.

2) 로버트 프로스트(Robert Frost, 1874-1963): 미국 시인. 시골 생활에 대한 진솔한 묘사와 미국 구어체의 구사로 유명하다. 그는 농장의 생활 경험을 바탕으로 소박한 농민과 자연을 노래해 현대 미국 시인 중 가장 순수한 고전적 시인으로 꼽힌다. 주로 20세기 초기 뉴잉글랜드 시골의 정경을 배경으로 했으며, 복잡한 사회적 · 철학적 주제를 시에 담았다. 케네디 대통령의 취임식에서 자작시를 낭송하기도 했으며, 퓰리처상을 4회 수상했다.

3) diverge: 갈라지다

4) undergrowth: 덤불, 관목

1 Because it was grassy and wanted wear;
 Though as for that the passing there
 Had worn them really about the same,

5 And both that morning equally lay
 In leaves no step had trodden black.
 Oh, I kept the first for another day!
 Yet knowing how way leads on to way,
 I doubted if I should ever come back.
10

 I shall be telling this with a sigh
 Somewhere ages and ages hence:
 Two roads diverged in a wood, and I —
 I took the one less traveled by,
15 And that has made all the difference.[5]

---

5) 마지막 연에서 작가는 자신이 선택한 길 때문에 모든 것이 달라졌음을 회상한다.

8

Do Not Go Gentle into That Good Night[1]

Dylan Thomas[2]

1　Do not go gentle into that good night,
　　Old age should burn and rave at close of day;
　　Rage, rage against the dying of the light.

5　Though wise men at their end know dark is right,
　　Because their words had forked no lightning they
　　Do not go gentle into that good night.

---

1)　이 시는 빌라넬라(villanella; 16세기 나폴리에서 생긴 성악곡의 형식) 형식의 시로, 시인이 가족과 플로렌스에 있었을 때인 1947년에 쓰였다. 그는 늙는 것과 죽는 것을 탐구하기 위해 죽음의 은유로 '밤'을, 삶의 은유로 '빛'을 사용하고 있다. 영화 〈인터스텔라〉(Interstellar)의 한 장면에 사용되기도 했다.

2)　딜런 토머스(Dylan Marlais Thomas, 1914-1953): 1930년대를 대표하는 영국의 시인, 작가. 『18편의 시』(18 Poems), 『25편의 시』(25 Twenty-Five Poems), 『사랑의 지도』(The Map of Love), 『죽음과 입구』(Deaths and Entrances) 등의 시집과, 시극 『밀크 숲의 그늘에서』(Under Milk Wood)가 있으며, 자서전적인 단편집인 『강아지 같은 예술가의 초상』(Portrait of the Artist as a Young Dog) 등이 대표작으로 알려져 있다.

1   Good men, the last wave by, crying how bright

     Their frail[3] deeds might have danced in a green bay,

     Rage, rage against the dying of the light.

5   Wild men who caught and sang the sun in flight,

     And learn, too late, they grieved it on its way,

     Do not go gentle into that good night.

     Grave men, near death, who see with blinding sight

10   Blind eyes could blaze like meteors[4] and be gay,

     Rage, rage against the dying of the light.

     And you, my father, there on the sad height,

     Curse, bless, me now with your fierce tears, I pray.

15   Do not go gentle into that good night.

     Rage, rage against the dying of the light.

---

3) frail: 노쇠한, 부서지기 쉬운
4) meteor: 유성, 별똥별